AMERICA'S
A Commemorative Portrait of the Mormon Tabernacle Choir
CHOIR

HEIDI S. SWINTON
Author of the Documentary Film by Lee Groberg

SHADOW MOUNTAIN
AND
MORMON TABERNACLE CHOIR

"It Is Well with My Soul"

——✦——

For all choir members
across the centuries,
in particular, my father.

Visit us at shadowmountain.com and mormontabernaclechoir.org

Library of Congress Cataloging-in-Publication Data

Swinton, Heidi S., 1948-
  America's choir / Heidi Swinton.
    p.   cm.
    ISBN 1-59038-282-X (alk. paper)
    1. Mormon Tabernacle Choir.   I. Title.
    ML200.8.S18T29 2004
    782.5'06'0792258—dc22   2004001368

Printed in the United States of America
Inland Press, Menomonee Falls, WI
10   9   8   7   6   5   4   3   2   42316-1003

Contents

COME, THOU FOUNT
OF EVERY BLESSING

Prelude

Prone to wander, Lord, I feel it,
Prone to leave the God I love;
Here's my heart, O take and seal it;
Seal it for thy courts above.

OR TWO YEARS I have been a member of the Mormon Tabernacle Choir. Mention of that brings a smile to the lips of anyone who knows me. I can't sing. But I love singing. I love what it feels like to listen to choral music; to hear the bells, the organ, the drums; to watch the Choir's command of the stage in "Betelehemu" and the drummer's enunciation of the beat. These are people who march today to a different drummer than most musicians who scale the charts. If you are keeping score. But the only measure that matters, I now recognize, is that the Mormon Tabernacle Choir sings from their very souls to the God who made them, from one end of the country to the other—one broadcast, one recording, one rehearsal, one wardrobe fitting, one tour, one prayer at a time. For them, that's all there is or ever will be.

They are America's Choir because they know America. They know the land, the people, and the promise that brought their ancestors here. They know the Almighty; they have placed themselves in His hands. They embody their signature anthem, "Come, Come, Ye Saints," for they are Saints in every sense of the word. Whether they are singing hymns or national anthems, folk songs or favorite show tunes, they are a noble breed born of obedience, reverence, authenticity, fidelity, and truth. I have sat at their sides, walked and worshiped with them. The Mormon Tabernacle Choir is the essence of grass-roots goodness put to the test. Time and again.

For many years I considered the Mormon Tabernacle Choir simply the backup to whatever was happening—from General Conference of The Church of Jesus Christ of Latter-day Saints to extravaganzas in stadiums, Olympic or otherwise. They were there; they were singing. I was not alone in that impression. When

To celebrate the Choir's seventy-five anniversary of broadcasting, Utah filmmaker Lee Groberg produced a national television documentary, America's Choir, *written by screenwriter Heidi Swinton. The documentary, and this companion book, spotlight today's Mormon Tabernacle Choir, its volunteer spirit, its worldwide recognition, and many significant moments in the Choir's history.*

I began studying the Choir, traveling with them, hearing them as their scores of devotees do outside their traditional setting, I saw a different choir. They hadn't changed; I had. Critics and presidents applaud the Choir as a "national treasure," and the locals nod their heads. Everywhere else, from London to Jerusalem to Tokyo, audiences stand on the benches and stamp their feet for just one more song. Curious.

To research and write about the Choir and its seventy-fifth anniversary of broadcasting has required more than hours in the library or in interviews. The primary source material has come from the Choir—when it sings, even in exercises, "one, two-a-tee." I have come to understand the Psalmist's words, "Make a joyful noise." I hear differently now; I hear angels.

Streams of mercy, never ceasing,
Call for songs of loudest praise.

The Choir is good, and getting better all the time. How is that possible? Craig Jessop and Mack Wilberg immediately come to mind. The first staff meeting I attended, I expected Mack Wilberg to sit down at the piano and play a stunning version of "My Shepherd Will Supply My Need." Craig would lead, and we would all sing along. It didn't happen. No one sang. No one talked about Brahms or Rutter. No one really even talked about music. They went

over the budget and plans for the upcoming tour. They talked about the copy machine and the royalties for recordings. I was surprised. "When do we sing?" I asked. They laughed at me.

Then I went to one of the weekly broadcast review meetings at Bonneville Communications. We watched the Sunday program, and I listened to the attendees point out camera angles, mishaps, and "Did you hear that?" They discussed ideas for *Music and the Spoken Word* and a message for an upcoming satellite broadcast. It was like being in the editing booth I know so well from documentary work, except that this was the Choir. I was surprised, and I asked, "When do we sing?" They kept talking.

I went to rehearsals on Thursday evening and early Sunday mornings. I stayed through the broadcast and attended concerts. That's when they sing. And I learned something. The Choir is all about singing praises to God and feeling the Spirit of the Lord reach out from inside and touch another. No matter what music the Choir was singing, I could hear "Here's my heart, O take and seal it, seal it for Thy courts above." And I wanted more. I was a regular at rehearsals and broadcasts. I started playing their recordings in the car, on my computer at home. I started to sing along.

Tune my heart to sing thy grace.

I loved what I felt when I sat in an obscure corner of the Tabernacle, observing, watching, listening. I loved sitting front and center in the choir loft, watching Craig Jessop do the backstroke and the butterfly all in the same song to bring everything out of 360 singers—music, feeling, message, and spirit—acting as one. His spirit encompasses the entire stage, all the way to the last seats in the choir loft, and pulls you in.

I remember tenor Ken Evans leaning over the railing and commenting, "How do you like death row?" That's what they call the front row. The choir members change seats twice a year. Far from coveted, a seat on the front row means just one thing: Time is up. Twenty years by anyone's count is not old, it's over. Choir members retire after twenty years of service or sixty years of age. Both come fast.

I love choir members' purity of purpose and their sense of being something far greater than one voice. Gracious, gifted, resilient, committed—these are their strengths, and they draw upon them even when they are sweltering on a stage in Virginia. I love their reverence for the Tabernacle, their home on Temple Square. Craig Jessop, spiritual leader of both the music and the moment, a man with a love for the Divine, says, "I never go into the Tabernacle that I do not feel the sacredness of that place and the spirit. I love that place. To me it is filled with those who have gone on before. To me, it is one of the most spiritual places on earth."

Lessons are learned in the loft, and lived there—

courage, humility, respect, patience, polish, and kindness. Talent, too, is in abundance. Talent to learn as well as sing, for their repertoire demands proficiency at more than 1,400 pieces, not counting masterworks. Every one of them is a favorite for someone. And most of them have grateful listeners writing letters of thanks because the words, the music, and most of all the feeling made a difference on an otherwise drab or dark day.

Teach me some melodious sonnet,
Sung by flaming tongues above.

Choir members are my friends. It was much easier for them to learn my name than for me to learn theirs. It didn't matter. We share something that has nothing to do with recognition and everything to do with connection. We share the rain at Tanglewood and the spectacular performance of Bernstein's *Chichester Psalms.* They sang; I listened. We share the wisdom of Craig Jessop as he encourages them to stay on pitch: "I'm going to have this needlepointed on your pillows, and then you will pray about it." We share the genius of Mack Wilberg, whose arrangements and musical scores are better than words could describe. "Majestic, dazzling, endearing, stirring"

In the re-creation of the 1929 broadcast, Jonathan Groberg (left) took the part of Ted Kimball; Dr. K. Newell Dayley (center) the part of Anthony C. Lund, choir conductor at the first broadcast; and Michael Ohman (right) the part of organist Edward P. Kimball.

The starting cue came by telegraph from New York to a telegraph operator, Weston Lee, in the local radio control room. With thirty seconds to go, Lee relayed it to John Cope in the basement of the Tabernacle, who in turn signaled by hand motion Louis Lacey, program director, who in turn gave the starting signal to Ted Kimball on top of the step ladder.

Dressed in period costume for the re-creation of the first broadcast, the Choir lip-synched to 1948 and 1939 recordings of "Gently Raise the Sacred Strain" and "The Morning Breaks; the Shadows Flee" for the one-hour film.

seem so pedestrian for music that is without match. And so is the man. We share the wisdom and peaceful countenance brought to the Choir week after week by President Mac Christensen. "Be good to yourself," he is always saying. He is good to everyone. He is the father, grandfather, uncle, next-door neighbor, and clothier-extraordinaire whom everyone invites to their inner circle. We share Lloyd Newell, whose heart is as pure as his voice. We share John Longhurst, a gentleman, a master at the organ and at life. His associates Clay Christiansen and Richard Elliott, Bonnie Goodliffe and Linda Margetts—their hands and feet, too, witness of the glory of God. We share the blessing of a seventy-hour-a-week staff who ostensibly work forty—Scott Barrick, Barry Anderson, Stan Parrish, Ann and Jim Turner, Julie Rohde, and dozens of volunteers, from choir historian Marene Foulger, choir medical team Dr. Richard Price and wife Lynn to Shirlene and Tom Thomas in the choir library to Gerry Avant, editor of the *Church News,* who has faithfully tracked the Choir from one corner of the globe to another. These people work days *and* nights more than occasionally, because that's simply what they do. They exemplify the idea that "Nobody knows what I did, but I did a lot."

This volume and the documentary that joins with it trumpet the Mormon Tabernacle Choir.

They deserve such applause. So does my husband, Jeffrey, for his help, encouragement, and good nature. For us, my researching and writing this book has been the experience of a lifetime.

How do you tell the story of a choir that began singing to sagebrush and is now courted by concert halls in the most sophisticated cities across the globe? Such fame and glory have never been their purpose or their satisfaction. Theirs is a history of volunteers who, year after year, from one century to another and then another, kept working, kept serving, kept singing. They have sung with a spirit that points to Almighty God. And there lies their secret to success. They are religious; they have found truth and take it to the world. Always, they bring with them the spirit of God. It is in them, each one. It is in their music, in their eyes. In their hearts. This is their story.

Come, thou Fount of every blessing,
Tune my heart to sing thy grace;
Streams of mercy, never ceasing,
Call for songs of loudest praise.
Teach me some melodious sonnet,
Sung by flaming tongues above;
Praise the mount; I'm fixed upon it:
Mount of thy redeeming love.

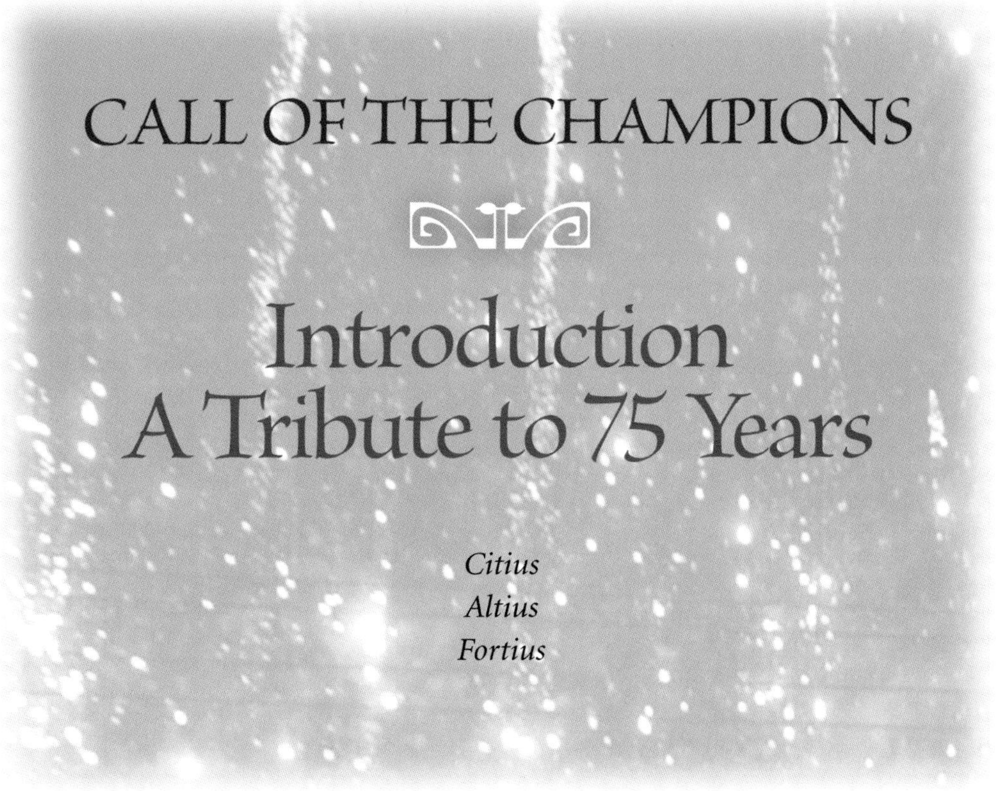

CALL OF THE CHAMPIONS

Introduction
A Tribute to 75 Years

Citius
Altius
Fortius

W HEN COMPOSER JOHN WILLIAMS conceived the idea of using a nineteenth-century Olympic motto for the words of the 2002 Olympic theme song, he imagined a celebratory feeling. "Before the orchestra played, we would hear the Mormon Choir proclaim these words," he later explained. *Citius. Altius. Fortius.* The Choir's performance of Williams's "Call of the Champions" at the opening ceremonies touched hearts and carried a spirit unique to their mission.

Citius—swifter. *Altius*—higher. *Fortius*—stronger. Little did Williams know that those words also describe the very essence of the Mormon Tabernacle Choir. It has been so for its decades of singing at General Conferences, broadcasts, concerts, rehearsals, recordings, celebrations, and even funerals.

The Choir's public-service broadcast, *Music and the Spoken Word*, turns seventy-five this year. July 18, 2004, will be the 3,910th continuous broadcast. No one else has

The Mormon Tabernacle Choir joined John Williams, Sting, Yo-Yo Ma, and others performing at the opening ceremonies of the 2002 Olympic Winter Games in Salt Lake City. The program was broadcast across the globe to an estimated audience of 3.5 billion.

In these days of political, personal, and economic disintegration, music is not a luxury, it's a necessity; not simply because it is therapeutic, nor because it is the universal language, but because it is the persistent focus of our intelligence, aspiration, and goodwill.

—Robert Shaw, choral and symphony conductor

such a record anywhere. Every week from the Mormon Tabernacle at the "Crossroads of the West" and occasionally from special tour locations, the Choir has welcomed its listeners, friends around the world, to the longest continuous broadcast in radio history. Well-aged and well-regarded, this program has become synonymous with what is right with the world.

Long before the airwaves of Sunday morning were flooded with evangelical hours, the Mormon Tabernacle Choir was communicating in the universal language of song. It began one well-baked July day with just the rudiments of radio and one microphone. Quickly, the broadcast penetrated the American conscience. In 1935 the press offered congratulations for the program's success: "America's oldest coast-to-coast, community-produced, non-commercial feature has winged its way on the

Following the prerecording session with the Choir for the Olympics, Sting said, "You make me very proud to be a member of the human race and one of God's children. I didn't know people were capable of producing such beauty."

airwaves for nearly six years." The broadcast has advanced—swifter, higher, stronger—to state-of-the-art control rooms in both the Tabernacle and Conference Center, to jib cameras and banks of lights that look more Broadway-bound than at home in one of the most unusual religious centers in the world. It has grown from thirty radio stations to hundreds. Television and satellite followed. The men's and women's wardrobes now fit a weekly color scheme; no more can the women wear hats; the printed program handed out to throngs of visitors includes the message of *Music and the Spoken Word*; and an orchestra adds trumpets and strings to the rich tones of the famous organ.

Much has changed since the beginning. Much has stayed the same. The broadcast still features singing and a sermonette designed to inspire and lift the listeners. The program is live and never routine. The format evolved quickly as the broadcast secured its place on the radio waves in the early 1930s and has been "something you could count

THESE ARE PEOPLE WHO ARE THERE FOR THE JOY OF MUSIC. IT'S NOT A JOB WITH THEM; IT'S A MISSION.

—*John Williams, conductor and composer*

The Choir's official home is the Tabernacle on Temple Square.

on" ever since. Awards and credits usually reserved for the world's highest-paid professionals line the pages of their history.

Being a religious entity, the Choir has purpose beyond good music sung in tune with appropriate, even exemplary, expression. Its mission is to share the love of Jesus Christ, His truths, His spirit, with all who will listen.

What the Choir communicates reaches far deeper than does a smile, a nod, or a high soprano trill. Gabriel Crouch of the King's Singers stated after a guest appearance, "Just standing there and allowing this wall of fantastic sound to wash over us—it really does make the hair stand up on the back of your neck." Hearts of listeners—everywhere—feel a spirit: uncommon, magnificent. Real. That spirit reaches out from the Choir, the conductor, and the announcer to hungry souls, one at a time. Applause from the audience at the end of a concert, a broadcast, or even a rehearsal not only congratulates the musicality but also speaks appreciation to the spirit that lifted them up. Lifting *higher* is what the Choir does best.

The heart of the Choir's message is simple: "Rejoice, the Lord is King." They don't sing words, they sing feelings. Hence, their rejoicing can naturally take the form of "Danny Boy" or the African

One of the Mormon Tabernacle Choir's primary responsibilities is to sing at LDS General Conference twice a year. In addition, the Choir sings at LDS Church First Presidency Devotionals and other special programs.

THE MAGIC OF THE CHOIR IS FIRST AND FOREMOST THEIR FAITH IN CHRIST. IT'S NOT SO MUCH ABOUT THE MUSIC AS IT IS ABOUT THEIR FAITH AND THEIR SERVICE TO THE CHURCH.

—*Craig Jessop, music director, Mormon Tabernacle Choir*

THE KING OF LOVE MY SHEPHERD IS

"The secret to choral music is in the scriptures," Craig Jessop explains. "It's in the Gospel of John, when the Savior is speaking to the apostles in the Upper Room, giving the Intercessory Prayer 'that they may be one, even as we are one':

> *As thou hast sent me into the world, even so have I also sent them into the world. And for their sakes I sanctify myself, that they also might be sanctified through the truth. Neither pray I for these alone, but for them also which shall believe on me through their word; that they all may be one; as thou, Father, art in me, and I in thee, that they also may be one in us: that the world may believe that thou hast sent me. And the glory which thou gavest me I have given them; that they may be one, even as we are one. (John 17:19–22.)*

"That is the essence of choral music, that many become one. And it is a metaphor for the journey of the human soul, our pilgrimage. What we want more than any other thing is to be one with God and with one another. We want to go back; we want to be embraced by him; we want to feel that we have returned to him and have come home. And become one.

"That is the secret of choral music—many people becoming one. And when they speak with one voice, when they're one, there is nothing else like it. To me, when the Choir is one, you can hear the voice of the Lord, and those moments when they are absolutely one in spirit, one in pitch, one in rhythm, one in diction, one in phrasing, when this instrument becomes one, it becomes a transcendent experience. Those moments are generally without compulsory means. They cannot be forced. They suddenly become organic. When those moments arrive, the conductor simply has to get out of the way."

I THINK THE MORMON TABERNACLE CHOIR HAS A GLOW ABOUT IT, AN INSPIRATIONAL GLOW. THEY ENJOY MAKING MUSIC THAT IS NOT COMMERCIALLY DRIVEN IN ANY WAY.

—*John Williams,*
conductor and composer

carol "Betelehemu," Handel's "Hallelujah Chorus" or the hymn "Come, Let Us Anew."

These 360 men and women are volunteers. But they are more than that. They are musicians, unselfish with the instrument—voice—given them by God. Each is someone's neighbor, employer, family, or friend. Choir president Mac Christensen states, "Ours is a volunteer organization. These people are singing for the right reason, and that

In its first major tour of the East Coast since 1976, the Mormon Tabernacle Choir presented a program that was nostalgic, stimulating, and fresh. The crowd-pleaser was clearly the Nigerian carol "Betelehemu," which announcer Lloyd Newell promised "won't be like anything you've heard from this choir." True. The Choir became an entire African village, singing, clapping, shouting, and swaying during the number, accompanied by a showy percussion band.

IT WAS AN EXTRAORDINARY EXPERIENCE TO HAVE BACKUP SINGERS LIKE THE MORMON TABERNACLE CHOIR. I HAVE NEVER EXPERIENCED ANYTHING QUITE LIKE IT BEFORE AND I WOULDN'T TRADE IT FOR ANYTHING IN THE WORLD. —*Angela Lansbury, guest artist, Christmas 2001*

makes it so easy. We don't have to demand; we don't have to threaten; we don't have to prod. We just have to be decent people and tell them that we love them and try to protect them—make sure we don't overwork them, whether it is the staff or the Orchestra or the Choir." Charles Osgood, composer and commentator, quips, "It does not surprise me that it is an all-volunteer organization, because how in the world would you pay that many people?"

They are faithful Latter-day Saints whose predecessors began singing in fledgling church choirs in Ohio and Illinois before ever crossing the plains. Their reach today extends from the Tabernacle to satellites in the sky and back down again to Australia, Europe, South America, the fifty states, and Canada. They serve without pay, donating their Sunday mornings week after week; many devote twenty years. They practice every Thursday evening and Tuesdays, too, when a concert or tour is looming. When recording—in a building constructed of wood lashed together with rawhide—they work four nights and all day Saturday. Then they return

Early on July 6, 2003, the Choir arrived at the Jefferson Memorial for a scheduled photo shoot, complete with Park Service permit. Then, visiting the inside of the Memorial, they broke into an impromptu "God Bless America," with Craig Jessop in the lead. Halfway through the second verse, a Park Service employee strode up the steps and demanded that the Choir quit singing. The Choir had a permit from the Park Service for the picture-taking but no permit for singing.

for the broadcast on Sunday. The schedule is grueling if time is the measure. But it isn't.

It happens in Michigan, England, Israel, and Russia. From the Tabernacle to the television, from Shepherds' Field in Israel to the Esplanade in Boston, on wax recordings and compact discs, from LDS General Conference to the steps of the Jefferson Memorial, the Mormon Tabernacle Choir has been there. And they will go back. While some may credit certain music or showmanship as their style, the core of the Choir is reliance on the Lord and His Spirit.

They will follow Craig Jessop—anywhere—and marvel at Mack Wilberg's genius as he completes yet another masterful arrangement for the Choir. They balance family, professional careers, and choir. They understand *swifter*. They use their vacations to tour with the Choir, most of the time on a bus. If glamour means being under the lights, the Choir will affirm that it feels more like being in an oven. They dress up for the camera in identical clothing that somehow fits every size and looks good on almost everyone. The Choir is "big." When

GOD BLESS AMERICA, LAND THAT I LOVE

The National Medal for the Arts was established by Congress in 1984. Following the ceremony in the Oval Office, the choir leadership attended a reception to honor all of the award recipients. (Left to right: Lloyd Newell, John Longhurst, First Lady Laura Bush, Mac Christensen, President George W. Bush, Craig Jessop, Mack Wilberg, Stan Parrish.)

The President of the United States of America

Awards this

National Medal of Arts

to

The Mormon Tabernacle Choir

for its extraordinary contributions to music and the art of choral singing; for the wide reach and impact of its music; and for inspiring audiences worldwide.

George Bush

November 12, 2003

The Choir has been invited to perform in Washington, D.C., at presidential inaugurals and White House concerts since the early 1900s. November 12, 2003, was the first invitation to the White House to receive "long-overdue" honors, President George W. Bush said when he awarded the Mormon Tabernacle Choir the National Medal of Arts in a special ceremony. Choir president Mac Christensen accepted the honor on behalf of the organization. The White House had invited each recipient to bring a handful of guests. Representing the Choir were Craig Jessop, music director; Mack Wilberg, associate director; John Longhurst, Tabernacle organist; Stan Parrish, assistant to the choir president; and Lloyd Newell, announcer for *Music and the Spoken Word.* The question everyone asked Jessop: "Where's the Choir?"

President Christensen confessed that when he walked into the Oval Office, he instinctively gave the president of the United States a bear hug. He later confessed to the Choir, "I didn't even think about the Secret Service. We just wish all of you could have been there." Then he said, "Let's have a hand for all of those who were here before we were." He concluded his congratulations by saying, "There are only a few of us who have this opportunity right now. Make the most of it." Speaking from his heart, he added, "The only time we are ever really happy is when we are quietly helping someone else."

Craig Jessop reported that while in Washington, he was asked where the Choir was going next. He replied, "Well, there's a rehearsal Thursday night and a broadcast Sunday morning."

"The great thing about the Mormon Tabernacle Choir," Jessop says, "is that it isn't built around an individual. It's built around an institution." He described his feeling of being with President and Mrs. Bush, of understanding "the symbolism behind what the president was

Pᴿᴇsɪᴅᴇɴᴛ Bᴜsʜ sᴀɪᴅ ᴛᴏ ᴜs ᴛʜᴀᴛ ᴛʜɪs ᴡᴀs ᴀ ʟᴏɴɢ-ᴏᴠᴇʀᴅᴜᴇ ʀᴇᴄᴏɢɴɪᴛɪᴏɴ, ɴᴏᴛ ᴏɴʟʏ ғᴏʀ ᴛʜᴇ Cʜᴏɪʀ's ɢʀᴇᴀᴛ ᴍᴜsɪᴄᴀʟ ᴄᴏɴᴛʀɪʙᴜᴛɪᴏɴ ᴛᴏ ᴏᴜʀ ɴᴀᴛɪᴏɴ ʙᴜᴛ ғᴏʀ ɪᴛs sᴘɪʀɪᴛᴜᴀʟ ᴄᴏɴᴛʀɪʙᴜᴛɪᴏɴ ᴀs ᴡᴇʟʟ. Tʜᴀᴛ ᴡᴀs ᴡᴏʀᴛʜ ᴇᴠᴇʀʏᴛʜɪɴɢ.

—*Craig Jessop, music director, Mormon Tabernacle Choir*

saying to the nation and to the world: 'We value the contribution of this organization that has remained steadfast for more than a century.' To be part of this choir is one of the greatest blessings of life."

To receive the honor, Christensen, Jessop, and Longhurst had flown to Washington from England, where they were on an advance trip for the Choir's 2005 tour. They announced the tour to the United Kingdom that evening as they shared the news of the National Medal of Arts award. They had little more than a week's notice that the Choir was to be recognized and had to wait for the White House to announce the prestigious award.

Mack Wilberg, associate director, described the experience as "magnificent," adding, "It was much more than I had anticipated, and you were on our minds during the entire period. Thank you to all of you and all who have come before us."

The Presidential Inaugural Committee requests the honor of your presence to attend and participate in the Inauguration of

Ronald Wilson Reagan

as President of the United States of America and

George Herbert Walker Bush

as Vice President of the United States of America on Tuesday the twentieth of January one thousand nine hundred and eighty one in the City of Washington

Co-Chairmen Robert K. Gray Charles Z. Wick

The Choir has sung for every president since Eisenhower and at many inaugurals since Lyndon B. Johnson. By special request the Choir's float in the Reagan inaugural parade stopped before the viewing stand to pay tribute to the new president with their famous "Battle Hymn of the Republic." The president and his wife joined in the singing.

Recipients for 2003 include (left to right) blues musician Buddy Guy, dancer Suzanne Farrell, children's author Beverly Cleary, actor/producer/director Ron Howard, President Mac Christensen on behalf of the Mormon Tabernacle Choir, arts educator Rafe Esquith, and Broadway performer Tommy Tune.

Stan Parrish, assistant to the choir president, told the Choir that the National Medal of Arts was first awarded by President Ronald Reagan. "It is the highest honor for artistic excellence in the country," Parrish explained as choir members passed the bronze disc around the choir loft. He read the citation of the award "to those individuals and organizations who have made extraordinary contributions to the creation, support, and growth of arts in the United States."

Soon after Charles Osgood, newsman and composer, completed his musical composition of the Pledge of Allegiance, he sent off a copy to choir directors Jessop and Wilberg to get their impression. They immediately added it in a new patriotic CD, Spirit of America, *and invited Osgood to perform with the Choir at Lincoln Center's Avery Fisher Hall to kick-off the seventy-five-year celebration of the broadcast. Said Osgood of the opportunity, "It's quite something to listen to 360 voices and a symphony orchestra perform something you wrote."*

writers, journalists, or cartoonists want an image that bespeaks "large," they often use the Choir.

President Ronald Reagan called them America's Choir. The name stuck. When they sing "Give me your tired, your poor," they can look back to ancestors or their own odyssey and understand the telling phrases "Send these, the homeless, tempest-tossed to me." Welsh, British, Irish, Polynesian, African, Scandinavian, Latin, Canadian, European— their heritage is uniquely "American." *Higher* to them is not above others; it is where they look to God.

At the tragedy of 9/11, the LDS Church First Presidency asked the Choir to shift an already scheduled concert to a memorial service. Craig Jessop and the Choir counted it an honor. "As we sang 'America the Beautiful,'" soprano Andrea Powell recalls, "the phrase 'thine alabaster cities gleam' reminded me that there were beautiful buildings still standing and that we are courageous and strong as a country."

Their music is never about them. It is about those who come to listen, to be filled, to find what they are missing—inside. Theirs is "soul" music that touches as well as sounds. It brings a spirit that feels *higher*. "The choir members come to this work with a high sense of purpose, a very strong unify-

ing sense of mission, and when they perform you can sense this spirituality, this deep inner commitment musically and spiritually to what they are doing," states John Longhurst, Tabernacle organist since 1977. "It's as pervasive as the music itself. People come to the Tabernacle and speak not only of what they hear but also of what they feel."

Broadcaster Walter Cronkite, who for decades presented the news to Americans from his anchor desk, said following a guest artist appearance with the Choir in December 2002, "Truly this experience touched my heart."

This is America's Choir on the road or on the air. *Stronger* because it is building on the foundation of singers, conductors, announcers, librarians, engineers, cameramen, writers, and composers who went before. *Stronger* because of the addition of the Orchestra at Temple Square and the Temple Square Chorale and its affiliation with Deseret Book, distributor for its new label. *Stronger* because of the leadership of President Gordon B. Hinckley, who for thirty-seven years has been the advisor to the Choir.

Heart, song, and spirit are the substance of the Mormon Tabernacle Choir.

Swifter, higher, stronger.

"I asked Jimmy Stewart why he was willing to do this small show," Michael McLean, director of Mr. Krueger's Christmas explains, "and he said, 'I have always felt that we needed to put the emphasis on what Christmas is really all about, and this story does that.' Then he smiled and said, 'The chance to stand in front of that choir that I have adored my whole life was just impossible to resist.'"

In the past three decades the Choir has sung with an impressive list of performers, including conductors Robert Shaw, Leonard Bernstein, Sir David Willcocks, Michael Tilson Thomas, Julius Rudel, John Williams, Rafael Frübeck de Burgos, and Keith Lockhart. Performers who have shared the stage with the Choir include Kiri Te Kanawa, Robert Merrill, Bryn Terfel, Marilyn Horne, Richard Stoltzman, Evelyn Glennie, Moses Hogan, Maureen McGovern, Gladys Knight, Roma Downey, Megan Follows, Walter Cronkite, Jimmy Stewart, the Canadian Brass, the King's Singers (pictured above), the U.S. Air Force Band, and the Singing Sergeants, to name a few. Says soloist Frederica von Stade, "I don't know if the public realizes this but, when these events take place, there are ducks that sail on the top of the water, and they are the soloists and the Choir and Orchestra, and then there are the feet that are going underneath the water, holding it all together and working like mad, and they are Craig and Mack."

Choir member Ron Gunnell has the assignment for special projects. He has arranged for guest artists Walter Cronkite, Angela Lansbury, Bryn Terfel, and others. He says of his experience with Walter Cronkite, "I told him that singing with the Choir was a life-changing experience for Angela Lansbury, and I assured him it would be the same for him." After three days in Salt Lake City, Cronkite said to Gunnell, "You assured me when we first met, this experience would change my life. My only regret is that I didn't do this earlier in my life. The way we were treated, the time we spent with the Choir, it was a truly life-changing experience."

ONE

COME, COME, YE SAINTS

A Choir Is Born

We'll make the air with music ring,
Shout praises to our God and King . . .
Oh, how we'll make this chorus swell—
All is well! All is well!

JULY 24, 1847. A vanguard wagon train of trail-weary Saints entered the Valley of the Great Salt Lake. Three weeks later, a ragtag chorus of men, their faces and hands worn from the quick work of putting down roots in the desert, gathered under the shade of a crude brush bowery to sing praises to God. It was an unlikely setting for worship. An unlikely choir.

Their raised voices were the only ones for thousands of miles, and their hallelujahs were not typical of the brash western adventurers or earnest homesteaders seeking land and promise. These were religious folk, driven from their homes in the East—again and again. Trekking to the wilderness of the Great Basin, they found only sagebrush, salt beds, mountains, and streams. The solitude was welcomed. Heartily. And they expressed their relief in an anthem that in the past century and a half has become the signature of this people: "Oh, how we'll make this chorus swell—All is well! All is well!"

The magic and genius of the Mormon Tabernacle Choir is that it is not built around a personality or an individual. Craig Jessop says, "We've seen great choruses—Robert Shaw, Roger Wagner, Norman Luboff—they've all come and gone. They've been built on personalities. But the Mormon Tabernacle Choir is not. It's built around faith in the gospel of Jesus Christ."

President Gordon B. Hinckley has worked with the Choir for more than half a century. He has encouraged the members time and again, congratulated them, and personally thanked many of the guest artists. "Without a doubt," he states, "this is the greatest choir in the world."

That simple choir is today the Mormon Tabernacle Choir. Nationally acclaimed and internationally respected, the Choir has sung its way into the American soul through radio, television, recordings, and concerts. "Choral music has everything to do with the spirit and quality of the soul that is engaging and generating the sound," Craig Jessop, the Choir's music director, contends. "The Choir is flourishing today because of its heritage and the sense of responsibility carried forward one choir leader, one member, at a time."

The Mormon pioneers fled the Union in 1846, taking with them only what would fit in their wagons. And in their hearts. Their luggage was the stuff of which they were made: courage, tenacity, reliance upon one another, faith in God, and grit. In the evenings, men, women, and children gathered by the prairie fires and raised their voices in song: "We'll find the place which God for us prepared, Far away in the West."

Early efforts to settle the desert basin of the Great Salt Lake no doubt distracted pioneers from singing much more than on Sunday. They faced hard-baked earth, not the rich farmland they had left behind in the Mississippi River Valley. They also faced crickets that gobbled up crops, a short growing season, and little extra to supply the constant stream of converts arriving with practically nothing. It was what many of the Saints had expected.

Come, come, ye Saints, no toil nor labor fear;
But with joy wend your way.
Though hard to you this journey may appear,
Grace shall be as your day.
'Tis better far for us to strive
Our useless cares from us to drive;
Do this, and joy your hearts will swell—
All is well! All is well!

Today, "Come, Come, Ye Saints" is recognized around the world and heralded. Doran K. Antrim, writer for the *Denver Post,* wrote in 1956 of the anthem's power: "Not long ago I heard the Choir sing in the Tabernacle. It seemed as though I were standing atop a hill with a strong wind blowing, blowing me and the world clean. From the powerful voice of the choir, I caught the undaunted spirit of 'Come, Come, Ye Saints—All is Well,' the spirit that keeps hoping when there seems no reason to

I LOVE THE SONG "COME, COME, YE SAINTS." NO MATTER WHAT OTHERS SAY, TO ME THAT IS THEIR SIGNATURE SONG. WHEN [THE LATTER-DAY SAINTS] HAD A LOT OF TOUGH TIMES, THEY KEPT SINGING AND KEPT GOING, AND THAT IS THE WAY IT IS WITH EVERYONE'S LIFE. I LIKE TO HEAR THIS CHOIR SING; I HAVE ALL THEIR RECORDINGS; AND IF THEY DON'T COME BACK EAST OFTEN, I'LL GO OUT THERE. —*Sue Coblentz, Iowa, 2003*

hope. This is the message that all people must get when they hear these lifted voices."

Music in the early Church also included bands, fifes, fiddles, and eventually orchestras. The Nauvoo Brass Band played at evening campfires and hired out for funerals and festivities at settlements they passed. Before a concert at a nearby community, William Clayton recorded, "One of the grocery keepers invited us to play him a tune, which we did. He then invited us in and offered to treat us to anything he had. We each took a little and then the next grocery keeper sent an invitation for us to play him a tune. We did so and he also gave us anything he had. A bee keeper next sent word that he did not want us to slight him and we went and played him a tune." They pocketed twenty-five dollars.

George James related another incident when "the band played the merriest airs, and all that could . . . engaged in the fun-making, which several Iowans, who were attracted to the camp out of curiosity went away saying they could scarcely believe their own eyes at seeing a people fleeing from civilization . . . thus passing away their time."

Colonel Kane

We'll make the air with music ring,
Shout praises to our God and King;
Above the rest these words we'll tell—
All is well! All is well!

Friend of the Saints Colonel Thomas L. Kane described the Mormon pattern of singing "sweet music winding over the uninhabited country, [as] something in the style of a Moravian death-tune blown at daybreak." In 1847, while visiting the Mormon encampments on the Missouri, German-

born traveler Rudolph Kurz observed, "I enjoyed, especially, . . . the singing of [their] choirs. When they met together for choir practice one evening in every week, I found real pleasure in hearing them sing. What made this particularly enjoyable was the fact that in the western part of the United States choir music was so seldom heard."

Welsh converts arriving in the Salt Lake Valley are credited with establishing the choral tradition. In the mid-nineteenth century, thousands who hailed from the Welsh coast of Swansea, the farm lands of Caermarthenshire, and the coal regions of Merthyr Tydfil grabbed hold of the new religion and began emigrating to what they called Zion. As their vessels pulled away from the dock of their homeland, the Welsh voices chorused a favorite hymn to the cheers of those yet to come.

Singing was far more natural for the Welsh

The Choir performed at the dedication of the rebuilt Nauvoo Temple, June 27–30, 2002. Divided into four choirs of eighty singers each, the group sang for ten of the thirteen sessions, which paid tribute to the Prophet Joseph Smith and the Saints who gave so much to that early era of LDS Church history. The Choir also broadcast Music and the Spoken Word *from Nauvoo and performed a benefit concert in Quincy, Illinois, in tribute to the early residents who took in the Saints fleeing the mobs in Missouri.*

harmony in their native tongue, he said, "I don't understand the words, but you should become the nucleus of a great church choir." Little did he know that these Welsh had crossed the Atlantic holding choir practice aboard ship. Sixty-year-old John Parry, a distinguished former preacher and stonemason from North Wales, had kept those who signed up for the choir to a practice regimen: 10:00 to 11:30 mornings and 4:00 to 5:00 afternoons. At Winter Quarters and then out on the plains, in the company of leader George A. Smith, Parry directed what they called the George Smith Company Choir.

Once in Salt Lake, Parry rehearsed the newly commissioned choir each evening, but the pressures of frontier life soon pushed the practices to twice weekly. The choir sang mostly patriotic songs and hymns and were regularly featured on programs for the two major holidays, the fourth and the twenty-fourth of July. The choir performed at General Conference and other Church gatherings, establishing a pattern and a purpose that is the core of the Choir's schedule today.

than driving a team of oxen across the heartland of America. One emigrant reported, "I was in the road part of the time and that was when I was crossing it." But in evening hours, music filled the barren plains. "As we sang the first part of the verse," William Morgan, a forty-six-year-old engineer from Merthyr Tydfil, reported, "we saw the English and the Norwegians and everyone . . . with their heads out of their wagons. With the second part the wagons were empty in an instant and their inhabitants running toward us as if they were charmed. . . . Some asked me where they had learned and who was their teacher? I said that the hills of Wales were the schoolhouse, and the Spirit of God was the teacher."

Their leader, Captain Dan Jones, wrote on October 12, 1849, "The Welsh are holding up under the difficulties of this journey, and are learning to drive oxen better than any expectations, and are winning praise from all the other camps of the Saints for their organization, their virtue and their skill, and especially for their singing."

In 1850 when Church leader Brigham Young heard the Welsh converts singing four-part

The first company of Welsh emigrants left for America in 1849 under the direction of Captain Dan Jones. He wrote of their departure from Liverpool, "On Monday, the 26th of February about two o'clock in the afternoon, we set sail from the port, and all the Saints, accompanied by the harp, sang 'The Saints' Farewell' as we left the dock. Their sweet voices resounded throughout the city, attracting the attention of and causing amazement to thousands of spectators who followed us along the shore as if charmed."

O GOD, OUR HELP IN AGES PAST

"The Spirit of God" was sung by the early Saints before the completion of the Kirtland Temple, but its majesty and spiritual significance was established when it was sung at the dedicatory services of that temple on March 27, 1836. The scene reflected the fervor of the dedication of the Temple of Solomon: "And it came to pass, as the trumpeters and singers were as one, . . . and when they lifted up their voice . . . and praised the Lord, saying, For he is good; for his mercy endureth forever; that then . . . the glory of the Lord had filled the House of God."

J. Spencer Cornwall

From its early days in upstate New York, The Church of Jesus Christ of Latter-day Saints has used singing as a means of drawing close to the Lord. The first services for the newly organized church on April 6, 1830, included hymn singing. Just months later Joseph Smith announced that the Lord by revelation had instructed Emma Smith—his wife and a musician—to make a selection of sacred hymns to be used in worship. Joseph announced that the Lord had stated, "My soul delighteth in the song of the heart; yea, the song of the righteous is a prayer unto me."

Emma's first hymnbook, published in 1835 with ninety hymns, included twenty-nine by LDS convert William Wines Phelps, who assisted in the production of the book. Looking back at that first hymnal, choir conductor J. Spencer Cornwall praised the effort, saying that the songs selected "are among the best of all Christian hymns." Included were Samuel Medley's "I Know That My Redeemer Lives," first published in 1789, and James Montgomery's "A Poor Wayfaring Man of Grief," which was immortalized in 1844 when John Taylor sang it for the Prophet Joseph Smith shortly before his martyrdom at Carthage Jail.

No music was included in the first volume of hymns, though editions that followed made reference to familiar melodies to accompany the lyrics. By 1844 seven other hymnals had been published, some of them in Great Britain. It would be 1889 before the Church would produce an official psalmody with verses and music.

Cornwall explained, "Music goes beyond words and carries one into the realm of mute feeling—which is so true of hymn music. Hymn singing is a cherished religious practice of both the high and the lowly." Popular in the Christian culture were "gospel hymns" that expressed fear, sorrow, lamentations for sin, incessant emphasis on the sufferings of the Lord at the crucifixion, and the inevitable eternal tortures awaiting sinners. In contrast, Latter-day Saints crafted hymns that expressed hope, love of God, joy, and gratitude for sins forgiven. LDS music "breathes optimism and not pessimism," Evan Stephens, choir director at the end of the nineteenth century, observed. It is "music in which the sombre must not predominate, but be used only as a means of contrast to heighten the effects of the bright." "Sacred earnestness touched with joy" characterized the new hymns of the Restoration. These songs connected the faith of the members to the Church's new doctrines and served as both spiritual companions and tutors. LDS Church historian B. H. Roberts later noted, "It would be expected that the highly religious emotions attendant upon the religious events of the Church of the New Dispensation, would be to give birth to a . . . music of a somewhat special kind."

In 1830 music was in its infancy in the United States. Public orchestras or singing societies, concerts, operas, and chamber-music recitals were few to non-existent. The music-publishing business had yet to be initiated. Yet in 1835 Joseph Smith established singing schools in Kirtland, Ohio, to teach note reading and vocal technique. In Kirtland the Saints built a grand temple that included four singers' galleries on the main floor. A "singing department" was organized on January 4, 1836, with Marvel Chapin Davis as singing master. The singers—qualified only by willingness and interest—met two nights a week. Joseph Smith, after a visit to a rehearsal, described the singers as having "performed admirably." Driven from Ohio to Missouri and then Illinois, the Saints may have carried a song in their hearts: "O God, our help in ages past."

Richard L. Evans, originator of the sermonettes in *Music and the Spoken Word,* said of that time, "Back in New England and New York and through Illinois, small congregations were beginning to grow up under the leadership of Joseph Smith and were becoming a singing people, fond of the art and deeply interested in the world's finest culture and music."

A choir tradition was born.

Choir members are both musical ambassadors and missionaries with the charge to open hearts and doors to Jesus Christ and his restored Church. With the leadership of President Mac Christensen and additional Church authorities—Elder Spencer Condie traveled with the Choir on the 2003 tour as did Elder Glenn Pace—the Choir exemplifies how a large volunteer group can continue to excel.

At the 1852 conference in the adobe tabernacle on Temple Square, the loosely organized choir adopted the name of its surroundings: the name "Tabernacle Choir" was born. The next year, 1853, President Young sent John Parry back to Wales on a mission to establish a choir among the members, and Stephen Goddard, choir leader from Nauvoo, Illinois, took over the Choir. James Smithies followed him, and then well-trained British conductor Charles John Thomas was handed the baton. Brigham Young had heard his choir—well-trained and engaging—and saw potential to improve the Tabernacle Choir under his direction. Reports indicate that C. J., as they called Charles John Thomas, inherited as few as twelve singers. Still, he left a legacy. Said one of his peers, "It may be said that his advent into these valleys marked an epoch in the early musical history of Utah."

More than a century later, the influence of the Welsh and English on the Choir is still visible. J. Spencer Kinard, then voice for *Music and the Spoken Word,* recalls, "In 1982 the Choir toured England, where the roots of the choir members go deep. The British contribution to the Choir was graphically illustrated at the conclusion of a concert in London's Royal Albert Hall. I stood and asked all members of the Choir with British ancestry to stand. The majority of the 350-voice choir rose to their feet."

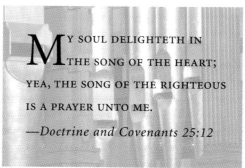

MY SOUL DELIGHTETH IN THE SONG OF THE HEART; YEA, THE SONG OF THE RIGHTEOUS IS A PRAYER UNTO ME.

—*Doctrine and Covenants 25:12*

Gird up your loins; fresh courage take.
Our God will never us forsake;
And soon we'll have this tale to tell—
All is well! All is well!

Tabernacle Choir directors helped shape the music tradition and culture of the new Zion. Of the first five choir directors, four of them emigrated from Great Britain. Collectively, they served two

decades and saw the Choir grow from a disparate band of thankful pioneers singing in a brush-covered hut to a chorus of hundreds singing in the great new Tabernacle, then the centerpiece of Temple Square. They offered melodious treatment of hymns and songs and introduced scores of listeners to the holy influence of song. Others expressed the music in their very souls and fostered musical talent throughout the territory. Communities outside Salt Lake—Huntsville, Plain City, Franklin, Grantsville, Ogden, Fillmore, Logan—sponsored choirs as well and were invited to join with the Salt Lake Tabernacle Choir, as it was initially named, on many occasions. Minutes of choir rehearsal in 1880 report that the conductor "spoke of a scarcity of singers during Conference and suggested that we adopt the plan of sending music to be sung in Conference out to the members of some of the country choirs, soliciting their aid."

In the pioneers' fight for survival, Brigham Young encouraged participation in music and theater to lift the spirits and bring added spiritual blessings. The first singing schools opened in the territory in 1851. In the years to come, names like John Park, John Tullidge, and David O. Calder left their imprint on early music training. Two

Praise to the Lord, the Almighty

Through the ages, music has given voice to worship of the Almighty. The ancients spoke of song and celebration of God with both reverence and spirit. Old Testament prophet Isaiah's poetic words have inspired hosts of believers through the ages: "The Lord Jehovah is my strength and my song." New Testament apostle Paul wrote, "I will sing with the spirit, and I will sing with the understanding also." The Psalmist recorded, "Let us sing unto the Lord: let us make a joyful noise to the rock of our salvation." That "rock" has generated musical tones that have lifted the spirits of a people and their nation. It has connected them to Divinity.

The Israelites of old asked, "How shall we sing the Lord's song in a strange land?" Another band of wanderers in another dispensation—Latter-day Saints—asked the same question as they crossed the frontier plains, fleeing their nation in the mid-1800s. Theirs, like the ancients, was a commitment born of belief in the Almighty. They knew that somehow, somewhere, God was there for them. Could they not have sung on such a perilous journey, "I sing the mighty power of God, that made the mountains rise"?

The Choir's repertoire is filled with singing praises to the Savior of the world. Invited to sing with the Jerusalem Symphony in the winter of 1992–1993, these Saints sang where angels had sung at Shepherds' Field. Soprano Carol Mahlum recalls "listening to the sound echo around the valley long after the Choir stopped singing." They sang at the Mount of Olives, the Garden Tomb, and the Sea of Galilee, places holy to all of Christendom.

hundred students registered in 1861 for voice instruction with the Deseret Musical Association, which taught tonic solfège notation; in 1871 the Philharmonic Society advertised vocal classes on Thursday evening for two dollars per quarter, payable in advance.

Nellie Druce Pugsley, who became a regular soloist with the Choir, wrote, "Many were the afternoons I listened at home to my mother and [others] singing through operas and oratorios." She made her first public appearance as a singer at fifteen and in the years to come received top billing:

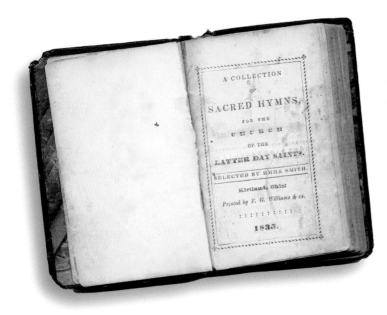

No religious movement has ever started without the aid of hymns. Fifty years after Emma Smith made selections for the first hymnal, Church president John Taylor directed Tabernacle Choir conductors Evan Stephens, George Careless, and Ebenezer Beesley, along with organist Joseph Daynes, to compose hymns specifically for the Tabernacle Choir. They responded with more than thirty.

"Nellie Druce Pugsley sang 'Gospel Restoration,' assisted by the Tabernacle Choir."

There were choirs in many of the fledgling settlements sprinkled up and down the corridor of Deseret, as the territory had been named. Early pioneers arriving in the Great Basin were often dispatched to outlying areas. The first groups settled 20 to 50 miles out, the next 100, and so on. The contingents were assigned according to skills and talents: carpenters, stonemasons, farmers, teachers, shopkeepers—and musicians. Early accounts speak of the hunger and devastations that plagued the people those first years. James Smithies recorded in his journal that on the advice of visiting Indian parties, several of the locals went in search of the sego lily, a wild plant, whose roots were said to be more nutritious than others. "I went out to dig roots, for this is our principal living," he related. "Roots and milk with a little meal."

Robert Sands, an Irishman, directed the Choir in the old Tabernacle and led the singing of an expanded choir for the dedicatory services of the Great Tabernacle when it opened October 6, 1867.

We'll make the air with music ring,
Shout praises to our God and King;
Above the rest these words we'll tell—
All is well! All is well!

IN THE HEART OF EVERY MEMBER OF THE CHOIR IS A RELIGIOUS CONVICTION. THERE IS FAITH UNWAVERING IN GOD OUR ETERNAL FATHER AND IN HIS BELOVED SON, THE SAVIOR OF THE WORLD. THEY SING ANTHEMS TO THE ALMIGHTY WITH A CONVICTION OF HIS REALITY AS THE FATHER OF ALL MANKIND. THEY SING PRAISES TO HIS BEGOTTEN SON WITH LOVE AND CERTAIN KNOWLEDGE OF HIM AS THE SAVIOR AND REDEEMER OF MANKIND.

—*President Gordon B. Hinckley,*
The Church of Jesus Christ
of Latter-day Saints

Simple Gifts

On the Choir's maiden tour—to American Fork—the members had prepared to honor George Careless, who had recently stepped down as conductor. On behalf of the Choir, C. R. Savage exhibited to the assembly a beautiful fifteen-inch baton that had been inscribed by the members of the Tabernacle Choir as a token of respect. The baton was made of mountain mahogany, heavily encased with native gold and rimmed with silver. The case was inscribed, "Presented to George Careless by the Tabernacle Choir. A souvenir of fourteen years of friendship."

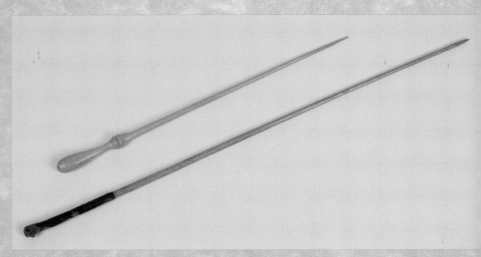

The choir minutes for Friday, September 10, 1880, "report that over $30 had been subscribed to the baton fund; that the letter and baton for Br. Careless would be ready in time."

Presentation of a baton came to be an expression of gratitude from the Choir, a tradition continued today. In 2002 guest conductor Walter Cronkite was presented with a baton etched on the end with the Choir's logo of the Tabernacle organ

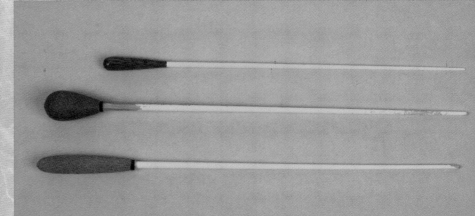

pipes and resting in a beautiful cherrywood case. In 2002 Charles Allyn crafted batons from the wood flooring for the reconstructed Nauvoo Temple and finished them as he had the building's windows and doors. They were presented to Craig Jessop, Mack Wilberg, and Barlow Bradford and used at the temple dedication. Jessop's joined his baton collection, which includes one from the wood of the Joseph Smith cabin, one from a shingle on the Carthage Jail, and one from a tree in Iowa near the riverbank where William Clayton wrote "Come, Come, Ye Saints."

Barlow Bradford was the first director of the Orchestra at Temple Square. In four years he built a remarkable ensemble, one capable of performing at the level of the Mormon Tabernacle Choir.

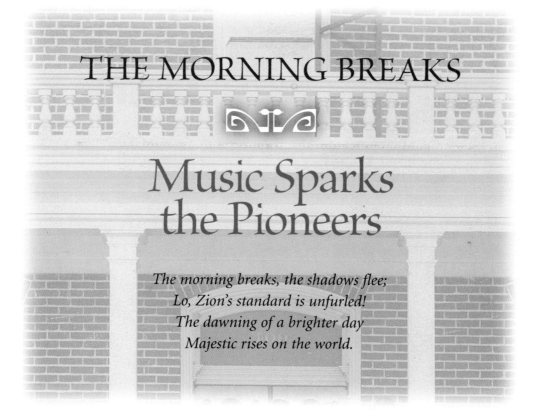

THE MORNING BREAKS

Music Sparks the Pioneers

The morning breaks, the shadows flee;
Lo, Zion's standard is unfurled!
The dawning of a brighter day
Majestic rises on the world.

WHEN PRESIDENT BRIGHAM YOUNG appointed George Careless as "Chief Musician for the Church" with the charge to take over the Tabernacle Choir, he directed him to "lay a foundation for good music." Careless was up to the task. He had studied violin, piano, harmony, counterpoint, instrumentation, voice-building, and conducting under some of the best in Britain. He was both a prolific composer and a gifted conductor. But the convert Careless had been counseled to put his religion ahead of his profession, and the young musician emigrated to Zion. Sailing to America on the *Hudson* in June 1864, he and his fellow Saints were a curiosity to the ship's captain, who had observed and listened to their singing during the ten-week crossing of the Atlantic. While unloading, the captain asked Careless for a song. He obliged, on the spot composing music to a poem by Parley P. Pratt, "The Morning Breaks." He then gathered his choir together, and they sang one last time for the captain.

In 1852 Brigham Young said, "Some wise being organized my system, and gave me my capacity, put into my heart and brain something that delights, charms, and fills me with rapture at the sound of sweet music. I did not put it there; it was some other being. As one of the modern writers has said, 'Music hath charms to soothe the savage beast.' It has been proved that sweet music will actually tame the most malicious and venomous beasts. . . . Who gave the lower animals a love for those sweet sounds, which with magic power fill the air with harmony, and cheer and comfort the hearts of men, and so wonderfully affect the brute creation? It was the Lord, our Heavenly Father, who gave the capacity to enjoy these sounds, and which we ought to do in His name, and to His glory."

Arriving in the Salt Lake Valley, Careless found that several other Brits had already set up music schools and secured the willing students. Careless gave himself two years to establish himself in the music field and hoped he wouldn't starve. Brigham Young recognized his talent and called him to direct the Tabernacle Choir. The two discussed potential music. President Young favored sweet and melodious music, while Careless pushed for music that represented the faith, courage, hope, and vigor of the Saints. President Young yielded. The Choir met in the Old Tabernacle, though it was too small to hold the Saints for services. A crude structure on the southwest corner of the Temple Block, it did house an organ brought over from Australia. But it was more like a potato cellar, built partially underground about six steps down. Uncomfortably cold and dark, it seemed a curious setting for singing the songs of Zion.

During Sunday services, Careless "composed a sacramental tune for the following Sunday which the brethren would copy for the Friday rehearsal and we would sing the next Sunday." A visitor from the East Coast commented after attending the 2:00 P.M. Sunday service at the Tabernacle, "A hymn is announced by some brother in a business coat whom you will meet in trade tomorrow, perhaps, and sung by the choir, for though the tune may be one of the old familiar ones, the audience does not

Edward P. Kimball, Tabernacle organist from 1905 to 1937, was at the organ for the first broadcast in 1929. Like those who also have sat at that keyboard, he understood that the organ is quite unlike any other instrument. The room in which it is housed serves as its soundboard and has a very significant influence on the effect of the organ. The Tabernacle organ is recognized as one of the largest and one of the most acclaimed in the world.

join in the singing." It was not until the demands of the weekly broadcasts, more than fifty years later, became so taxing that the presidency of the Church relieved the Choir of singing for the Sunday afternoon services. At first other choirs were invited to participate, but it was not long before those gatherings were discontinued altogether in favor of local ward meetings.

On July 4, 1873, the *Deseret News* reported the first concert held in the new Tabernacle "outside of Church services, . . . at 4:30 in the afternoon as there was no lighting in the building." Appropriately, the program was intended to "do justice" to the anniversary of national independence and included "a rare and rich musical treat" with a guest cantatrice, Madame Anna Bishop, and her troupe, assisted by the "regular Tabernacle Choir." George Careless conducted the concert with Frank Gilder at the organ. Tickets cost twenty-five and fifty cents.

The glory bursting from afar
Wide o'er the nations soon will shine.

The Tabernacle had no lights. It also had no heat, prompting relocation of rehearsals in the winter. The choir minutes noted, "The temperature of the weather having made it too cold to meet in the Tabernacle for rehearsals on Friday evenings, on this date an adjournment was had to Social Hall, arrangements having been made to hold rehearsals there until the approach of warm weather next spring."

The choir rolls in the 1870s listed some eighty-five members—absences were common—and Careless augmented those numbers by regularly inviting more than a dozen local groups to join his chorus. Conference sessions often featured more than 300 voices in the combined choir.

Careless was restless, not content to simply sing the songs of Zion. In 1876 he produced and directed one of the first performances of Handel's *Messiah* west of the Mississippi. A remarkable feat, the performance required extensive rehearsals and the combining of Salt Lake's Tabernacle Choir with many non-Mormons. The Salt Lake Theatre was

Lead, Kindly Light

Charles John Thomas

"The personality, sincerity, and musical background of the conductor of a choir ultimately decide the failure or success of the whole organization," Frank Asper, Tabernacle organist, observed in 1941. "Every conductor must love the work, and he must have the power to make the choir love it as well. He must possess full confidence in himself and thus inspire confidence in those under his direction. He must know within himself that he can make this chorus of voices sing to such good purpose that they will reach to the inmost thoughts and hearts of the congregation."

Each conductor has brought a certain style, sought a certain sound, and developed a discipline. Craig Jessop believes that "every conductor has a different choral aesthetic. You cannot separate what the conductor's ear is drawn to and wants to hear. I've always preferred an enlarged lower sectional sound. Consequently, I have increased the second alto and second bass sections of the Choir. I conceive choral music

Jay E. Welch

as much like the shape of a pyramid, with a broad-based lower end and a lighter top."

Highly acclaimed Tabernacle organist Alexander Schreiner was acquainted with a century of choir conductors, from George Careless to Jerold Ottley. He spoke of

Donald H. Ripplinger

Careless as one who "wrote many hymn melodies, many of them still loved and sung by our people in church." Evan Stephens "led only with up-beats, vigorous and inspiring. It was impossible then to sing flat; the singers appeared to be hypnotized." Lund, said Schreiner, favored a "symphonic clip" that brought out the perspiration and happiness of the singers and the smiles of Lund. J. Spencer Cornwall had a "very artistic expression in slight variations in tempo, avoiding the metronomic dullness sometimes used." Richard P. Condie "drove the choir to great accomplishment" in Columbia recordings. Jerold Ottley, said Schreiner, will be remembered for his "ever-increasing artistry and stirring conducting."

The Tabernacle Choir has had fourteen conductors, assistant conductors, and a host of guests who have stepped up to

Richard P. Condie

wave the baton. Keith Lockhart, conductor of the Choir's neighbor, the Utah Symphony, and of their Independence Day stage partner, the Boston Pops, describes conducting the Choir: "The most amazing thing about the Choir, especially when you get to work with them as I have the last few years, is the sound that they produce. It is an amazingly well-blended sound that comes from a lack of egos, really, 350 people who are committed to singing together, and a large enough body that no one has to force to be heard, so the sound is just enveloping, it's all-surrounding, and it's frankly just wonderful to be in the middle of when you are conducting."

Conductors who have led the Mormon Tabernacle Choir since its creation include:

John Parry (1849–1854)

Stephen Goddard (1854–1856)

James Smithies (1856–1862)

Charles John Thomas (1862–1865)

Robert Sands (1865–1869)

George Careless (1869–1880)

Ebenezer Beesley (1880–1889)

Thomas C. Griggs, assistant

Evan Stephens (1889–1916)

Horace S. Ensign, assistant

Anthony C. Lund (1916–1935)

B. Cecil Gates, assistant

Albert J. Southwick, assistant

J. Spencer Cornwall (1935–1957)

Albert J. Southwick, assistant

D. Sterling Wheelwright, assistant

John R. Halliday, assistant

Richard P. Condie, assistant

Richard P. Condie (1957–1974)

Jay E. Welch, assistant

Jay E. Welch (1974)

Jerold D. Ottley, assistant

Robert C. Bowden, assistant

Jerold D. Ottley (1975–1998)

Donald H. Ripplinger, associate

Craig Jessop, associate

Craig Jessop (1999–)

Mack Wilberg, associate

Barlow Bradford, associate (1999–2003)

filled to capacity for the presentation, and the concert received rave reviews: "To musical adepts who understand what a worthy execution of a complete oratorial composition means, this performance of the 'Messiah' in Salt Lake City may fitly be considered as one of the capital events in the musical history of America."

In 1877 Careless bid farewell to the Church leader who had given him his start, President Brigham Young, who had passed away in August at the age of seventy-six. The Tabernacle "was entirely filled, as were the aisles and doorways, and every available standing place. The congregation within the building numbered at least 12,000, while thousands of persons unable to obtain admission were in the grounds of the Tabernacle, or in the streets outside." The funeral services began at noon with Careless leading the choir of 220 voices in two numbers: "Hark, from Afar, a Funeral Knell" and "Thou Dost Not Weep to Weep Alone." Joseph J. Daynes was at the organ. The Tabernacle Choir began the long tradition of singing tributes at the funeral services of Church presidents and leaders.

By 1880 Careless had resigned from the Choir and turned his attention to his own orchestra and a bold touring schedule.

Twenty-year-old Agnus Olson arrived in Salt Lake on July 16, 1879. She wrote, "On the first Sunday after arriving in Salt Lake City, I attended the services in the Tabernacle; it was all so wonderful to me and I was wondering if I ever would be permitted to become a member of that wonderful choir." At her retirement from the Tabernacle Choir she said, "I have had the privilege and pleasure to sing in the Tabernacle Choir for fifty years, from February 14, 1881 to June 1931. I never stayed away without good cause."

Ebenezer Beesley took over the Choir in 1880.

Ebenezer Beesley left his imprint in conducting, composing, teaching, and compiling a hymnal. A singular force in music in the Church for decades, he was known for his precision, talent, direction, and discipline. The November 4, 1881, minutes of the Choir report his instructions: "At this practice it was carried by motion that in the future those members absenting themselves four practices of the Choir without sending a sufficient excuse would have their names stricken from the roll and that to rejoin they must be represented for membership."

I HAVE HEARD THE HISTORY OF THIS CHORUS, SO IT WAS NOT A SURPRISE THAT IT WAS GOOD. I WOULD NOT HAVE EXPECTED ANYTHING ELSE.

—*Rafael Frübeck de Burgos, Tanglewood Music Festival, 2003*

When the Choir moved into the Tabernacle on Temple Square, the building's acoustics were far from the reputation enjoyed today. Sound quality improved with the addition of the galleries before the Tabernacle was dedicated in 1875. "I love how the acoustics shoot the women's voices across to us," states Steven Hendricks, baritone. "You actually hear them coming from behind you."

By that time Latter-day Saint hymns included both music and lyrics. Singers shared copies, if they had music at all. Until the hectograph was developed, sheet music had to be tediously hand-copied, each part. Beesley inherited a choir library with 182 hymns. Missionaries in England and Europe had purchased much of the Choir's music and contributed it when they returned home. Beesley's longtime efforts in compiling music and lyrics with those of Careless, Evan Stephens, and Joseph Daynes, produced a much-needed psalmody in 1889.

He also introduced new standards to the Choir, adding professionalism to the all-volunteer chorus. Wrote the *Deseret News*, "The Choir contains . . . the elements for much pleasure, being composed of good singers, some excellent instrumental per-

formers and a host of friendly, companionable and whole-souled Latter-day Saints."

Jehovah speaks! Let earth give ear,
And Gentile nations turn and live.
His mighty arm is making bare
His cov'nant people to receive.

Following General Conference in 1884, Beesley noted, "The Choir kept well in tune in every piece, but lacked in execution in some pieces. . . . The latter point of course is due to the incapability of some of the members of the Choir who though they have been recommended by other members are not up to the standard of proficiency that they should be. This defect I shall endeavor to rectify by testing the voice and capability of each new applicant for

On the last day of LDS General Conference, April 6, 1892, the temple capstone was laid. One spectator who staked his place early noted, "As soon as the temple block gates were opened the multitude pressed in and filled the Tabernacle." The aisles and doorways were crowded, and the thousands unable to get near enough to hear the proceedings from the pulpit "got in position to witness the ceremonies" when the Tabernacle services ended.

LAYING THE CAPSTONE OF THE GREAT TEMPLE AT SALT LAKE CITY, UTAH APRIL 6th 1892 — S & J PHOTO SALT LAKE

HOSANNA, HOSANNA TO GOD AND THE LAMB

On April 6, 1893, the Choir sang at the long-awaited dedication of the Salt Lake Temple. It had been forty years in the building. Thomas Griggs, a member of the Tabernacle Choir, arrived at the south gate at 8:20 A.M., but the line was so long, he wrote, that "it was 9:55 A.M. when I was ten feet from the [gate]. Getting desperate I pushed forward and being well known as a soloist of the choir got into the yard and was taken to the south west entrance and hurriedly passed through the rooms, some magnificent, crowding along the jam and reached Bro. E. Stephens who passed me a [choir] book . . . and directed me to be sent into the gathering."

An organ had been set up in the assembly room to accompany the 300-voice choir during the services. The women of the Choir were dressed in white, and the men in dark suits. Annie Wells Cannon wrote, "During the temple dedication the people of Utah had a wonderful and beautiful revelation concerning the divine art [of music]." She continued, "Did any of us really know before the talent of our musicians? From the morning of the first meeting, when the 300 trained voices, under the baton of our admired Evan Stephens, pealed forth those beautiful anthems and hymns . . . there was a continual and delightful surprise."

Noted pioneer photographer and member of the Choir C. R. Savage recorded, "Sang with the choir in the first dedication ceremony in the Temple. Never in my life did I feel an influence like unto the one I felt during the ceremony—every heart was touched with the divinity of our surroundings, . . . my soul was filled with peace, and my whole nature replete with satisfaction."

Guest conductors are a familiar sight before the Choir, but Eagles football coach Andy Reid was a bit out of his element when he accepted the baton from Conductor Jessop and led the Choir at Philadelphia's Mann Theater on July 7, 2003. He told the Church News, *"It was the thrill of thrills. I've been to the Super Bowl; this was right up there."*

membership hereafter." He also noted that the choir loft was crowded, so he implemented a system of "issuing tickets to all singers and having someone appointed to admit only those who have tickets to the seats allotted to the choir." Beesley divided the Choir into eight vocal parts—first and second soprano, alto, tenor, and bass, but he thought of more than just musicianship. At his funeral in 1906 his close associate Augustus W. Carlson paid him tribute as "a man of evenness of temper and of the utmost kindness of heart," noting, "His soul was filled with harmony, which not only found expression in the music that he produced, but it was manifest in everything that he did."

In 1890 Evan Stephens was handed the baton, and a new era for the Tabernacle Choir began. Many choir members retired to give attention to businesses and families, so Stephens, having run a music school, encouraged many of his former students to join. He increased the numbers from 200 to 300 voices.

Self-taught in reading music and playing fife, accordion, and organ, this diminutive Welshman's experience as a choir leader in northern Utah and as organist for the Logan Tabernacle set him on a path to major musical contribution. When he served as a professor of music at the University of Deseret in Salt Lake City, more than 900 people were enrolled in his courses. But it was his composing that distinguished him and left his name and his music in the annals of LDS hymnody to be chorused for generations to come. Born in South Wales, Stephens renewed with the Choir the Welsh flare for choral music with remarkable energy and personal style. His stirring composition "Let the Mountains Shout for Joy" reflected his exuberance for life and music. He was both philosopher and musician: "If mystery is an element of sublimity, as I believe it is claimed, and rightly in literature, our songs are wanting in that element, but they make up for it in practical

MUCH OF THE TEXTS OF THE GREAT ORATORIOS, ESPECIALLY OF HANDEL AND MENDELSSOHN, FIT OUR MODES OF EXPRESSION, AND EVEN THE EXPERIENCE, TRIALS, AND HISTORIC INCIDENTS OF OUR CHURCH SO GENERALLY THAT ONE MIGHT THINK THEY WERE SPECIALLY WRITTEN FOR OUR USE.

—*Evan Stephens, conductor, Mormon Tabernacle Choir*

clearness, devotion, and fervor. Yesterday was the dreamer's day. Today belongs to the active, wide-awake worker, and our religion is pre-eminently in harmony with today, and its unparalleled activity. Our songs and music, to a degree at least, are here again in harmony with our religion, as they should be; and, true to its active, optimistic character, our young people sing:

"'We will work out our salvation, We will cleave unto the truth,

"'We will watch and pray and labor, With the earnest zeal of youth.'"

Karl G. Maeser, German-born educator at the Brigham Young Academy in Provo, Utah, and Tabernacle organist, observed the growing strength of the Choir: "The impetus which the celebrated Tabernacle Choir of Salt Lake City is giving, is felt already to a greater or less extent throughout all . . . of Zion."

Evan Stephens observed his sixty-second birthday on June 28, 1916. Three weeks later he sent a letter to the First Presidency stating that he had served twenty-six years as leader of the Choir, and that he felt his place should now be filled by "a suitable and younger man." The First Presidency accepted his resignation.

Under his care the Choir entered a new era, as did the Church. In 1893 the Church completed the massive, forty-year building project to construct a temple of God next to the Tabernacle but far more grand and expressive of the Saints' reach to heaven. The Choir had sung on Temple Square in the Bowery, the Old Tabernacle, and the new one as the workmen hauled the granite for the temple and lifted it into place. The choirs for the groundbreaking and the laying of the capstone were now singing at the dedication. One of their members was Fred Graham, who years earlier had served as a

WHEN YOU THINK ABOUT PRODUCING CEREMONIES IN ANY LOCATION, YOU LOOK FOR INSTITUTIONS IN THE COMMUNITY THAT ARE STRONG CREATIVELY, THAT REFLECT THE CULTURE AND THE VALUES. . . . I HAVE NEVER HEARD HUMAN VOICES SOUND THE WAY I'VE HEARD THE MORMON TABERNACLE CHOIR SOUND. PART OF IT IS JUST THE ETHIC, THE WORK ETHIC. WHEN YOU GET THAT MANY VOICES, IT IS JUST AMAZING TO HEAR THE CLARITY OF THE ENUNCIATION AND THE PURITY OF THE TONES.
— *Don Mischer, executive producer of the opening ceremony of the 2002 Olympic Winter Games*

water boy for the singers, carrying a bucket with a dipper to choir members during rehearsals.

Evan Stephens prepared the "Hosanna Anthem" for the long-anticipated event. Combined with "The Spirit of God," composed for the Kirtland Temple dedication, the "Hosanna Anthem" is sung at every LDS temple dedication. From the nineteenth century to the twenty-first, the Choir would participate in other history-making temple dedications: in 1955 in Switzerland, at the dedication of the first temple in Europe; and in 2002 at the dedication of the rebuilt Nauvoo Temple in Illinois.

By the close of the century, Stephens had positioned the Mormon Tabernacle Choir to grow in national attention. He is considered by many "the father of Mormon music."

Angels from heav'n and truth from earth
Have met, and both have record borne;
Thus Zion's light is bursting forth
To bring her ransomed children home.

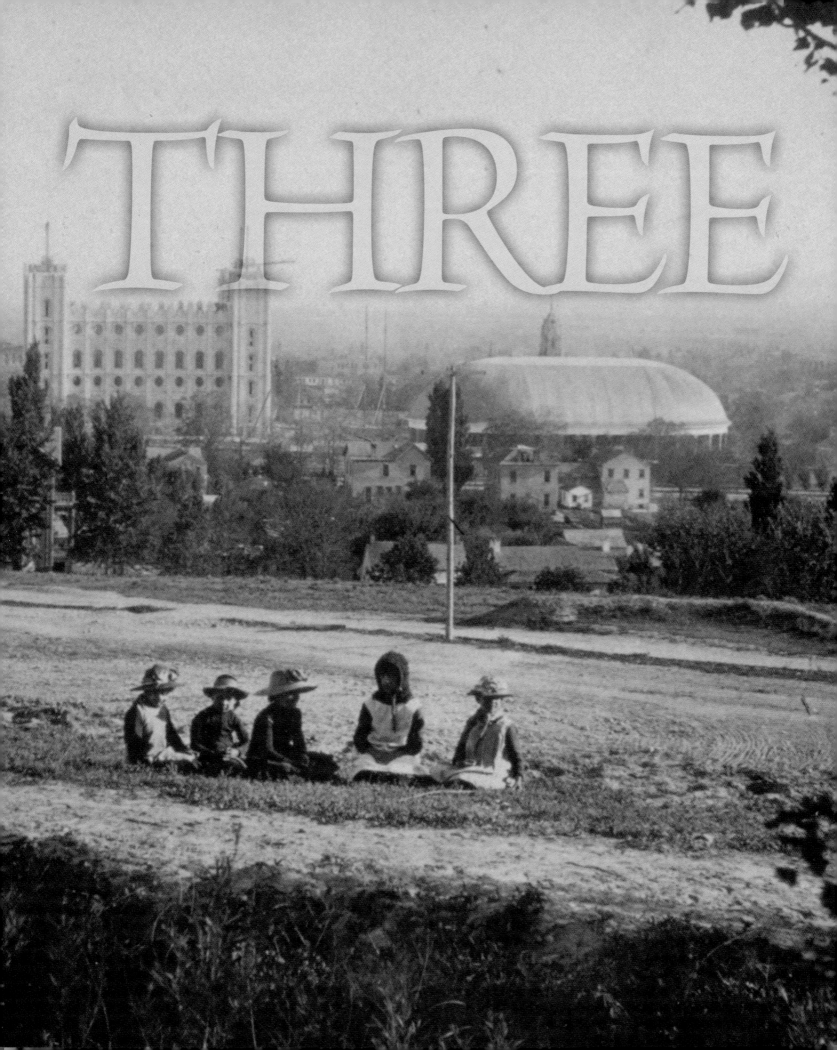

THREE

THOU, GOD,
ART PRESENT THERE

The Tabernacle on Temple Square

I sing the mighty power of God, that made the mountains rise,
That spread the flowing seas abroad and built the lofty skies.
I sing the wisdom that ordained the sun to rule the day;
The moon shines full at God's command, and all the stars obey.

FOR MORE THAN 130 YEARS, the Salt Lake Tabernacle has served as the platform for spreading God's teachings both in music and in word. This unusual pioneer structure is today wired for sound to stretch around the world, yet its rafters are still strapped with the original cowhide like mighty pythons clutching their prey. Its purpose has not changed, though its reach has broadened from a congregation of hopeful and gritty Saints to listeners around the world who prize the good word and goodwill of the lofty tunes. A century after its completion, a visitor to the Tabernacle described it as "a pleasure dome dedicated to God and the souls of men."

The Tabernacle is, in purpose, like the platform designed two thousand years ago in ancient America. In LDS scripture, King Benjamin, in order to speak to the multitudes near the temple in the land of Zarahemla, erected a platform that the multitudes

"might rejoice and be filled with love towards God and all men." The Tabernacle has served as such a setting "that the mysteries of God may be unfolded."

"This pulpit has never been any one man's forum," Stephen L Richards, counselor in the First Presidency, proclaimed in 1952, the 100th anniversary of an earlier Tabernacle structure. "Rather it has been the oracle of a divine dispensation where the cause has overshadowed the man, where humility has higher rating than self-assurance, where worship is measured in deeds rather than protestations."

Worship in tabernacles reaches back to ancient times. Brigham Young in 1846 led God's covenant people on an exodus into the wilderness to escape

The Tabernacle today is home to the Mormon Tabernacle Choir, the daily organ recitals, and the two new music entities, the Orchestra at Temple Square and the Temple Square Chorale.

THE TABERNACLE VAULT, THAT SACRED VAULT, HAS HAD MUSIC MADE IN IT ALMOST EVERY DAY FOR OVER A CENTURY. I DON'T KNOW THAT THERE IS ANOTHER SPACE ON THE PLANET, EVEN SOME OF THE GREAT CATHEDRALS, WHERE MUSIC IS MADE EVERY SINGLE DAY WITHOUT EXCEPTION.

—Craig Jessop, music director, Mormon Tabernacle Choir

oppression, as had Moses dispensations earlier. Both built tabernacles for worship. The Israelite tabernacle, designed to be portable, served as a holy temple; the nineteenth-century Temple Square Tabernacle, designed as a meetinghouse, served the spirited pioneers and today reaches a worldwide broadcast audience.

In April 1844 Joseph Smith talked of building a tabernacle in Nauvoo to provide shelter for the Saints when they met together. The proposed

The first tabernacle in Salt Lake City, on the left, was erected in the southwest corner of the temple block. It stood north and south, and the doors opened on the ends. A traveler described the entry with steps descending, the inside resembling a theatre, "benches rising one behind another until the outer row is a great way from the pulpit."

On the right is the bowery, a gallery of rough timber and wattles that was one of the first buildings raised in the Salt Lake Valley. It was used for sacred worship, public assemblies, music, and theatrical performances. In June 1851 the foundations of the Tabernacle were laid, and theatrical entertainments were presented by the Deseret Amateur Choir, William Pitt, captain and manager.

structure was to stretch 250 feet on the west side of the Nauvoo Temple, then under construction. That dream was not realized before his martyrdom. But on June 8, 1845, Orson Hyde went east to raise funds to purchase canvas for an elliptical tabernacle. His account records show $1,415.38 collected in donations. The more than 4,000 yards of Russian duck canvas cost $1,050.56; the surplus was applied to the Nauvoo Temple expenses. Church leaders abandoned plans for construction of the Nauvoo Tabernacle, but the canvas was put to good use as covers for wagons and tents in the exodus west.

Arriving in the Salt Lake Valley, Brigham Young saw the immediate need for a shelter for worship in the desert Zion. Within a week, men had erected the first of a series of open-sided boweries on Temple Square, with wooden posts supporting a roof of leafy boughs and branches. Poles were chopped in the mountains and drummed into the ground to support the simple structure. Hastily constructed, the first

Joseph Smith

bowery provided sanctuary for two years until a second—much larger—was placed on the same ground. Again, the sides were open, though a much larger roof was supported by 100 upright poles. For three years the Saints worked at sustaining life and shaping a community, meeting in the crude quarters, weather allowing.

The Old Tabernacle, the first major building on the temple block, was finished in 1852 on the southwest corner, where the Assembly Hall now stands. One year in construction, its footprint measured 126 feet long and 46 feet wide, and it could seat about 2,500. Like many of the hastily constructed pioneer shelters scattered about the area, it resembled a giant dugout. The walls were adobe brick covered by a gabled roof of native white-pine shingles, and the floor sat below ground level. But it was not without ornamentation. Both gabled ends featured triangular panels of carved rising suns, which curators have supposed symbolized the restoration of the gospel, a theme expressed in

The roof structure of the Tabernacle has undergone little structural change since the pioneers built it in 1867. When the supporting scaffolding was removed in 1867, skeptics thought the roof might collapse because of its unique design. But it held, and the original wood rafters are still in place today.

The Tabernacle was a massive building project that drew masons, carpenters, and plasterers from different parts of the territory. Sandstone blocks for buttresses were hauled from quarries just east of the city on two wheeled drays. An average of seventy men worked on plastering the building.

The wood shingles have been replaced with metal, but still in place are the wooden beams secured with wooden dowels, split with wedges.

the traditional hymn "Morning has broken . . . praise for the singing!"

On April 6, 1852, at General Conference, Willard Richards dedicated the building. The record states that a choir performed "soul-inspiring music and hymns, composed for the occasion by W. W. Phelps and Sister Eliza R. Snow, [which] enlivened the Saints." Regular Sunday services that followed included administration of the sacrament of the Lord's Supper. President Brigham Young presided, one or two of the Church authorities spoke, a missionary reported on his service, and President Young gave concluding remarks. This Tabernacle's life was short. With Saints pouring into the valley, its capacity of 2,500 was inadequate by the time it was completed. Two years later, at President Young's instruction, the 7,500 attending the April conference met out of doors, and a third bowery went up. Already a temple was under construction just to the northeast on the square.

In April 1863 Daniel H. Wells announced at General Conference, "Right here, we want to build a tabernacle to accommodate the Saints at our general conference and religious worship that will comfortably seat 10,000 people." Only sixteen years had passed since the pioneers had rattled down Emigration Canyon in trail-weary wagons with little but what they were wearing and could carry. The First Presidency was proposing to build an auditorium that would be among the largest in the world at the time and to build it in a desert settlement 1,500 miles from railroad access for building materials—nails in particular. It was a bold undertaking. Some would have called it foolhardy; Brigham Young considered it a project

CALLED BY THY NAME

The summer of 1866, Truman Angell toiled on the Tabernacle, particularly on the cornice. That winter he and his wife, Polly, left their Gilmer Park farm three miles southeast from the domed oval under construction and moved into a little shed thrown up between two of the forty-two sandstone piers supporting the Tabernacle roof. Here he took up his pencil and began sketching details for the two buildings—the Tabernacle and the Salt Lake Temple—that would become recognizable symbols of The Church of Jesus Christ of Latter-day Saints. The temple walls were not yet above ground; the Tabernacle shell was nearly in place. But the interior was bare. Angell designed the seating arrangements, the stand and pulpit, the choir section, the doors and windows. He also supervised the workmen. And he was exacting in his attention to detail. If he found that a

Truman Angell

window sash had swayed from the designated curving, he corrected the error himself. But he took no credit. His satisfaction came in pleasing President Brigham Young. "I feel a blessed spirit always when I can suit the president in anything," he said.

The Tabernacle held special significance for Angell. There he was sustained again by the conference as Church architect. He recorded in his journal, "God grant I may do my duty and the voice of the spirit of revelation be on me in the same."

The Salt Lake Tabernacle, positioned at the center of the city on Temple Square, was a marvel when it was built. The Tabernacle's sturdy presence in the community symbolized both permanence and pioneer ingenuity. Today it is a venerable, trusted friend and home to the Choir.

whose time had come. He wanted a structure with a roof unsupported by interior posts or pillars so that nothing would obstruct the view of the pulpit—or the Choir.

Brigham Young named a triumvirate as the building committee—Henry Folsom, then Church architect; Truman Angell, former Church and temple architect; and Henry Grow, a Pennsylvania bridge builder. All three had worked on the Nauvoo Temple. Folsom, a New Yorker, superintended construction of the Salt Lake Theater and the Manti Temple and directed the design of the Tabernacle's exterior. Angell, one of those in the first pioneer company to enter the Salt Lake valley, was a skilled

carpenter who left his imprint on the design and crafting of many pioneer structures, from the Council House to homes for many Church leaders, including Brigham Young. He is most noted for directing the construction of the Salt Lake Temple and supervising the interior work of the Tabernacle. He also sang in the Tabernacle Choir. In 1853 Grow had built the first suspension bridge in Utah across the Weber River, followed by another across the Provo River and one across the Jordan River. He then tackled the daunting task of putting a roof on the Tabernacle—clearly a remarkable structure.

This undertaking, coupled with the temple, harnessed the ingenuity and work ethic of the desert settlement. Said Church architect Truman Angell, "It is the gospel that has brought us here. I take comfort and joy when I reflect that I have volunteered with you to serve the Lord Almighty."

The immense auditorium, a remarkable feat of engineering for its time, was a massive public-works

EVERY TIME I SING IN THE TABERNACLE, I FEEL LIKE I'M SINGING WITH THE THOUSANDS WHO HAVE PRECEDED ME THERE. —*Janine Green, soprano*

project for the Saints. The $300,000 cost was covered by donations that came in building materials, bread, vegetables, labor, jewelry, and clothing.

Lord, how thy wonders are displayed
Whene'er I turn my eye;
If I survey the ground I tread
Or gaze upon the sky.

The structure is simple: a great dome supported by buttressed walls. Because construction materials would have had to be hauled from the Missouri River by ox team at a prohibitive cost, the builders turned to the surrounding hills and canyons to provide supplies. The red sandstone blocks were quarried in Red Butte Canyon to the east of Temple Square, the lumber cut in the Wasatch Mountains. Men harvested and hauled by ox team more than 1.5 million feet of lumber for the construction project, which included an intricate scaffold inside and out.

Grow adapted his bridge-building expertise to construct the roof, putting in place lattice trusses to shape the massive, elliptical arches. Each piece of the arch was twelve to fourteen feet long, twelve inches wide, and two to three inches thick. The trusses were assembled on the ground and raised by pulleys to rest on the sandstone buttresses, which stood ten to twelve feet apart around the circumference of the building and measured nine feet deep and three feet thick. They were joined together and secured with wooden dowels, and wrapped with green rawhide that shrank as it dried, pre-

venting cracks in the beams from further splitting. The truss work occupied ten feet from the inside of the plastered ceiling to the outside roofing. When finished, the arch's unique trestle-type design created an unsupported interior space 150 feet wide, 80 feet high, and 250 feet long. The twenty doors circling the perimeter, all opening out, were designed to clear the hall in five minutes.

Grow contended that the Tabernacle was the largest hall in the world unsupported by columns. Brigham Young told the Saints it would "stand through the millennium."

"Plans do not exist for the Tabernacle; rather, it is thought the building was laid out on the ground

The interior of the Tabernacle was originally designed by Truman Angell. The rostrum was redesigned in 1882, 1933, 1977, 1986, and 2000 when General Conference was moved to the new Conference Center and the Mormon Tabernacle Choir and the Orchestra at Temple Square became the historic structure's primary tenants.

President Mac Christensen has the mind of a businessman and the heart of a saint. The sixth president of the Choir, he understands his role: "I've always found that if something is going to be successful, you build, and you keep building, and you build it strong."

Choir President Mac Christensen is a retailer in the men's clothing business. He built his highly successful chain from the trunk of his car. Nearly. "I'd get up at 6:00 in the morning," he remembers, "and work until 9:00 at night. I started with a little store in Bountiful, Utah. We had a delivery truck that we fixed up, and we would drive into Salt Lake every morning and sell to people we knew. We would sell our suits right out of the truck. Hopefully, you were always fair; you had to run a tight ship; you had to love your people."

That work ethic translated quickly to the Mormon Tabernacle Choir.

Recently returned from directing the LDS Temple Visitors' Center in Washington, D.C., he was enjoying retirement in 2000, his sons running the hugely successful business, when President Gordon B. Hinckley asked him to be president of the Mormon Tabernacle Choir. The call caught this long-time clothier off guard. "President, I am a monotone," he entreated. President Hinckley responded, "Mac, we aren't calling you to sing." When Mac Christensen stood before the Choir to be introduced, he didn't know directors Craig Jessop, Mack Wilberg, or others on the staff. He didn't know anyone in the Choir. But his humor and wit were quickly revealed. When asked to say a few words, he quipped, "I am sorry, I don't know your names, but I know your suit sizes."

His formula for directing the operation, which includes the directors, the organists, the staff, the Chorale, the 360 members of the Choir, the 110 members of the Orchestra, and more than forty additional volunteers, is to treasure the talent, the willingness, the camaraderie, and the spirituality of the organization. His favorite words—"unbelievable . . . brilliant . . . take care of yourself . . . thank you . . . genius"—translate into attitude and actions. His respect for others is shown in his willingness to listen: "We hear more criticism about the dresses than the music. We listen. How can we make it better?"

Christensen learned that lesson when he was young: "I remember in my days down in Ephraim, Utah. I had a horse I was going to show, and I wanted a new bridle. We couldn't afford it. My dad said, 'There isn't anything we can't make better.' He took shoe polish and worked the bridle, and we went to the show. There isn't anything we can't make better."

without the aid of formal drawings," a Harvard professor summarized after a visit to survey the much-acclaimed structure. The building remains very much as Brigham Young designed it, though he would have contended, "God is the Supreme Architect. We owe all our inspiration, our love of beauty and the knowledge of how to express our views to the Father in Heaven who gives to His children what they ask for and what they need."

The Tabernacle was usable by October 6, 1867, but was not dedicated until October 1875. Saints sat on temporary seats, and President Young quickly

recognized that the capacity was inadequate. The horseshoe-shaped gallery seating was added in 1870. The 400 pine benches—still in use today—were finished to look like oak with a special Old World graining process applied by artisans who had emigrated from Germany and Holland.

The west-end stand included the pulpit, organ, and choir section. The Choir originally occupied seating at the same elevation as the audience but inside a railing that also surrounded the speaker's platform. The steep choir loft, so recognizable today, was not added until years later, nor were lights and heat. In 1891 Evan Stephens added 200 voices to the Choir, requiring "a new choir platform" to be constructed at the base of the organ. A February 1891 concert program described the improvements: "Chairs of the latest pattern were ordered, and all are now in their places. Twelve tiers of seats, rising one above the other, extend from the President's stand which has been brought forward about ten feet up to the gallery in the rear. Six of these are arranged in front of the great organ, while

the other six extend up each side of it. By this arrangement the singers all face the congregation." The improvements cost "upwards of $2,000."

At the turn of the century, the roof's hand-hewn shingles were replaced with copper sheeting, and in 1947, at the 100th anniversary of the settlement of the valley, the roof was covered with aluminum. A basement was added in 1968, and the west end rostrum was reshaped in 1882, 1933, 1977, 1986, and 2000.

At the first General Conference in the Tabernacle, choirs from Springville, Spanish Fork, Payson, Brigham City, and Smithfield joined with the seventy-five Tabernacle Choir members. Of

THE TABERNACLE SEEMS TO HAVE THIS WONDERFUL SOUND THAT CONTRIBUTES TO THE LOVELY SOUND THAT THE CHOIR MAKES. IT ISN'T JUST THE SINGERS; IT'S ALSO THE SPACE WITHIN WHICH THEY PERFORM AND THE HISTORY OF THE CHORAL SINGING THERE OVER MANY, MANY YEARS.
—*David Hurley, King's Singers*

that occasion the record states, "The gates to the Temple Block were opened at nine o'clock and the people flooded in. Long before ten o'clock, the time for the commencement of the conference, the seats in the great Tabernacle were filled, the aisles and doorways were crowded, and many were left outside. The stand was filled with the Church officials and the various choirs who were present to take part in the service."

Heber C. Kimball, counselor to President Brigham Young, said to those gathered, "I have seen a great many people assembled out of doors, but never have I seen so many in one house before." In reading the prayer of dedication of this now-famous domed structure, he put before the Lord "the mortar which binds the foundation stones together . . . the nails, bolts and straps of iron, of copper, and the brass, the zinc, the tin and the solder wherewith the metal is soldered together . . . all the lath and the nails and the sand and the lime . . and all the ornamentation . . . both within and without."

> SINGING IN THE TABERNACLE IS LIKE JOINING VOICES WITH EVERYONE WHO HAS SAT IN YOUR SEAT BEFORE YOU. IT'S YOUR FAITH AND TESTIMONY JOINING IN WITH THEIRS TO PRAISE GOD. —*Kristen Olsen, alto*

The Tabernacle has been called a "colossal whispering gallery" because of its remarkable acoustics. The drop of a pin at the front can be heard at the back of the hall. The large hall, oversized for its time, was built so the audience within could both see and hear. It was decades before electrical amplification of sound would be invented. Choir members will attest that "there is something about how the sound moves around" that they have never experienced in any other hall, including the great ones in Europe. "When you sing in the Tabernacle," Vance Everett, baritone, explains, "you hear sounds that keep coming back around. I honestly believe there are extra voices singing with us sometimes." Soprano Janalee Free from across the loft agrees: "I have sung with angels."

Seventy years after its construction, Stephen L Richards, counselor in the First Presidency, praised the foresight in building the Tabernacle: "This great structure, enormous at the time of its building, is the physical embodiment of a mighty concept that the work of God is expansive, all-embracing, with room for all who will come and listen and receive."

The building was a great curiosity. One Church authority described it as "Noah's ark turned bottom side up." Visitor Joseph L. Townsend suggested, "You must climb to some eminence where you can look down upon its huge fungus-like form. Elevate it sixty feet, or set it on a hill, and . . . it would be as grand as the Parthenon at Athens."

Two of the first guests to visit the dramatic structure were President and Mrs. Ulysses S. Grant, whose train stopped in the Utah Territory for a tour on October 3, 1875. "Gentlemen conducted me through [the] great [Tabernacle]," Julia Grant explained, "had the magnificent organ play for me, and, as the great volume of solemn sacred music filled the [Tabernacle], I could not help kneeling with bowed head and my heart, always so susceptible to the power of music, full of tenderness, to ask God's blessing to these people. The gentlemen asked if I had offered a prayer for them. 'Yes . . . a good Methodist one.'"

While all that borrows life from
thee is ever in thy care,
And ev'rywhere that we can be,
thou, God, art present there.

ALL THINGS BRIGHT AND BEAUTIFUL

Craig Jessop's energy is contagious. It encourages even those "in the wings" to break into song.

President Christensen says of Craig Jessop: "So much ability and such a great organizer. Craig Jessop is one of the greatest communicators that the Church has today, not only through his music but also through his words."

Choir members enjoy working with Craig Jessop. Lou Ann Crisler, known by Choir members for her special arrangements of birthday songs and tributes, mimics the classic Jessop conducting style.

Jessop listens to a just-recorded number. "I am trained to hear mistakes," he explains.

AS THE DEW FROM HEAVEN DISTILLING

The Grand Organ

Let our cry come up before thee.
Thy sweet Spirit shed around,
So the people shall adore thee
And confess the joyful sound.

To so many, the organ, the Tabernacle, and the Choir are one. Together they stand for everything the Mormon pioneers were seeking—religious expression, permanence, majesty, identity, and praise to God. Over the years the three have shaped a signature sound—which has yet to be packaged for the road. Because of *Music and the Spoken Word*, the organ has been heard by millions, more people than any other organ, prompting the Church magazine to call it "the Golden-toned Missionary—one missionary that has always been gratefully received and which has never been maligned or misunderstood." Daily, year-round recitals and numerous performances at Church conferences, concerts, and services have only increased the visibility and recognition of the famed instrument.

"One would think after twenty-five years at the organ bench that one would be jaded to the sound of the Choir and its music," says Tabernacle organist John Longhurst

John Longhurst has been part of the weekly broadcasts and daily organ recitals since 1977. The constant pressure makes the organ bench "the hot seat." He and his associates, the Choir members, and the Orchestra musicians have taken to heart the counsel of President Hinckley, "You're good, but you can still be better."

(who has been at the console since 1977). "But very frequently, I get that huge shiver running up and down the spine, just absolutely thrilling, and again that is the result of their musical expertise coupled with their spiritual strength."

His associate Clay Christiansen agrees: "This organ gives not just a signature sound, but a sound with soul. It has a warmth, power, and finesse found in very, very few organs in the world."

Longhurst describes the building as a great companion to the organ and "so sympathetic to organ music." He states, "An organ is quite unlike any other instrument; the room in which it is housed serves as its soundboard and has a significant influence on its effect." Organists of similar

instruments have concurred, suggesting, "The acoustics of the historic Tabernacle are unique and give the organ the advantage that no other organ in the world has." Monumental by any standards, the five-keyboard instrument is made up of 11,623 individual pipes organized into 147 voices and 206 ranks. The massive casework is both an icon and a frontispiece for the thousands of pipes, which range in size from a speaking length of thirty-two feet to three-quarters of an inch long. The pipes are even taller when the length of the foot is included.

For many years in the late 1800s, organ recitals were given only sporadically. John J. McClellan increased the frequency when he became organist in 1900. At April General Conference in 1909, an announcement was made that noon organ recitals would be offered daily throughout the year at no charge.

Daily organ recitals as well as *Music and the Spoken Word* have kept the organ in the public eye. "Whatever we happen to be playing," Longhurst states, "we try to make it absolutely exciting and beautiful. For the moment, it's the only piece that matters." The organists try to play music that is

The original ten speaking pipes still in place today were originally finished in gold paint, not nearly as luminous as the gold leaf on those wooden pipes today. A varnish has been applied to keep the luster.

Angels from the Realms of Glory

For more than fifty years, Dr. Alexander Schreiner walked up to the Tabernacle organ and took his seat. Visitors, even those with no musical background, knew they were in the presence of greatness, for Schreiner was one of the most popular organists of the twentieth century. Schreiner appeared to be something of a sage. Confident. Brilliant. Cheerful. He could easily have passed for the "chairman of the board," his silver hair and distinctive eyebrows fitting his distinguished countenance. He considered engineering as a profession but chose to become an organist and was revered the world over in music and Church circles.

He was born in Nuremberg, Germany, on July 31, 1901, to Johann Christian and Margarete Schemer Schreiner. At five years old he played in public for the first time; at eight he was appointed organist for the Nuremberg LDS branch. He had already learned most of the hymns in the hymnbook. In 1912 the family emigrated to America and settled in Salt Lake City. He was immediately appointed as organist for meetings of the German Saints, and, soon, as organist in the Cannon Ward. His musical studies in piano, harmony, and organ were continued under the tutelage of Tabernacle organist John J. McClellan, who recognized the talent of this eleven-year-old boy.

Dr. Alexander Schreiner left a legacy of thousands of daily noontime and evening recitals in the Tabernacle and hundreds of nationwide broadcasts with the Mormon Tabernacle Choir. For seven consecutive years, 1944–1950, Dr. Schreiner was voted one of the outstanding organists of the Musical America annual radio polls.

At the age of sixteen, Schreiner was playing the organ at the American Theater, then the most important playhouse in Salt Lake City. By the time he finished high school, he had a similar offer in Oregon for $300 a week but turned it down to accept a mission call to California. Upon his return he was appointed a Tabernacle organist. In the years to come, he would study in Europe with great masters, teach at UCLA, and receive his Ph.D. in music from the University of Utah. In addition to his Tabernacle organ duties, he performed on the world's finest organs, and he lectured, recorded, composed, and toured in the United States and abroad. One year he logged performances in 109 cities and thirty-five states. On tour, he went from the sacred works of Bach to the century-old pioneer anthem "Come, Come, Ye Saints," receiving resounding applause for his performances.

In addition to his duties at the keyboard, he directed the rebuilding of the Tabernacle organ from 1946 to 1949 and chaired the Church Music Committee. He retired in 1977. At his death in 1987, the First Presidency stated that Alexander Schreiner had "left a legacy which will continue to lift those who love beautiful music."

Sing unto God

Mastering the massive organ has always required both training and touch. Not just anyone sits down and plays the Tabernacle Organ. Those who have sat at that seat over the years include the following:

Joseph J. Daynes (1867–1900)
John J. McClellan (1900–1925)
Edward P. Kimball (1905–1937)
Walter J. Poulton (1907–1908)
Tracy Y. Cannon (1909–1934)
Moroni B. Gillespie (1911)
Frank Asper (1924–1963)
Alexander Schreiner (1924–1977)
Wade N. Stephens (1933–1944)
Roy M. Darley (1947–1984)
Robert Cundick (1965–1991)
John Longhurst (1977–)
Bonnie Goodliffe (1979–)
Clay Christiansen (1982–)
Linda Margetts (1984–)
Richard Elliott (1991–)

Assistant organists have included Henry Giles, Katherine Romney Stewart, Fanny Young Thatcher, Dr. Karl G. Maeser, Orson Pratt Jr., Sarah A. Cooke, William Poulton, and John H. Chamberlain.

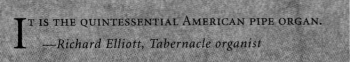

IT IS THE QUINTESSENTIAL AMERICAN PIPE ORGAN.
—*Richard Elliott, Tabernacle organist*

what Longhurst calls "approachable." Nothing overtly avant-garde finds its way into the noon performances or the Sunday-morning broadcast. "You can hear them walk out of the Tabernacle during your performance," Longhurst chides, "because the floor squeaks." Richard Elliott, Tabernacle organist, says, "It is not a typical organ job. There is a lot of pressure here. You have to pick up music very, very quickly." Familiarity with the music is as important as the melodic character and the melody. "A lot of people in the noon organ-recital audiences have never set foot into any kind of concert hall, or in some cases a church, in their life. So we try to keep that in mind and play mostly accessible works, although we play one longer piece per program, or one piece like a Bach prelude and fugue, which might be a little less accessible," says Elliott. They play John Philip Sousa marches on Sousa's birthday and "Danny Boy" for nostalgia, well-known hymns that reflect the religious roots of the LDS Church, and pieces like "Sheep May Safely Graze" or "Air on G String" by Bach that come from the classical repertoire but are familiar.

Tabernacle organist Elliot explains, "There are a few, maybe fifty organists in the country, who do a regular recital, though very few of them play every single week. But on the other hand, a lot of these organists are playing in big churches where they're expected to provide a fifteen-minute prelude, a fifteen-minute postlude, or something comparable, so it's almost like a recital every week. Plus they're accompanying the choir and hymns during the service, so they probably have as much performing time in front of their audience as we do. Although it's a little bit different—the environment isn't quite as critical as the audience filling the Tabernacle."

When Longhurst first came, "the Choir could hardly sing a verse of a hymn without organ accompaniment because they had difficulty maintaining the pitch. The Choir is now able to produce a high degree of nuance that is not just a big thunderous sound, which at one point seemed to be its major appeal." And the Choir values its setting. "Where else can a person of modest talent sing under the direction of world-class conductors

Pipes are arranged by ranks. A rank is a complete set, one pipe for each note on the keyboard. An organ pipe's pitch is determined by the length of the pipe.

Top photo: Igor Gruppman performs with the Orchestra at Temple Square. Above photo: The 110-member Orchestra at Temple Square functions as both an independent concert orchestra and a companion to the Choir. Before the Orchestra's formation, acclaimed groups such as the Philadelphia Orchestra and the Utah Symphony occasionally accompanied the Choir.

The Orchestra at Temple Square has transformed and reinvented the Mormon Tabernacle Choir. "They have brought a whole new dynamic, a new freedom to repertoire that is being felt and seen," Craig Jessop believes. The Latter-day Saints have sponsored choruses and choral classes, orchestras and band ensembles since their early days in Ohio. In 1999 when choir president Wendell Smoot announced the creation of the Orchestra at Temple Square, the new entity had a foundation on which to build.

Craig Jessop functions as music director of the entire Tabernacle Choir organization, which includes the Orchestra. Igor Gruppman, internationally acclaimed violinist and conductor, has succeeded Barlow Bradford, associate director from 1999 to 2003, as conductor of the Orchestra. Meredith Campbell, concertmaster of the Orchestra, contends, "The Choir's desire to do their best flows down to each member in the Orchestra. It's a world-class situation."

Creating an orchestra had two purposes: First, to broaden the repertoire of the Choir, giving the singers an opportunity to consistently perform the great choral masterworks, those compositions conceived for the combination of voice and orchestra. Prior to the Orchestra, the Choir relied on organ accompaniment and guest orchestras. Second, to establish its own concert series and further strengthen musicality in the Church. The timing was right for just such an initiative.

For years the Choir had been joined by such notables as the Philadelphia Orchestra, the New York Philharmonic, the Utah Symphony, and most recently the Boston Pops and Boston Symphony. The challenge was to attract orchestra members as volunteers rather than as paid musicians. Says Meredith Campbell, "We are still feeling our way, but the Lord absolutely wants this orchestra, and we know it will be successful."

Like the Choir, the members of the Orchestra are volunteers. John Williams, who conducted the Choir and Orchestra at Temple Square for the Olympics, said, "There's a spirit there that's different from a studio group or hired

ROBIN, BRING YOUR FIFE AND COME

players; these are people that are there for the joy of music or for their own spiritual need to live through music. And one feels that."

The first steps were tentative, but percussionist Trent E. Christensen, who signed on in 1999 and now juggles the Orchestra with law school forty miles from Temple Square, says, "We are all giving to the Lord what he has given to us. What a chance of a lifetime!"

The Orchestra has played on recent choir recordings under the Telarc and the newly created Mormon Tabernacle Choir labels, provided music for Church media productions, and accompanied the Temple Square Chorale as well as presenting its own concerts three times a year.

Flutist Tiffany McCleary appreciates the spirit she feels while playing the music: "The arrangements that we play invite the Spirit to be with us. It's the Lord's orchestra, and the spirit that comes with that is what makes this different from other orchestras."

The orchestra members feel more and more a part of the choir experience. Much of that is due to the efforts of Barry Anderson, administrative manager, with his responsibility to manage the 110 musicians on the orchestra's roster. "It tests my organizational skills," he says. "I like that."

Did the Orchestra put the Tabernacle organ out of a job? Not at all. The organ can provide an accompaniment for just about anything. "But an organ is not an orchestra," Longhurst explains. For Mack Wilberg, the addition of the Orchestra is a glorious opportunity for new arrangements and works for the Choir.

An orchestra ensemble travels with the Choir on tour. In addition to the concerts, flutist Jeannine Goeckeritz provides music for special tour receptions, as does harpist Tamara Oswald.

accompanied by a world-class organ with other fine singers?" says Mike Stevens, baritone.

The story of the first organ in the Salt Lake Valley began halfway around the globe in Australia. British-born Joseph Ridges arrived in the valley in 1857 with a small, seven-stop pipe organ he had constructed while mining for gold "down under." He reassembled the instrument, which had been packed in soldered tin shipping cases for crossing

Today, on national tours, the Choir takes an electronic organ to provide, as closely as possible, the Tabernacle organ sound. In many locations, pipe organs are used. Organists John Longhurst and Richard Elliot also play piano as accompaniment, even in the rain. President Christensen protects them as much as possible.

the Pacific, in the Old Tabernacle. Brigham Young had dispatched fourteen mule teams to bring the organ from the California coast.

But its tenure was short-lived. With the approach of Johnston's Army and the threat of violence, the organ was disassembled and carted south along with most of the population of the Salt Lake Valley. When the Saints returned, so did the organ.

With the announcement of the building of the massive Tabernacle, Brigham Young determined that the hall needed a grand organ: "We can't preach the gospel unless we have good music," he said. He commissioned Ridges to build another organ, one befitting the size and scale of the dramatic new structure. President Young insisted that with the organ, "We can sing the gospel into the hearts of the people." To purchase and ship a comparable instrument from the East Coast would have cost far, far more than the pioneers could spare.

Ridges fashioned the organ from great yellow pines in Pine Valley, far to the south. The wood, ranging in size from two feet to thirty-two feet in length, was ideal: straight and free of knots, pitch, and gum. A load of logs to Salt Lake City, a distance of 300 miles, took three weeks to transport. At one point Ridges and his party narrowly escaped from hostile Indians.

Ridges had to purchase other items in Boston and New York, spending about $900—all that could be spared from Church funds. John Longhurst, Tabernacle organist, suggests that Ridges patterned the Tabernacle organ after one "being installed by the German builder E. F. Walcker in the Boston Music Hall."

Ridges worked from a shop inside the Tabernacle walls. The organ's weight required reinforcing to support its size. The gleaming gold pipes of the facade—a hallmark so easily recognized—

are shaped from laminated wedges fit together to form a cylinder. The outsides were covered with plaster and painted gold. Ridges and his crew had to make their own glue to be used in the construction by setting up kettles on the street outside the temple wall and boiling cowhides. They used calf skins to create the great bellows.

> *Lord, behold this congregation;*
> *Precious promises fulfill.*
> *From thy holy habitation*
> *Let the dews of life distill.*

The organ wasn't finished when the Tabernacle first opened its doors on October 6, 1867, for the Church's thirty-seventh semiannual General Conference. But the organ was playable. Only 700 of the 2,683 pipes were completed. The casing, intended to stand forty feet high, was about fifteen feet and was covered with a loose drape. "Brother Ridges and those who have labored with him, have done the best they could," President Young explained. "I am pleased with it."

Two years later when the scaffolding was dismantled, the *Deseret News* hailed the organ's grand appearance: "Its cathedral-like shape, with the immense towers and symmetrical proportions, now stand out beautifully." In 1901, at special services honoring the new century, the Tabernacle Choir and organ were featured on the program. Joseph Ridges, seventy-four, received a standing ovation from the crowd and choir. At his funeral in 1914 LDS Church president Joseph F. Smith fittingly called him "an instrument of God."

The new organ demanded a skilled organist. British-born Joseph J. Daynes, who was the regular organist in the "Old" Tabernacle, was appointed organist for the new Tabernacle at age sixteen. He served under five choir conductors—Sands, Careless, Griggs, Beesley, and Stephens. Daynes, who made his living as a teacher, served as organist from 1867 to 1900. He played for the choir, played at recitals, and kept the organ in repair and in tune. He occasionally received contributions when the hat was passed at special performances or recitals. The hymn "As the Dew from Heaven Distilling," for which Daynes wrote the music, is the closing theme for *Music and the Spoken Word*.

Further changes to the organ were made in

THE ORGAN HAS BEEN ENLARGED AND REBUILT SEVERAL TIMES SINCE, TAKING ADVANTAGE OF VARIOUS MODERN THINGS LIKE ELECTRIFICATION OF THE CONSOLE AND ELECTRIC BLOWERS, AND EVEN NOW IT CONTINUES TO BE A STATE-OF-THE-ART INSTRUMENT.
—*John Longhurst*

1885 by Niels Johnson, who had assisted Ridges in building the organ.

In 1901 the organ was rebuilt by the Kimball Organ Company of Chicago, which installed a complete pneumatic action and electric blowers. The console was detached from the organ and moved up to the front of the choir loft. Renovations to the organ were simplified by access to the rail lines. The Oregon Short Line carried some of the freight but returned a check for $2,176.20 for their bill, stating "that the organ recitals and the many courtesies extended to tourists by the Church prompted the action." The updated instrument was touted as one of the best pipe organs in the world.

In 1915 the Austin Company of Hartford,

They, the Builders of the Nation

When President Brigham Young directed the building of the Tabernacle, he was building for the future. That history was repeated in 1996 when President Gordon B. Hinckley announced the building of a Conference Center four times the size of the Tabernacle. It would seat 21,333.

The new LDS Conference Center includes an organ about two-thirds the size of the Tabernacle organ in terms of the number of pipes. John Longhurst, who described it as a "project of immense proportion," received direction for the new pipe organ from President Hinckley just as Ridges had been directed by President Young. Recalled Longhurst of the charge, "The President said to me, 'Now, John, I don't want you to attempt to eclipse the Tabernacle organ. That is to remain the premiere instrument of the Church.'"

Longhurst and his associates took that to mean that the new Conference Center organ should be smaller than the Tabernacle organ. "What a challenge to put a smaller instrument in a space that is four times larger and make it work," Longhurst said. "No one had ever put an organ in a space that size before."

The organ case and the facade pipes were in place for the opening of the Conference Center at General Conference in April 2000, but the organ was not completed until 2003, six years after construction of the facility began. The Conference Center pipe organ includes 130 ranks of pipes as compared to 206 in the Tabernacle, and 7,708 individual pipes. The pipes had to be much larger in scale and speak under higher wind pressure than those in the Tabernacle to project the sound.

Longhurst recalls thinking, "With this huge space, what is it that makes an organ seem grand and large and impressive to

The Choir's second home is across the street at the Conference Center, where LDS General Conference is now held. The 21,000-seat facility is staggering to guest artists, who are often featured in programs for Christmas, Easter, and other special occasions.

match the scale of the room?" He says, "And the thought struck me that when I hear an organ, the thing that speaks size and power to me is its ability to produce bass effectively throughout the room. The Conference Center organ has a pedal department that is really something quite incredible, and apart from that the entire organ is on a much larger scale than the Tabernacle organ."

Work on the organ consumed Longhurst and his associates. Schoenstein & Company, who had done the rebuilding work at the Tabernacle in the 1980s, were brought in to construct an organ for the monumental space—still just on paper. Work on the organ went ahead in order to have it ready fairly near the completion of the building project. The finished organ was introduced to the community in a special inaugural concert in June 2003.

The Conference Center organ is described as an American Romantic instrument, while the Tabernacle's is American Classic. The difference was purposeful. Longhurst explains, "First of all, we wanted the organs here at Church headquarters to represent different tonal philosophies. We have the mechanical action instrument in the Assembly Hall that represents the European and particularly German organ-building tradition. We have a modest organ in the chapel of the Joseph Smith Building that speaks with a French accent. We wanted something a little different for the Conference Center."

President Gordon B. Hinckley dedicated the building and its organ, saying, "We dedicate this magnificent hall, unique in its design and size, constructed to house the thousands who through the years will gather here to worship . . . and to be entertained in a wholesome and wonderful way. . . . May it be a thing of beauty to the beholder both inside and out. May it be a house of many uses, a house of culture, a house of art, a house of worship, a house of faith, a house of God."

Connecticut, replaced the tubular pneumatic action, which had been less than reliable, and installed a new console and new chests. The most visible and dramatic change was the addition of two fifteen-foot wings, which extended the width to sixty-one feet. The organists were delighted with the advancements. Said Tabernacle organist John J. McClellan, "We feel that in the newly reconstructed organ we have an instrument that will compel the admiration of the musical world." In 1926 twenty-two sets of pipes were added. This was the organ used for the first two decades of radio broadcast.

Today's Tabernacle organ dates back to 1948, when the Æolian-Skinner Organ Company rebuilt and enlarged the instrument. In announcing the plans, Church officers promised that care would be taken not to change its outside appearance, including its distinctive color. Tonal designer G. Donald Harrison, regarded as perhaps the leading proponent of what is called the American Classic style of organ building, directed the rebuilding, with Alexander Schreiner at his side. The Tabernacle Organ is viewed by many as the pinnacle of his work, a true all-American instrument pulling from European and English traditions. The American Classic style, Longhurst explains, "is a tonal approach that incorporates elements from the various European organ-building traditions and synthesizes them into a single instrument that can play a wide variety of music acceptably though not with complete authenticity. The American Classic organ was a reaction to the romantic, orchestrally conceived pipe organ that had evolved in America during the first three or four decades of the twentieth century." A few souvenir pipes from Ridges's original organ and the center portion of the organ case are still in place.

All divisions of the organ are located behind the massive casework on the west except the antiphonal division, which sits in the lower attic at the east end and speaks through openings behind the seats in the center balcony. Today's pipes are made of wood, zinc, and various alloys of tin and lead.

Between 1985 and 1989, Schoenstein & Company of San Francisco led the last major renovation to the organ. They regulated the pipework, installed seventeen ranks of new pipes, and replaced the combination action with a solid-state system and relays to take advantage of the latest technological innovations.

In 1971 the Tabernacle was recognized by the American Civil Engineering Society as a landmark of American civil engineering. In 1994 the Organ Historical Society recognized the Tabernacle organ as "an instrument of exceptional historic merit, worthy of preservation."

For generations this much-beloved organ has touched the hearts and souls of millions of people around the world with its musical magic. It stands as a reminder of a people who built better than they knew and as a testimony to future generations of the broad sweep of the language of music.

Let our cry come up before thee.
Thy sweet Spirit shed around,
So the people shall adore thee
And confess the joyful sound.

ONWARD, YE PEOPLE!

The year 1999 brought major changes to the music programs offered on Temple Square. The Temple Square Chorale was added in 1999 to further develop choir members and prepare new applicants for choir membership. The Chorale adds further dimension to the music programs offered on Temple Square.

With the announcement of the Chorale, the training school, the choir leadership also lowered the minimum age to audition for the Choir from thirty to twenty-five. The Mormon Youth Chorus was disbanded at the same time, and it was expected that many of the singers in that chorus would apply for the Chorale. Length of service remained at twenty years maximum or age sixty, whichever comes first. Membership in the Chorale is required for admission to the Choir. Applications are made twice each year, the first of July and the first of January. The screening is a three-step audition process: a written application and taped submission, a music-skills inventory test, and, if the applicant passes the first two phases, a live audition. Those selected rehearse and perform for three months under the direction of Dr. Wilberg and then, assuming satisfactory performance, are eligible to join the Choir. Experienced choir members also rotate through the Chorale to fine-tune their skills. Many Choir members choose to sing with the Chorale on a continuing basis. Past performances have included such works as *King David,* by Arthur Honegger; the Mozart *Requiem;* and Handel's oratorio *Saul.*

"There has to be a decided and different mindset when singing with a smaller ensemble like the Chorale," says Mack Wilberg, associate director of the Choir, who has direct responsibility for the Chorale. "Many of our qualified applicants and indeed many current members of the Choir have had limited experience singing in a finely tuned smaller ensemble. Those who give themselves completely to the experience come out being able to make better individual contributions to the larger Choir."

The new audition process caught the interest of a local television station, which saw the possibility of a story: "How do you get chosen for the Choir?" After calling Ann Turner, choir executive secretary, for details, the station reporters broadcast the particulars of how to get into the Mormon Tabernacle Choir and gave the choir phone number for further information. In the next few days the choir office fielded 800 requests for applications.

"We are constantly trying to attract the best singer-musician possible," observes Wilberg. "With the Choir's unrelenting performance schedule and limited rehearsal time, we are in need of those who not only have a good voice but also have excellent musical skills and instincts. We need singers who can sight-read a moderately difficult piece almost perfectly the first time through. Unfortunately, we don't have the time to spoon-feed notes and rhythm."

Upon retirement from the conductor's podium, Jerold Ottley and his wife, JoAnn, volunteered to develop the Choir Training School. Temple Square organists Bonnie Goodliffe and Linda Margetts now manage the Training School, with Dyanne Riley as voice coach.

Mack Wilberg conducts the Temple Square Chorale. Like the Orchestra, the Chorale has its own concert season offering a repertoire of masterworks. Wilberg is also known at Choir rehearsals for conducting with one hand and playing the piano with the other.

WE, YOUR PEOPLE, EV'RYWHERE

A National Presence

Till we rest when day is done;
May we tell our hearts' own story,
Hearts that honor and believe,
Through our care for one another,
For this life and land we love.

THE TABERNACLE CHOIR was touring before they were ever on radio. The first official performance outside the Tabernacle was at the dedication of the Salt Lake Theater on March 6, 1862. Fifteen hundred attended the dedication. The theatre was a massive undertaking for the upstart community, and no such structure of its size or up-to-date construction was found elsewhere in the West for many years to come. On the program "an orchestra of twenty members performed, assisted by the Tabernacle Choir."

The Choir began out-of-town touring on September 29, 1880, taking a two-hour train trip to American Fork, just thirty miles south of the Tabernacle. The 150 choir members and the Tabernacle Orchestral Band joined with the American Fork Choir for a 10:00 A.M. performance in the local meetinghouse. The local religious leader "made a few remarks of welcome in his usual happy style, expressed his gratification at the 'honor' conferred by a visit of the Salt Lake Tabernacle Choir, and referred to the Prophet

Joseph Smith as the organizer of the first choir in the Church of Jesus Christ in this dispensation. The program featured choir numbers, an organ polka, solos and quartets and a final number, 'Glory to God in the Highest.' As the train rolled out of the station, [the Choir] was greeted with prolonged cheers and cries of 'Come Again!' by the warm-hearted inhabitants of that place."

Other short tours soon followed. The Choir visited surrounding settlements, performing in local tabernacles and meetinghouses in Provo, Logan, Ogden, Brigham City, and Nephi. After expenses, the Choir showed a profit, following the 1884 Nephi event, of $11.90. The *Salt Lake Herald* reported of a concert in Tooele, "They gave a free concert in the meetinghouse, seating 500. It was filled a long time before the concert began, with many assembled outside the windows." A brass band led the wagon-loads of singers to the train depot.

One of the more unusual performances was a trip in the 1870s to the Utah Penitentiary. Choir director Ebenezer Beesley later recalled, "I took the Tabernacle Choir up to the penitentiary and gave the prisoners a concert. We got there soon after 10 o'clock and when I went up on the wall I saw for the first time the inside of a penitentiary. There was a large square surrounded by high, thick walls, and we could see groups of men all dressed alike except for their hats. . . . When the choir all arrived we were led through the large gates and shown into the dining room; and when we were all ready the prisoners were let come in. . . . The visitors with the 180 prisoners filled the room to overflowing. Brother Dunbar played them a tune on the bagpipes. I asked permission for some of the prisoners to take part in the exercises, which was granted." Some of the prisoners were former choir members, incarcerated not for robbery but for practicing polygamy.

The choir was applauded for their outreach. An 1883 news report stated, "The choir contains . . . the elements for much pleasure, being composed of good singers, some excellent instrumental performers and a host of friendly, companionable and whole-souled Latter-day Saints."

We have loved you for your rivers,
We have loved you for your shores,
Ev'ry treasure you have shown us
Ev'ry seed that you have sown.

The Choir took the train for all of its out-of-town touring, beginning with a venture to American Fork in 1880. Not until 1962 with the Telstar broadcast at Mount Rushmore did the Choir fly to a location to perform.

The Choir launched a major tour in 1911 covering 5,500 miles, presenting fifty concerts in Ogden, Cheyenne, Omaha, Chicago, Detroit, New York, Washington, Toledo, Richmond, Indianapolis, St. Louis, Topeka, Denver, and Colorado Springs.

"The singing choir numbers about 350, and it is being led by a Welshman from Pencader, Carmarthenshire, South Wales by the name of E. Stephens. And I can assure you that the singing is good," asserted William D. Davies, a Welsh emigrant, in 1891 after having toured various parts of the country, including Colorado and Utah.

And it was a Church choir. The Tabernacle Choir at the turn of the century had been singing for LDS General Conferences for fifty years, its primary assignment even today. In addition, over the years, the Choir helped raise funds for worthy causes such as Deseret Hospital, Brigham Young Academy, and This Is the Place Monument, as well as smaller efforts, raising $500 to construct a new meetinghouse in Stockholm, Sweden, with a fifty-cent charge for seating in "all parts of the house."

But it was destined to step onto a larger stage. Opportunity came in 1892. The Choir's Welsh con-ductor, Evan Stephens, recognized opportunity when the Choir was extended an invitation to the Eisteddfod, the renowned Welsh choral competition, at the Columbian Exposition, the 1893 World's Fair honoring the 400th anniversary of the landing of Christopher Columbus in North America. The Eisteddfod, designed to encourage artistic instruction and expression, dates in modern times from 1771. The Choir was enthusiastic over the prospective contest, particularly because of choir members' reverence for and family ties to the Welsh choral tradition.

I T IS LIKELY, THAT THE CHOIR OF THE TABERNACLE IS THE BEST CHURCH CHOIR IN THE WORLD.

—*William D. Davies, Welsh Journalist, 1891*

OUR MOUNTAIN HOME SO DEAR

Evan Stephens, conductor of the Tabernacle Choir, prolific composer, and writer of hymns reached the pinnacle of musicianship in the LDS Church. Said biographer John Evans, "There is nothing small about Stephens, except his stature." Often called the "Father of Mormon Music," this Welshman conducted the Tabernacle Choir from 1890 to 1916. He retired at age sixty-two. Of his life this diminutive bachelor and masterful musician said, "I have found my greatest joy and my greatest usefulness to others to be one and the same thing." At his funeral, his successor, Anthony C. Lund, said, "Evan Stephens has done more than any other one person toward musical progress of the Church and this state. . . . May he rest in peace and be loved and remembered."

His life had not been easy. He crossed the plains on foot at age twelve with his family in 1866. He was the youngest of ten. The Stephens family, from Pencader, Carmarthenshire, South Wales, were poor. He had received little schooling in Wales, and that didn't change in Willard, Utah, where the family settled. He herded sheep and cattle, hauled lumber, taught himself to speak English, and worked as a section hand on the Utah Northern Railroad for $37.50 a month. When he stumbled upon a book of music, his life changed. He taught himself the music scale, picking out notes from the song "Jerusalem, My Glorious Home." He later took organ lessons in the Tabernacle from Joseph J. Daynes.

In 1871 he was made choir leader in Willard and included in their programs compositions of his own. A year later, his chorus sang with the Tabernacle Choir at General Conference. He served as organist for the Logan Tabernacle, taught both adults and youth vocal lessons for two, three, and four dollars per quarter of ten weeks. Two hundred students enrolled in his courses. Ogden wanted him one day a week; there he trained 500 youth. Springville added another 500 to his student list. In 1883 Dr. John Park of the University of Deseret, later named the University of Utah, courted him as a teacher. Evans balked at the request, claiming, "My language is too poor. I make too many mistakes in grammar." Dr. Park retorted, "I don't want you for grammar. I want you to teach music." Stephens took the job.

In 1890 he was selected to lead the Tabernacle Choir. From his singing schools, Stephens was able to increase the numbers in the Choir quickly to more than 550 members, though nearly 40 percent were absent at any one time, keeping the number of performers near 300.

He expected great things from his choir members. A musician, he believed, "should tingle to his finger tips with a passion for music. He should be saturated with music, without losing the spirit of the gospel. He should have an intense love for the community. He ought to be endowed abundantly with that all-pervading desire to lead the choir to prominence on the national scene."

Stephens was prolific, writing more than ninety hymns and anthems, with a propensity to showcase his own work in Tabernacle Choir programs. His hymns include several favorites, "True to the Faith," "Let Us All Press On," and "The Morning Breaks." He also wrote the anthem "Utah, We Love Thee" for the 1896 statehood celebration. It was later designated as the state song.

At a General Conference in 1905, LDS Church president Joseph F. Smith described choir conductor Evan Stephens as "a man gifted of God, talented in music, in poetry and in song, and above and beyond all that, a man gifted with humility and with faith in the Gospel of Jesus Christ; who is not only diligent in his labors here with this great choir, but who is faithful in his soul to the cause of Zion."

The Choir's departure for Chicago drew crowds of well-wishers to the train station. Of Utah, the Chicago Guide to the Exposition *stated, "Utah, as a Mormon refuge, dates back so far as 1847. The discussions of Mormonism and the Mormons have been so frequent as to relieve us from all necessity for considering the subject."*

Thousands thronged the Salt Lake Union Pacific station on August 29, 1893, to salute the 400 travelers; 250 of them were members of the Choir. At 3:10 in the afternoon, the ten-car train inched out of the station to begin the six-day, 1,500-mile journey east. Historian E. A. McDaniel observed, "The fact that the great Tabernacle Choir was to take part in the choral contest, together with the Utah Day exercises, was telegraphed all over the United States, and almost immediately inquiries began to pour in from all parts of the country . . . so that they could time their visit to the Exposition in order to hear the concert."

For the Choir and the Church it represented, the trip was a return to roots. Among the singers and guests making their way across the country by rail were a handful who had walked across those same plains decades earlier in pioneer companies. The Choir performed in Independence, Missouri, where the Saints had been driven from their homes

half a century before; in St. Louis; and on the return home in Omaha—places familiar to the Saints from their earlier settlement efforts.

Arriving September 3, the Choir rehearsed daily. The music was not for the faint-hearted: "Worthy Is the Lamb" from Handel's *Messiah;* "Blessed Is the Man Who Fears Him," from Mendelssohn's *Elijah;* and "Now the Impetuous Torrents Rise," from the oratorio *David and Saul,* by David Jenkins. The contest for the great national prize took place in Festival Hall on September 8, the contestants being two choirs from Scranton, Pennsylvania—the Scranton Choral Union and the Scranton Welsh Choir; one from Ohio, known as the Western Reserve Choir; and the Tabernacle Choir. "I had the wonderful opportunity of going to Chicago with 250 members to contest at the World's Fair in 1893," seventeen-year-old Irene Merrill wrote of the excursion. "We were just a bunch of unknown Mormons from out west.

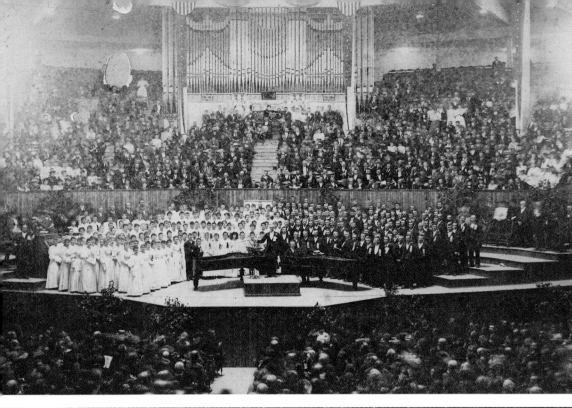

The Choir's Welsh roots made them natural competitors in the Columbia Exposition's Eisteddfod. Soloists Robert C. Easton, Nellie Druce-Pugsley, and others were well received, though many contended the Choir was denied first place not by musical performance but by politics. The Choir's appearance at the Exposition was a turning point for the Church's public image. The Choir became a valued representative and resource for the American-born religion.

The Columbia Exposition covered twenty-two acres, with buildings representing the architecture of different countries as well as industry, agriculture, mining, women, and the arts. Choir members visited many of the exhibits.

Grandmother Smith sent my sister, Maud, to chaperone me. We had a wonderful time."

Choir member Thomas C. Griggs reported Evan Stephens's final instructions to the Choir: "Pay no attention to your competitors until you have sung, be not eager to excel them. Simply be calm, earnest, and see to it that we do ourselves justice, and I for one, will be satisfied, prize or no prize."

The Choir performed for about twelve minutes and then joined the other contestants in a finale of the "Hallelujah Chorus." Evan Stephens was invited to conduct the combined chorus.

"In giving their verdict the judges were constrained to say that it was in reality very difficult to determine who were the victors, the Scranton or the Tabernacle singers, the contestants being so nearly equal, and the degree of excellence with each

on all points being of such a high standard." The judges awarded the prize to the Scranton choir. The Utah participants considered "that in a contest of such magnitude, to be almost if not equal to the best talent the country could produce, was something for the West to be proud of." Second place came with a $1,000 cash prize.

Conductor Evan Stephens, often called Professor Stephens because of his years directing the Department of Music at the University of Utah, said to a *Deseret News* reporter, "Am I satisfied? I cannot be otherwise. A nicer, more faithful lot of singers never sang together than my 250 proved to be. Not one absentee at any concert during the trip (only by permission, when we had no room for them). Soloists and chorus members did everything reasonable, and within their power, to make my labors as conductor, and the one in charge of the artistic side of the tour, successful and pleasant. I have nothing but love and gratitude to them, one and all."

Utah Day at the Fair was September 9, the sixty-third anniversary of the creation of the Utah Territory. The day was "one long to be remembered, and attracted more attention than was accorded the observance of most State days." Following the address of the Fair's president, the Choir "rendered a choice selection, at the close of which the vast audience almost went wild with enthusiasm. Thousands were present for the express purpose of listening to this famous company of musicians from the far West. In many respects it was a critical audience, many having an idea that as musicians Utah people were not

THE SPIRIT OF GOD

When Wendell Smoot was released as president of the Choir, President Gordon B. Hinckley, to whom Smoot reported directly, paid tribute to his service. His words were praise for all who have led the Choir as volunteer presidents, keeping up with the choir schedule and keeping ahead of it: "The fact that we kept him there for seventeen years speaks for itself. He's done a really masterful job, a wonderful job. We'll always be indebted to him. We're so grateful for his service."

Craig Jessop noted, "Wendell knows how to run a business, and he has left this choir on a firm foundation of financial security through very hard work and being a wonderful steward. Second, he's an administrator. He knows how to take charge, he knows how to give direction, he knows how to listen. There is never any question that we would follow our leader. Third, and most important of all, he's a priesthood leader and knows how the priesthood of God functions."

Wendell Smoot

Presidents of the Mormon Tabernacle Choir have included the following:

David A. Smith (1908–1938)
Lester Hewlett (1938–1962)
Isaac M. Stewart (1962–1975)
Oakley S. Evans (1975–1984)
Wendell Smoot (1984–2000)
Mac Christensen (2000–)

entitled to the praise that had been lavished on the Choir after the choral contest."

A prominent Easterner commented to the press, "Deep down in my heart there was a strong prejudice against the people of Utah as a whole, but after listening to the music of your great choir I have changed my mind. I am only one of thousands here today whose sentiments in regard to Utah and her people have changed."

The Choir's reception at the World's Fair gave the media and the nation a new look at the Mormons and their faith. Church officials recognized that the Choir could do much to soften stony hearts and remove the prejudice that existed. The Church's First Presidency had accompanied the Choir on the tour. Second counselor Joseph F. Smith called the Choir's performance "a glorious triumph" and "a good seed sown." He observed in a letter home, "To get the 1st prize . . . would have put them at once at the top of the ladder of choral singing. This was too much honor to confer upon Utah and the Mormons."

With the Choir's national success in 1893, it was poised to become an emissary for the LDS Church and the region. In 1896 Utah was admitted to the Union. The Mormon Tabernacle Choir was on hand to join in the celebration.

On Monday, November 6, 1911, Utahns gathered at Brooklyn naval yard to formally present a silver tea service for the battleship Utah, *one of the world's largest battleships, 510 feet in length, 88 feet in breadth. From the deck of the battleship, the Choir sang "Utah, We Love Thee," including two verses written especially for the "queen of the ocean wave."*

I CONSIDER IT HAS DONE MORE GOOD THAN FIVE THOUSAND SERMONS WOULD HAVE DONE IN AN ORDINARY OR EVEN IN AN EXTRAORDINARY WAY.

—*Joseph F. Smith, president, The Church of Jesus Christ of Latter-day Saints, 1893*

The event marked the first great public success of this budding American musical institution—the Mormon Tabernacle Choir—and its role as emissary for the Church. The touring of the Choir had purpose far beyond exposure and fine singing. As one music editor noted, "The program was varied, but the ideal was apparent in the words of all: a religious idealism, a challenge to modernists, and an exhortation to the faithful." No matter the venue, the Choir's efforts reached far beyond the music in their hearts and hands.

We have loved you for your mountains,
For your prairies, for your fields,

All these gifts we have been given
All these glories that we share.

The choir members crisscrossed the country by train from New York to California: Denver in 1896, the San Francisco World's Fair in 1902, the Alaska Yukon Exposition in Seattle 1909. The Choir balked at a seventy-five-cent admission fee at the Seattle Fair, waiving the opportunity to compete in the choral competition. The chorus did sing before 20,000 in a stadium performance for the Exposition. "The audience tired itself encoring the numbers," the *Seattle Post Intelligencer* reported of the 1909 performance. Church leaders were pleased with the Choir's growing number of engagements but counseled them to avoid becoming "a common troupe of minstrels."

The *Deseret News* encouraged the Choir to go abroad in 1910, making the case that participation in the Eisteddfod in Wales would bring international stature: "Musical people all over the world understand the importance of these Eisteddfods. Choirs

For the Beauty of the Earth

At General Conference in 1869, fifteen-year-old Evan Stephens visited Temple Square. He wandered in the west door of the Tabernacle, where George Careless, choir leader, noticed the boy in his shirt sleeves. Evans wrote, "He came up quietly and patted me on the shoulder and asked me where my coat was. 'I have a coat but I thought I would not need it.' 'I think you had better go and get that coat,' he said. So I realized dress had something to do with it." Stephens later became director of the Tabernacle Choir, and his chorus sang in whatever clothes they had.

With touring and broadcasts, that changed. The first costumes were choir robes sewn by sisters in Relief Society. As styles changed, so did the Choir's wardrobe. Men's suits have long been the standard, but the color of the jacket and the tie has varied. Over the years they have ordered jackets—blue, black, white, tuxedo—through manufacturers. Interestingly, the men have strong opinions about their clothing. Asked about their current favorite look, the "new black" suit stands out because "it isn't polyester." Others dislike the bow ties, and some take issue with the colored jackets.

The women donned satin dresses in the 1950s and then wore black skirts. The women bought their own; the Choir bought the blouses. The gold blouse never garnered a following. One choir member retiring in 2000 described the costume changes over the years: "We have gone from the 'old, white brocade calf-length' dresses and salmon blouses to the fine wardrobe we now enjoy. I survived the sausage wrapper dress, gold blouse, and short rose dress," she said with satisfaction. In the 1950s the women were required to have their hair no longer than shoulder length. One woman, refusing to cut her hair, tucked her long tresses under a wig.

In 1974 choir member Virginia Peterson was charged with heading up the women's wardrobe committee. She served twenty-eight years organizing committees of choir members to research fabrics and suggest dress designs. Peggy Becker and Margot Marler worked with her; all three were volunteers. At first the Choir bought some of the women's clothing from manufacturers, who were only too happy to provide 150 dresses plus extras. But it became apparent that most women are not a perfect size, and reorders were complicated. The wardrobe committee determined to design and produce their own and to expect a dress to last twenty years. Varied hem length prompted full-length gowns, and tests on camera determined colors.

The public sees the finished product: the aqua, the fuchsia, the white, the cream, the black skirt and beaded top, the royal blue. But there is much going on behind the scenes. Three women work in the basement of the Tabernacle, unstitching,

cutting, sewing, hemming, measuring, and cleaning. Theirs is unsung service—in this case, underground Temple Square.

Valerie Jensen, recently retired from the Choir, was asked to head up the wardrobe committee in 2003. Peggy and Margot are still serving. To see them at work—"Add this to the sleeve, a little more here, put a tuck there"—is to see a fine-tuned operation. Virginia developed a system for measuring that makes it possible to customize each dress. Peggy sews each one; Margot cuts and hems. One black sequined top takes all day to make. The task seems daunting to everyone but them. They start with a sample dress and make notes of adjustments. They fit and refit as needed. "Someone is always here when the Choir meets," Valerie explains. "We are fitting, sewing, and fixing all the time." They travel with the Choir, mending, adjusting, and cleaning as they go.

Their biggest push was to sew dresses for the 2002 Winter Olympics. The royal blue had been designed, but they didn't start sewing until October 21, 2001. They finished the dresses with two weeks to spare before the Choir began performing its Tabernacle concerts for the many visitors in February 2002.

"Our job," they chime, "is to make the women in the Choir beautiful."

At first, choir members wore what they had in their closets. Then, for uniformity, they had the Relief Society make them choir robes, but with changing tastes, fashions, and television audiences, colors in the choir loft became popular. Jewelry also adds to the look. The wardrobe is always a point of discussion.

The Church constructed tabernacles in many communities. In the late 1800s there were choirs up and down the state—the Ogden Tabernacle Choir, the Logan Tabernacle Choir, the Provo Tabernacle Choir—but the Salt Lake Tabernacle Choir was the most consistent and had the largest "stage." While others were invited to sing at General Conference and were well respected in their towns, the Salt Lake Mormon Tabernacle Choir became the LDS Church's musical voice to the world.

There is fire in their eyes, and thunder in their throats."

In the fall of 1911, the Mormon Tabernacle Choir took a 5,500-mile tour to the American Land and Irrigation Exposition held in New York's Madison Square Garden. The Choir visited twenty-three cities and gave twenty-six concerts in addition to the ten days of appearances each afternoon and evening at the New York Exposition. Favorable comments by music critics again boosted the image of the Latter-day Saints.

As the Choir's Oregon Short Line train pulled out on October 23, 1911, loaded with "two hundred sweet singers of Zion," their president, David A. Smith, reported, "To take a look into the train, as it left Salt Lake City, one would wonder at the excitement, but upon closer scrutiny, he would find that dress-suits and white shirts were being unpacked by the men, and adjusted to their persons, as fast as possible, in the small dressing rooms of the cars. The ladies likewise were clothing themselves in white, and preparing for their first concert away from home."

Following the highly successful concert, the *Omaha Excelsior* declared, "If the aim of the Mormon choir in this its swing around the

competing there will receive attention from music journals and judges throughout the world." The pleas went unanswered another forty years.

The *St. Louis Post Dispatch* commented in 1910, "They sing in entirely different fashion from any other chorus. In the Mormons' song there is a magnificent note of religious frenzy, a diapason of devotion, an echo of deeds of fanaticism and of grappling with the desert, to make it blossom like a rose. . . . Their song has the note of triumph over difficulties and dangers overcome. It is the note of the pioneers, the roadbreakers into the wilderness; and indeed, they do not in looks belie their ancestry.

THE MUSIC OF THE CHOIR JUST SQUEEZED MY HEART.
—*Barbara Turner, Chautauqua, 2003*

eastern circle is to make propaganda for its Church, it certainly could not have enlisted a more powerful instrument than its great choir."

The *St. Louis Star* commended, "To the skeptical who went prepared to see beings of strange

On September 25, 1909, President William Howard Taft visited Salt Lake City, attended an organ concert in the Tabernacle, and the next day spoke from the hall's pulpit. Two years later the Choir performed for ten days at New York's Madison Square Garden and on the return trip presented a special concert in the East Room of the White House for President and Mrs. Taft and invited guests.

physique and of peculiar tone production, the performance proved a great revelation, and those in the audience who expected to be amused were much edified. This contingent will testify that there were no horns or feathers visible, while, on the other hand, the entire audience will long recall the occasion as one of the rarest musical delight."

In Philadelphia, the clergy circulated a petition decrying the appearance of the Choir as "Mormon propaganda" and calling for a boycott of the performance, but the effort failed. Judge Edward, who had led one of the Welsh choirs in Chicago in 1893, attended the concert and thrilled the Choir with his congratulations, stating that "this was the greatest singing he had ever heard."

The Choir's first appearance in New York elicited a congratulations from the *New York Musical Courier:* "The visit of this organization from Salt Lake City gives evidence that there is sincere earnestness in artistic matters in the remotest parts of the United States. All the good things in music are not concentrated in the metropolis of New York."

> *Now, we thank you for these blessings,*
> *We, your people, ev'rywhere.*

At the invitation of U.S. president William Howard Taft, the Choir performed in the East Room at the White House, beginning a tradition of singing for presidents that would reach through the 20th century. And into the next. One of the choir members who sang for Taft in 1911 was one of 125 choir members who sang for President Eisenhower in 1958.

The 1911 tour was the last for choir director Evan Stephens. He was released five years later. Stephens bid farewell to the Choir in a stirring poem:

> *My Father has work which I yet may do,*
> *In his vineyard great and wide;*
> *Just some little thing, either old or new*
> *On this, or the other side.*
> *And tho' today I unburden the load,*
> *I've been carrying along,*
> *'Tis only to rest by the side of the road—*
> *Just a pause in the midst of a song.*

I JUST KEEP MOVIN' ON

❧❧

Touring Far

Goin' home, goin' home,
Been so long away;
Wander'd far down the road,
Goin' home to stay.

ANTHONY C. LUND was chosen by LDS Church president Joseph F. Smith to
lead the Choir after Evan Stephens. Within the year, Lund would direct the
Choir at the graveside service for President Smith, the last LDS president to
have known the Prophet Joseph Smith. On that solemn occasion, Lund also performed a solo, "I Know That My Redeemer Lives," a hymn adopted early by the
Latter-day Saints for their first hymnal. Lund would serve for nineteen years.

He would also lead the Choir to a totally new venue—radio. On July 15, 1929, he
directed the first radio broadcast, launching a whole new means of "touring" to the
choir schedule.

In 1934 Professor Lund took the Choir back to Chicago, where it had made a name
for itself four decades earlier. The manager of the 1911 New York Tour, George D.
Pyper, was tapped to direct the Chicago venture. Stopping first in Denver, Colorado,

In 1977 the Choir was honored for "its contributions to a better life," as part of World Gratitude Day. In the next decade, the Choir's globe-trotting tradition took them to Russia (above), in 1991. The Choir also performed in such diverse locations as Brazil (1981), England, Scandinavia, Europe (1982), Canada (1984, 1986), Japan (1985), Hawaii, New Zealand, and Australia (1988).

Choir conductor Anthony C. Lund directed the Choir in a pageant. He noted that "The Message of the Ages," celebrating "century one of the History of the Church of the New Dispensation, came to its close with this evening's pageantry in a blaze of glory." The theme drew from the words of Tennyson: "I doubt not through the ages, one increasing purpose runs." The west end of the Tabernacle was converted to a huge stage divisible by immense curtains for the event, which featured the organ, an orchestra, and music by the Choir.

the 268 members of the Choir sang to an audience of 7,000 in the City Auditorium and were applauded by the *Denver Post* as "the singing saints of Salt Lake City."

The Choir presented sixteen concerts—a different program each time—at the Chicago Century of Progress sponsored by Ford Motor Company. The manager of the exposition wired his applause to Salt Lake City, saying, "Critics and laymen alike

A music professor, Anthony C. Lund enhanced the vocal training of the Choir and often highlighted the Choir's celebrated vocalists, including Jessie Evans Smith, wife of apostle Joseph F. Smith, who was later a president of the LDS Church.

consider its concerts one of the most successful entertainments offered during the entire year." The Choir received national recognition for their participation as witnessed by reviews in the *New York Herald*, which applauded their "dashing brio and deep reverence."

In August 1935 J. Spencer Cornwall was asked to take up the baton. He was handed a choir with touring and broadcast experience, and he built upon both in the years to come. In his era, the Choir took the Sunday morning broadcast on the road, albeit infrequently. They produced shows from Zion's National Park and Sun Valley. He and the Choir again toured California, where the music editor of the *Los Angeles Times* wrote, "Cornwall's work with this choir is as solid as the 16-foot foundation that supports the temple in Salt Lake where the Tabernacle Choir lives and moves and has its being."

In addition to touring, the Choir began hosting

AGAIN WE LEAVE YOU . . .

From 1930 until his death on November 1, 1971, Richard L. Evans was the sole voice of *Music and the Spoken Word*. He was welcomed every Sunday morning in homes across America as a friend and wise counselor, his words prompting new direction, hope, or solace: "It sometimes seems that we live as if we wonder when life is going to begin. It isn't always clear just what we are waiting for, but some of us sometimes persist in waiting so long that life slips by—finding us still waiting for something that has been going on all the time. . . . This is life and it is passing."

Producer, writer, and announcer, he continued in his choir service and his weekly assignment on radio and television and as the announcer on tour even after his calling as a member of the Quorum of Twelve Apostles. He was

a man of vision, a philosopher, a believer that Jesus Christ and his gospel can ameliorate any difficulty, heal any wound. Said Evans of his role, "I've tried to keep in mind that radio, no matter how impersonal it may sometimes seem, creates an intimate relationship between the broadcaster and the listener—a relationship whereby the listener permits us to come into his home, which is a sacred trust of which we are at all times mindful."

Each of his short sermons is masterfully crafted and presented, as illustrated by the following given on October 2, 1949:

"There is a lesson sooner or later learned by almost all of us, and that is that there are some things we have to leave to time. If we were to call for self-confession, we might well have a large showing of hands from those who have sometime planted seeds but who couldn't wait for shoots to show above the surface and so have dug them up to see what they were doing. But we can't dig up the seed and have a harvest or break open a bud and have a flower. We have to leave some things to time. When someone is confined with illness or injury, his first question is, 'How long will it be?' The seasoned physician will sometimes say, 'A few days,' when he knows full well it will likely be much longer, but he tries to fit the forecast to the endurance of the man who is down. We can help the healing process; but, despite the pressure of our impatience, there is much we have to leave to time. Sometimes we see someone who seems to be 'getting away with something' without prevention or punishment, and we may feel that justice is unreasonably slow as well as blind. But time overtakes all offenses and offenders—sometimes sooner than we suppose. Sometimes we see people we are impatient to improve. But we can't force the minds of men. We can teach, persuade, and persevere, and set before them a convincing example—and leave the rest to time. Of course we can't leave everything to time. We can't condone complacency. We must actively oppose the intrusion of every evil. We must earnestly be about our business and be anxiously engaged in a good cause. We must plant when it is time for planting or we shall have no harvest. But having done the best we can do, we must learn to leave what we can't do to the growing, developing, mending, mellowing process of time. And if we have faith enough, patience enough, perseverance enough, time will work many wonders. It will reveal truth and discredit untruth. It will silence slander. It will soften many sorrows. It will heal many wounds—wounds of the flesh, of the heart, of the mind and of the spirit. It will right many wrongs. It will bring compensation, retribution, vindication. And even if in our time we don't find all the answers, immortal men can afford to have faith in the limitless future—if we do each day what can and should be done and leave to time what time alone can do."

The Choir sang in the great European art centers: Glasgow, London, Copenhagen, Amsterdam, Berlin, and Paris. They sang to sold-out houses, and in Paris, the demand for tickets so exceeded seating that the French carried the two-hour concert on radio.

dramatic musical events in the Tabernacle. On May 5, 1936, the Great Philadelphia Symphony Orchestra, with Leopold Stokowski as conductor, gave a concert at the Tabernacle and invited the Choir to sing the "Hallelujah Chorus" from Handel's *Messiah*. Not in all the decades that this chorus has been singing in Salt Lake has there ever been heard such a rendition." The "Hallelujah Chorus" has marked many important milestones in the Choir's history.

The next year, the Philadelphia Orchestra returned, this time under the baton of its new conductor, Eugene Ormandy. A friendship, trust, and musical alliance was formed. Ormandy is quoted as saying, "I wish we had such a chorus in Philadelphia."

In 1955, under the direction of Cornwall and with the blessing of LDS Church president David O. McKay, the Choir took a leap to the world stage with a six-week tour of Europe. It required "Herculean effort" from all involved. They would sing in Glasgow, Manchester, Cardiff, London, Amsterdam, Scheveningen, Copenhagen, Berlin, Wiesbaden, Bern, Zurich, and Paris; at the dedication of the LDS temple in Bern, Switzerland; and at the groundbreaking of the London Temple. It had been more than fifty years since the Choir's participation in the dedication of the grand Salt Lake Temple.

The party of nearly 600 Choir members and staff sailed from Montreal to Scotland on a Canadian

liner, the S.S. Saxonia. Church officers bid adieu to the singers with the charge to go "as ambassadors of the greatest nation and the greatest cause that any group has represented." Travel costs exceeded $400,000.

Richard L. Evans, an apostle and longtime voice of *Music and the Spoken Word*, counseled the travelers, "Keep close to one another; . . . keep close to your standards; . . . keep close to your Father in Heaven." The lord provost of Glasgow, Andrew Hood, greeted them with a bagpipe band and "a thousand welcomes," but a bold headline in the Glasgow daily questioned, "Can they sing?" Their first concert settled the matter.

Cornwall later related, "The faces of the audience exhibited neither friendliness nor unfriendliness. They were neutral but curious. They greeted the entrance of the choir with applause, but it seemed to be simply concert deportment." "God Save the Queen" was the opening number, followed by Scotland's most beloved hymn, "Crimond," a Scottish psalm tune with the text versified from the Twenty-third Psalm. As the Choir began to sing the third stanza, the audience joined with them:

> Goodness and mercy all my life
> Shall surely follow me,
> And in God's house for evermore
> My dwelling-place shall be.

President McKay observed, "The dignified attitude of the group as a whole, their comely deportment, their evident sincerity of purpose, their responsiveness, won the audience even before they started to sing."

> *That's the place ' want to see,*
> *Now my work's all done;*
> *That's the place ' want to be,*
> *That's where I belong.*

President David O. McKay (center), accompanied by his wife, Emma Ray McKay, and (left to right) Elders Matthew Cowley, Richard L. Evans, and Spencer W. Kimball, officiated at the groundbreaking of the London Temple, the first in the British Isles, and the dedication of the Swiss Temple, the first on the European continent.

At nearly every concert, choir members reported the audience demanding six or eight encores and applauding mightily for songs performed in their native tongue—most often their national anthem—and for the Mormon anthem, "Come, Come, Ye Saints." The words "All is well" resonated with countries who had put the ravages of war behind them. In Paris, the demand for tickets so exceeded the seating that French radio broadcast the full two-hour concert. Of the concert in the Netherlands a young man wrote, "The sound of your choir was like God's own voice, who calls to the world because his Son will soon come back. In your choir I heard his voice calling me."

Elder Richard L. Evans, master of ceremonies, implemented an introduction that has become a tradition on tour. At each performance he asked choir members who traced their origins to that country or region to stand. The impact was dramatic, for these Americans were, for the most part, returning "home." One European newspaper captured the significance of the moment, headlining its article "In the Land of their Fathers." Rave reviews were printed

THE IMPOSSIBLE DREAM

Composer and conductor John Williams calls Craig Jessop "fabulous," suggesting that this music director of the Mormon Tabernacle Choir "ranks with Robert Shaw and the other great American choral conductors." His singers appreciate him, describing him as tireless, passionate, a firecracker with a waltz, driven, professional, a dynamo. Marcie Alley, longtime choir member states, "You can find the ictus of the beat in his hair. His whole body is full of rhythm."

He grew up in Millville, Utah, a little town in northern Utah. "None of us had anything, and we didn't know it," he says. But they had a youth choir—started by sixteen-year-old Craig Jessop. His career didn't begin there; it began in the horse corrals and farm fields he worked as a young man. His work ethic underpins what choir members call "their phenomenal experience" with this dynamic conductor.

"What I love about being a conductor is that I love people," he says with that ever-present twinkle in his eye. "And as a conductor I can stand in front of the Choir and they allow me to see who they really are. They drop all facades. I love having the opportunity to see the beauty of who each individual is. And I try to be aware of where they are, and if Ryan Bateman isn't there, I feel a hole. If Kristen Olsen isn't there, I know the family circle is not complete."

For him, rehearsal is the ultimate choral experience: "The moments that I treasure more than any other are the insignificant moments in rehearsal. It might be warming up the Choir a cappella on 'Abide With Me, 'Tis Eventide' and just hearing that sound float in that sacred space. It's just me and the Choir and God. The music isn't for an audience. It isn't sung for applause. It is sung to make it as good as it can possibly be."

He is quick with lighthearted quips and encouragement. He's firm and focused yet known for his kindness. Rehearsals bring out vintage Craig Jessop: "Let's give it a read; here we go." "I know you are tired. I feel your pain. Pinch your cheeks, run around the block, but don't get out of your chair. Sprint to the finish line." "Warm it up ever so little; it's a little sterile. Split the difference with me." "I dare you to go sharp." "This has to have such joy, such youthful exuberance." "If you look down at the end and the beginning of a phrase, the middle will take care of itself—just like tomorrow."

Louisiana-born Moses George Hogan was a conductor, pianist, and arranger of international renown. Hogan recorded and conducted several of his arrangements with the Mormon Tabernacle Choir on their release "American Heritage of Spirituals."

"Craig is an orator," states Julie Sessions, soprano. "He can change the sound of the Choir by sharing a few thoughts on the meaning of a song."

Craig Jessop has loved the Choir since he was small. When he was four, his mother took him to Temple Square. He remembers the event vividly: "I was in the back seat of our car, looking out the back window. My mom was driving around and around, and there were just people all over. It had to have been Conference. And I could see the spires of the temple and hear the Choir in my mind."

When he was a little older, he still loved the Choir: "I would go to my first Sunday meeting, priesthood meeting, then I would run home, because if I ran quick enough I could get part of the broadcast on the radio and still make it back in time for Sunday School. I can just see myself running back to my bedroom, turning on my clock radio to listen to the broadcast. I never missed. Ever."

After graduating from Utah State and while pursuing a master's degree at BYU, he wanted to join the Choir. The procedure was less formal than it is today. He called and made an appointment for an audition with choir conductor Richard Condie. It was set for the next Sunday after the broadcast. Jessop recalls, "I went up after the broadcast, and I said, 'Brother Condie, I am Craig Jessop. You told me to come audition today.' He looked at me and said, 'Well, I can't hear you today—

it's Memorial Day,' and he turned away. My friend in the Choir said, 'Don't move. Stand right there and don't move.' I was gutsy enough to do it. A long line of people shook his hand, and when he saw me still standing there, he said, 'Okay, come on.' We went down in the basement. He had me sing 'O My Father,' and then he looked at me and said, 'By golly, you can sing. Come Thursday night and bring a letter from your bishop.'" In hopes of being accepted, Jessop had already gotten the letter.

He was a member of the baritone section for four years, assigned to a seat next to Ken Rodgerson, who sang in the Choir more than fifty years, including the first broadcast in 1929. Jessop left to get his doctorate from Stanford. Years passed before he made his way back to the Salt Lake Tabernacle and the position seemingly made in heaven for him.

Jessop's first experience conducting in the Tabernacle came as a guest conductor in November 1975 at a Veterans Day concert with the Granite High School chorus. He was a guest conductor several times for the Mormon Tabernacle Choir in the years to come. He then served as associate director for the Choir from 1995 to 1999, when he was named the Choir's music director. He brought with him experience gained as a member of the U.S. Air Force conducting the highly applauded U.S. Singing Sergeants, the Band of the United States Air Forces in Europe, and the Air Combat Heartland of America Band. He toured with the Robert Shaw Festival Singers throughout Europe and performed with them at Carnegie Hall. He credits Shaw as the biggest musical inspiration in his life. "Robert Shaw told me the tone of Craig's voice was a gift of God," recalls Westin Noble, conductor of the Nordic Choir at Luther College and a good friend of the Mormon Tabernacle Choir. He expressed his own impression of choir director Jessop, saying, "His depth of dedication, his depth of stewardship to his Church and to the Choir can't be overstated."

Mack Wilberg, associate director, joined Craig soon after his appointment as music director in 1999. "I came here because of Craig Jessop," says Dr. Wilberg. "His generosity of spirit and his vision are remarkable. We are just beginning to see the effects of his organizational genius."

in London, Paris, Berlin, Wiesbaden, and Zurich. *Time* magazine reported, "Everywhere they are stirring up waves of good feeling and applause. Salt Lake City's Mormon Tabernacle Choir is a smash hit in Europe." The Dutch paper *Telegraaf* said, "They have disarming naiveté and a cordial and honest expression."

Cornwall captured the essence of the Choir's efforts: "When loyalty was asked for, you gave it. When faith was needed, you exercised it. When fortitude was imperative, you had it." President David O. McKay reported at the October General Conference, "Every member of the Choir deserves the highest praise." He quoted the Paris correspon-

dent of the *New York Herald:* "The whole program was sung by heart, in the most literal sense."

Just a year later, after the Choir sang at the Denver Symphony's summer music festival at Red Rocks Amphitheater, a *Denver Post* columnist wrote, "This great choir sang songs of faith and spirit, making proclamations of divine import, casting on the gathered throng the unforgettable sense of being joined together in celebration of life and its great mysteries."

Since its grand European tour, the Mormon Tabernacle Choir has made regular out-of-state appearances. They have traveled up, down, and across North America, visiting Canada, Texas,

THIS IS HIS CHOIR, AND EACH OF US IS BUT A TRANSIENT, OCCUPYING A CHAIR FOR A SEASON AND FILLING WITH DEDICATION A PLACE IN THE GREAT FLOWERING OF HIS ETERNAL WORK. . . . YOU ARE A PART OF THE GREATEST CAUSE IN ALL THE EARTH. YOUR ANTHEMS OF PRAISE TO HIM, SUNG WITH SUCH POWER BEFORE THE BEAUTIFUL PEOPLE THAT SOME OF US HAVE LONG LOVED AND WHOM ALL OF YOU HAVE NOW COME TO LOVE, WERE HEARD AND ACKNOWLEDGED BY HIM WHO "WATCHING OVER ISRAEL, SLUMBERS NOT NOR SLEEPS."

—*President Gordon B. Hinckley, The Churchof Jesus Christ of Latter-day Saints*

Colorado, Missouri, Illinois, California, South Carolina, Tennessee, Washington, and Massachusetts, to name a few. Following a concert in the East, a reviewer wrote, "Their fortissimos, when called for, were the expected rafter-rattlers." Not until 1970 did the Choir travel the 110 miles to its sister state Idaho for a concert.

For the nation's 200th birthday, the Choir toured the East with a bicentennial salute that climaxed at the Kennedy Center in Washington, D.C. It was the Choir's seventh venture to the nation's capital.

In the next quarter century, the Choir would repeat its sweep of Europe and visit Asia, Japan, Korea, Australia, New Zealand, Mexico, Brazil, Scandinavia, Eastern Europe, and Israel, adding not only stamps in passports but also scores of new Mormon Tabernacle Choir enthusiasts. The Choir has performed at music festivals and historic commemorations and toured every continent but Africa. At music festivals, they've been on the summer schedules with grand opera companies, dance and ballet companies, major symphony orchestras, and theater companies, always as a favorite of those attending. They have kept their purpose firmly in their programming and their performing.

On June 2, 1988, as the Choir set out for Hawaii, New Zealand, and Australia, Church president Gordon B. Hinckley remarked, "This is the longest trip the Choir has ever made it in its history. You won't make another one so far, I think, until you become heavenly angels singing in a heavenly choir. And I have no idea how far that journey is."

In 1991 the Choir bused or flew 4,200 miles across eight European countries—Germany, France, Switzerland, Hungary, Austria, Czechoslovakia, Poland, and Russia. In each country the Choir sang

Richard Condie, Richard L. Evans, and Ed Sullivan on the set of the popular television variety show, which aired from 1948 to 1971. Sullivan saw his role as talent scout and cultural commissar for the entire country, introducing thousands of performers, including the Mormon Tabernacle Choir.

THE HOLY LAND JUST SEEMED TO DRINK IN OUR MUSIC. IT BELONGED THERE—PERHAPS LIKE THE BIBLICAL ACCOUNTS OF CHOIRS OF ANGELS.
—*Robb Cundick, tenor*

a selection in the native language. Choir Director Jerold Ottley explains, "We made it a point a long time ago not to try to carry coals to Newcastle by trying to sing the literature of their own culture that they know so well, except for maybe a national hymn or a national song or at least a folk song. We try to sing it simply so that they can understand it and feel the communication of it, rather than try to do some of their masters which they could do better. And that has allowed us to move into the hearts of a lot of people."

Voice coach JoAnn Ottley was in the audience when the Choir began just such a song in Poland.

In Israel, the Choir was in the land of the Savior. Choir member Julie Rhode recalls when they sang at Shepherds' Field, "It felt as if I had been there before with a choir in the heavens." Others agreed, "We've done this before."

She notes, "There was a bit of a gasp as it started, and then in the dark I just saw one figure stand and then another figure stand and then another figure stand, and it just kept growing and expanding, and then the tears. You could see the tears coming down. And to watch that, knowing how oppressed these people had been—their city is so majestic yet so untended, their clothing that was very old and very tired." She will never forget the significance: "They had been given a return of something that was more precious to them than anything."

The tour of the eastern European countries was filled with such moments. "The curtain went down three times in Budapest before we could get off the stage," choir president Wendell Smoot recalls. "Literally, the curtain came down and the

Wendell Smoot

people were still clapping. We had to raise the curtain and sing another song. We did that three times. They wouldn't let us go."

Visiting Israel in late December 1992 and January 1993, the Choir performed at concerts, broadcast *Music and the Spoken Word*, and filmed segments for a television documentary featuring the Choir in the Holy Land singing Christ-centered songs in several locations, including Shepherds' Field and the Garden Tomb. The *Church News* reported that Reverend Peter Vasko, director of pilgrimages at St. Savior's Monastery, commented, "I often wondered what the angelic chorus of long ago sounded like when they sang to shepherds in the fields of Bethlehem. I need wonder no more." Showpiece concerts with the Jerusalem Symphony Orchestra, billed as "A Classical

Touring is a lot of standing, lining up, waiting, sitting, and sleeping on buses, trains, planes, and floors. The Choir travels light, if light is one suitcase, clothes for nineteen days, wardrobe and music for thirteen concerts, and sensible shoes.

On an eight-nation tour, the Choir sang numbers in the language of the countries they were visiting. In Russia they performed in Moscow's famed Bolshoi Theater and Leningrad's Philharmonic Hall. The programs featured religious hymns and anthems as well as folk and show tunes. At both concerts, the Choir sang an old Russian prayer, "God Bless Us." The song had not been sung in public for many years and brought a tearful response from many in the audience. The official photograph of the tour was taken in front of the famous St. Basil's Cathedral in Moscow.

Winter in Jerusalem—Liturgica 92," featured Berlioz's *Requiem Mass,* Opus 5.

In 1998 the Choir toured Europe, and again they were more than well received. Ottley asked Craig Jessop, then his assistant, to conduct the Choir in a British favorite, "Jerusalem," at the concert in London's Royal Albert Hall. "He knew I had been a missionary in England, and he also knew I loved that song," Jessop recalls. "When the Choir sang, you could feel the emotion in the room." They were asked to sing it again as an encore. "Everyone in Albert Hall stood. It was a great moment as we sang it again."

That tour itinerary averaged one concert a day, including twelve formal concerts, one outdoor performance, three Sunday meetings, and four evening devotionals. The words "He has sounded forth the trumpet that shall never call retreat" well described the cadence of the Choir.

The magazine *American Organist* caught the vision of the Choir's work ethic, volunteerism, and spirit in this 1989 tribute: "In its 140-year history, the Tabernacle Choir has performed for royalty and heads of state from the world over, but never has it lost the common touch, the ability to stir the hearts of all mankind as it lifts its collective voice in singing of the values we all cherish and in praising the God who created us all."

Steady down the road keep movin',
Soon these weary eyes a-soothin'
When I look on home.

Land of the Free, Home of the Brave

It was Ronald Reagan who dubbed the Mormon Tabernacle Choir "America's Choir." He said of them, "At my first inauguration as president of the United States, I wanted very much to re-ignite the fires of liberty and re-inspire the American Spirit. And no one sings the anthems of America quite like the Mormon Tabernacle Choir.

"It isn't just your inspirational singing that moves us, it's also the heritage of faith and self-reliance you represent, a heritage handed down from your pioneer forebears who carved homes out of a barren wilderness.

"The Choir's singing was a highlight of our inauguration, as we knew it would be. I'm sure I speak for all Americans when I say thank you for saying so well what all of us feel about this land of the free and home of the brave. There is no more inspirational moment for any American—and that includes Ronald Reagan—than to hear the Mormon Tabernacle Choir sing 'Glory, glory, hallelujah, His truth is marching on.'"

News commentators agreed. A CBS anchor said of the Choir's performance in the Reagan inaugural that if it were possible to "bring the house down at an outdoor parade, the Mormon Tabernacle Choir just did it."

The Choir has a long tradition of singing for U.S. presidents—nearly every one since Dwight D. Eisenhower and several before. Some have come to the Choir; some have had the Choir come to them.

Lyndon B. Johnson had the stand at the Capitol rebuilt to accommodate choir members for his inauguration. Johnson later acknowledged at a White House concert the great influence of the Choir, its heritage, industry, and service. He explained that President Thomas Jefferson once wrote to a friend "that it was difficult to employ musicians because of—as he put it—the economy which we are obliged to observe. Jefferson's solution was simple. He decided he could hire persons to fill the house with music if they would agree to work part-time as gardeners." President Johnson then added, "I know folks from your part of the country have done very well through the years farming new ground. . . . No stronger fabric of America has been woven from many threads," he claimed, "and no thread is stronger than that thread of religious devotion and religious freedom which runs through all our history."

The Choir has sung for many U.S. presidents. In 1958 the Choir was welcomed at the White House for a "memorable evening" performing for the Eisenhowers. Richard L. Evans cautioned the Choir, "Remember this, success is never final. That which you could do in the past isn't nearly as significant as that which you can do or do better. This is the conclusion of a great triumph and achievement, but only the beginning of great and meaningful things yet to come." In 1963 President John F. Kennedy (above) spoke in the Tabernacle with the Choir providing the music. In 2002 the Choir sang with President George W. Bush at a program at the Utah State Capitol.

For the inauguration of Richard M. Nixon, the Choir sang "This Is My Country." A local news reporter stated of the chorus's parade performance, "The final curtain of this affair that has gone a little Hollywood, is the Mormon Tabernacle Choir. Quite an ending to a parade with them singing, 'America, a New Beginning.'"

Choir members recall that in 1989 George Bush sang "Battle Hymn of the Republic" along with them when the float stopped at the stands.

Of their 1999 appearance for the second President Bush? The weather was cold. Had it been the broadcast, it could have been called *Music and the Frozen Word*.

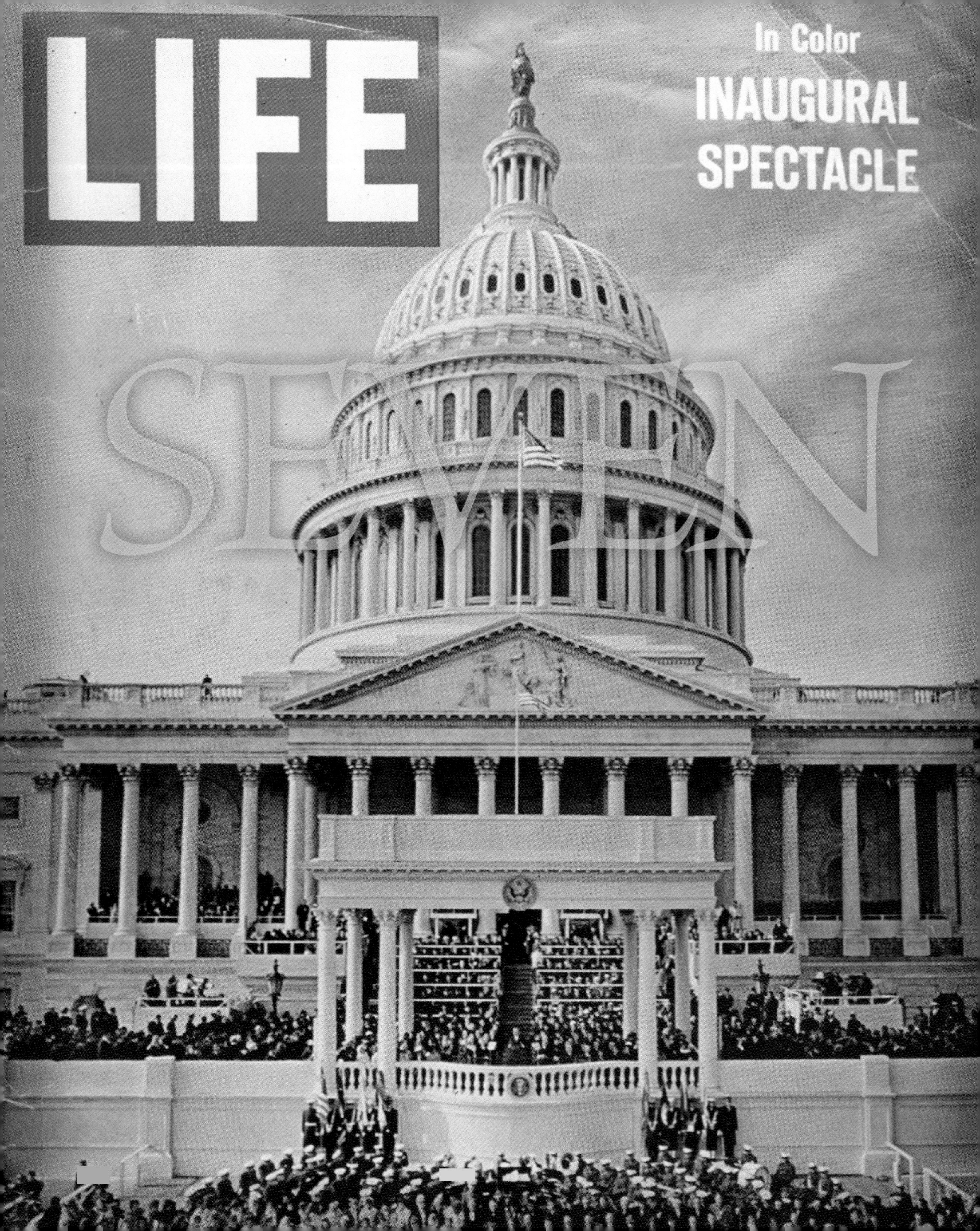
LIFE
In Color
INAUGURAL
SPECTACLE
SEVEN

AMERICA, THE DREAM GOES ON

The Country Applauds

America, America, and the dream goes on.
There's a song in the dust of a country road.
On the wind it comes to call.
And it sings in the farms and the fact'ry towns,
And where you'd think there'd be no song at all.

"IT'S LIKE TRAVELING WITH A SMALL ARMY," administrative manager Barry Anderson says of the weeks on the road worrying about chicken dinners, bus schedules, and room keys. He chuckles as he adds, "Traveling with the Choir fits the statement from an old western, 'You've come far, Pilgrim,' and the response is quick: 'Feels like far.'"

The Choir launched its northeastern states tour on June 24, 2003, to commemorate the seventy-fifth anniversary of continual network broadcasting of *Music and the Spoken Word*. Six states, ten cities, nineteen days, eleven concerts. Ten busses with friendly drivers. Three charter airplanes left Salt Lake International Airport at staggered times. Fifteen hundred pieces of luggage were pulled from midnight to 3:00 A.M. by strong-armed volunteers—who double as tenors and basses at concerts. Three hundred thirty-five singers, twenty-five instrumentalists, two organists, two

conductors, and even the volunteer seamstresses, librarians, and historian were on board. Each woman traveled with three concert gowns, each of the men with a tux and a suit. Hotel rooms for 565, scrambled eggs, and box lunches; all-night trains to make back-to-back engagements; sightseeing from a bus as it pulls into the parking lot of the concert hall. Rain, hail, and heat in midsummer. That's a Tab Choir tour.

Rock stars they are not. But sometimes they feel the fanfare. Police with flashing lights escort them through city streets. They get standing ovations, whistles and clapping. More often than not concert-goers return home with a new resume item: "I sang with the Mormon Tabernacle Choir."

Remember the voice of Jefferson
and the sound of Thomas Paine.
Lincoln sang at Gettysburg about America.
Listen well to the wind, and you can hear
from Oregon to Maine,
America, America.

The Choir flew into Grand Rapids, Michigan, and hopped (it was early in the trip) busses for the two-hour trip to Interlochen. It was a first for the Choir at the famed Interlochen Music Festival. With Green Lake as backdrop and birds chirping for accompaniment, the Choir opened a nineteen-day tour to some of America's most prestigious music festivals and concert halls, a prelude to the seventy-fifth anniversary of the broadcast. "Dedicated to the promotion of world friendship through the universal language of the arts"—Interlochen's purpose was a perfect fit for the Choir. Other engagements were outdoors, but the music was not one bit casual. Nor was the grand

Fourth of July celebration on the Boston Esplanade with the Boston Pops.

The Choir sang in the premier concert halls— the New Jersey Theater for the Performing Arts, Avery Fisher Hall in Lincoln Center. The tiered concert hall of New Jersey, resembling the great halls of Europe, was filled. The sponsors wished they'd booked two nights. But there were no two-night engagements. Craig Jessop said, "We were singing the songs of the masters in halls that could receive such power. And then we were on the road in the morning." Though Grand Rapids could only offer its sports arena, "It was grand, and the Choir nearly filled it," Anderson observed. They sang at the most prestigious music festivals in the east— Interlochen, Chautauqua, and Saratoga Springs in New York, Wolf Trap in Virginia, Mann Theatre in Philadelphia and Tanglewood in Massachusetts.

The Choir traveled with an instrumental ensemble from the Orchestra at Temple Square. A semi-truck with a forty-eight-foot trailer carrying the instruments and organ kept ahead of the Choir. Two organists—Longhurst and Elliott—played the touring electronic organ at those venues that didn't have their own. Traveling with the Choir's technical crew were two organ technicians, David Bagley and Jeff Hanson, whose responsibility was to set up the organ, pack it away, and voice it to the acoustics of

Two American musical icons combined on July 4, 2003, to present an Independence Day spectacular for 600,000 gathered on the Boston Esplanade. Millions more across the country watched on television.

SAINTS BOUND
FOR HEAVEN

Tours are all about bus travel. The Orchestra bus on the 2003 tour specialized in playing "bus twister." Coaches with more subdued passengers rode farther back in the posse of ten. And then there was Newark. You had to have been there to experience ten busses circling the airport in search of the Marriott Hotel. We could see it, but we couldn't find it. No road. No markers.

For an hour, the intrepid drivers split off, thinking they had found the way, only to cross the freeway waving to one another—no closer to the Marriott sign in the center of the maze. Perhaps it was the 1:30 A.M. hour at the end of a long day and halfway to morning that prompted the hysterics. Our bus had been lost most of the night, so retracing our tracks around the ring-road time after time, up and down, around and through, and meeting Bus 7 and then Bus 2 seemed standard procedure. Even the bus driver (we were in the lead bus and hopelessly lost) was laughing. Laptops with everything but On-Star had kept us going in the right direction but hadn't yet gotten us there. It was one of those times always to be remembered, worthy of mention in an obituary: "Traveled with the Choir in 2003, participated in unscheduled search, no rescue, at Newark airport. Safe at last."

each venue. To replicate the sound of the Choir on the road is a major challenge because the Tabernacle organ and the acoustics of the Tabernacle itself are part of that sound. Richard Elliott recalls a reviewer of a choir tour to Minneapolis a few years earlier "expecting the signature Mormon Tabernacle Choir sound, which is the Choir with the organ. And he was disappointed that he hadn't heard that." It was the first time Elliott had realized there was a signature Mormon Tabernacle Choir sound, which included the sound of the organ.

The five-man crew would break down the show; load lights, sound equipment, organ, and large instruments into the semi-truck and van in the order of what would be needed for the next concert; drive to the next venue; and begin setting up again in time for a sound check in the early afternoon. Sleep was optional. Work began long before the Choir took to the stage and averaged four to five hours for each concert setting. Alex Morris, stage manager for the Orchestra, had the packing of the truck designed for each concert depending on the equipment needed. In New York City and other metropolitan areas, he says, "negotiating the streets with the truck takes great skill." Wolfgang Zeisler, stage manager for touring, coordinated the effort of moving the Choir and setting up the stage. For him, the headache was fitting the 360-member choir, the orchestra ensemble, and the organ onto a stage. It always is. The Choir is an anomaly in touring circles, concert circles, any circles.

Zeisler takes an advance trip with the Choir directors to scout the halls, including the sound and lighting capabilities. A last-minute venue change in Houston in 2001 was what he calls "a disaster." "We walked into a hall the day we were

While 100 choir members went on ahead to rehearse in Boston, 200 dressed in performance attire walked from Times Square to Rockefeller Center to perform outside on the Today Show—*in the rain.*

performing, essentially, and had to put it together." Somehow it worked.

For international tours, the five-man crew takes only minimal equipment, renting most of what they need at the sites or in the towns. Still, things happen to shatter the schedule. On an eastern European trip in 1998, the truck carrying all the equipment was stopped at the border for twenty-four hours. Hiring local drivers who understand the culture and expectations always makes a difference in foreign lands, Zeisler explains.

Most venues do not have the sound quality of the Tabernacle. "When the acoustics are good, the audience feels good, and the Choir feels good because they can hear themselves. It's one thing for the audience to hear the Choir. It's just as important for the Choir to hear the Choir," explains sound technician Lynn Robinson. Out in front, the sound technician is controlling the sound for the audience. Backstage, the work is to balance for the Choir. "It's two audiences," Robinson adds. "The better the venue, the less we have to do."

And then there are lights. The Choir needs to see the conductor, but the audience needs just the right light to frame the Choir. In some locations, a bank of lights is rented; in others, they come with the hall, though they are rarely configured to light a 360-voice choir, Lorin Morse, lighting technician, explains.

And the words are the words that our fathers heard
As they whistled down the years.
And the name of the song is the name of the dream,
And it's music to our ears.
America, America, and the dream goes on.

July 3, 2003 was typical of a choir tour. Busy. Quick-thinking. Patience. Following the concert at Lincoln Center the night before, 100 singers boarded busses for a midnight ride to Massachusetts and

Choir members are used to sound checks and bag checks at airports. But security checks—by dog, prior to boarding the bus for the performance at the Boston Esplanade—was a new wrinkle.

an early practice call for the Fourth of July on the Boston Esplanade. It was the only way to be in two places at the same time. At 7:15 A.M. the remaining choir members gathered in the foyer of the Marriott Marquis for a quick tribute in song to the hotel staff—and guests who hung over the interior balconies.

Most of the Choir, 235, stayed behind for an 8:00 A.M. appearance on NBC's *Today Show.* They walked the six blocks, a string of women in their long, fuchsia dresses—conspicuous even for New York streets. The gray clouds spilled light showers

WE TRY TO PUT THINGS IN THE TOUR THAT MAKE IT MAGIC—LITTLE, SIMPLE THINGS SO THE CHOIR CAN JUST SING, EAT WELL, FEEL GOOD ABOUT BEING THERE, AND BRING THE SPIRIT.
—*Barry Anderson, administrative manager*

as the choir members assembled on the outdoor risers. Then, with ten minutes to air time, came the downpour. Spontaneously some choir members broke into "Singin' in the Rain," which was quickly added to the show schedule. And they sang in the pouring rain, a plastic cover over the piano running rivers to the ground, as Elliott and Longhurst reached inside the folds to the keys. The hair coiffed especially for the national broadcast matted, the makeup ran, and the choir members sang and smiled their way into hearts and homes across the nation.

They walked back to the hotel, picked up box lunches, boarded busses, and headed north in caravan for the Boston Pops July 4 performance. Of course, they got caught on the turnpikes in holiday traffic. Arrival was pushed back once, twice. And again. Those going to a reception with Governor Mitt Romney, friend of the Choir from Olympic days, missed their engagement. But the Choir arrived in time to sing at the evening rehearsal and

THIS DAY

The Choir sang once before in 1967 at the Chautauqua Institution, in the town of Chautauqua, New York, near the Pennsylvania border. Two members of the Choir—Steve Stoker and Diane Miller—had been members on that tour, which also took them to Omaha, Nebraska; Montreal and Expo '67; Narragansett Park, Rhode Island; Saratoga Springs, New York; Detroit, Michigan; and Tulsa, Oklahoma.

One Chautauqua audience member commented, "This place was made for them." That place was a 5,000-seat auditorium with a roof but no sides, somewhat reminiscent of the Old Bowery on Temple Square. A genteel place, Chautauqua is idyllic in its setting on a lake and distinctive in its focus—a retreat dedicated to rejuvenating and lifting those who come for a week, a month, or the summer. Adults attend classes and concerts and participate in discussions. Chautauqua. The setting is of a bygone era—porches with residents rocking in the summer sun; flags, flowers, and an aura of peace that has sought distance from a hectic world. Craig Jessop calls it "a place of renewal."

Ticket holders stood four deep in lines two blocks long just to get a seat—a hard bench at that—but they weren't there for the benches. This sophisticated, concert-going crowd pounded on the backs of their wooden seats to cheer the Choir on to one encore and then another. They clapped along to "This Land Is Your Land," they sighed at the strains of "Climb Ev'ry Mountain," and they joined in the familiar "Battle Hymn" chorus of "Glory, glory, hallelujah."

At the end of the evening as the choir members made their way to waiting busses on the edge of the quaint Victorian community, these summer residents congregated on the porches of their gracious homes that edged the narrow lanes leading out of town. All that was missing was confetti as the residents clapped, waved, and sought promises of a return. The Chautauqua performance and scores of others point to the Choir's outreach to the world. They not only walked the streets—no cars allowed—but they also talked and exchanged addresses with residents. For one afternoon, they called Chautauqua home.

President Theodore Roosevelt said that Chautauqua, New York, was "typically American in that it is typical of America at its best"—a fitting venue for the Mormon Tabernacle Choir. The audience lined up for blocks, more than two hours early, to get seats.

A patriotic sing-along with "Yankee Doodle," "This Land Is Your Land," and "You're a Grand Old Flag" brought cheers and tears from the audience.

again at the splendid fireworks show broadcast live to America. *The Dream Goes On.*

With a twist.

Picture the nation's celebration of the Fourth of July: 600,000 people lining the Charles River for music and fireworks, rows of red dresses, blue suits, and beaming smiles of the Mormon Tabernacle Choir, with the Hatch Shell in the background. "It occurred to me that the Pops and the Choir had never performed together," Pops conductor Keith Lockhart explained, "and I thought it would make a wonderful grand visual and musical statement if they could come here for July Fourth, and that was the incentive for putting this tour together." With the

familiar shell seen often as backdrop to Keith Lockhart and the Boston Pops, the Choir sang as one of their numbers the anthem that made them famous, "Battle Hymn of the Republic." Grand. Spectacular. Fireworks and flashing cameras. But the sound came not from the Choir front and center

While the Choir on camera sang, the voices of the Choir in the tent went out over the airwaves to all America.

I FELT SO STRONGLY THERE WERE "OTHER" SINGERS WITH US THAT I WANTED TO TURN AROUND AND SEE WHO ELSE WAS SINGING. —*Rita Felt, alto*

with the cameras but from the 100 choir members sitting in a tent behind the stage where microphones and sound engineering matched the assembly of fireworks outside. While the Choir on camera sang, the voices of the Choir in the tent went out over the airwaves to all America.

Those not in costume sang the "glory, glory, hallelujahs" as if Uncle Sam were watching them himself. The scene was the essence of the Choir: selfless, talented, united, generous, and good. Selection for the "tent choir" was made by director Craig Jessop. No one appealed for center stage. Choir president Mac Christensen was proud of his people: "This is a choir of one voice and one heart, no matter the setting—even in a tent backstage."

And the words that we read on the courthouse walls
Are the words that make us free.
And the more we remember the way we began,
The closer we get to the best we can be.

Wolf Trap was sizzling for the Choir. With the singers packed two deep on each tier of the stage risers; "melt-down" took on new meaning. The *Washington Post* wrote, "It must have been sweltering on stage at Wolf Trap Saturday evening. Several hundred choristers and musicians packed onto the boards, yet the sea of white dresses and shirts remained pristine. The precise enunciation and attentive delivery achieved by this enormous choir is a testimony to the discipline and leadership of its music directors." The evening was most poignant for Jessop, whose associates from his U.S. Air Force days were scattered about the outdoor setting. With his tribute and applause to his former fellow officers, Jessop took the entire audience into his arms.

At Philadelphia's Mann Theater, Eagles coach Andy Reid stepped up to the podium for a surprise addition to the program. He conducted the Choir in his team's fight song. "It was exhilarating," the "guest" conductor said, "thrill of thrills." He ranked his experience "right up there" with the Super Bowl. So did the cameramen from the seven local stations who filmed the fight song and played it on the late news. It was a first for the Mormon Tabernacle Choir—their first time as a sports story.

President Mac Christensen noted, "There are twenty-four hours in a day; we've been going twenty-six. We have not had an extra second. Nor have we touched so many hearts in such a short period of time."

Early One Morning

The bags of each choir member and fellow traveler on tour—more than 1,500 pieces of luggage—are sent on ahead to be waiting in the rooms. That means setting aside everything that will be needed in the morning for the four-, six-, eight-hour bus ride to the next venue. Such planning ahead is learned.

Choir member Stephen G. Stoker, tenor, wrote home to his family of an incident on his second night of the 2001 Southern States tour. It was his first tour since rejoining the Choir from membership in the 1960s:

"One of the drills we go through on this trip is to put our luggage out in the hall at night for our luggage-handling team to pick up. We only keep our carry-on luggage. The problem with that is that you have to take the clothes you will wear the next day out of your suitcase before you set the bags out in the hall, or you will not have any clothes in the morning. This was our second night at doing this, and, as we had the first night, my roommate Phil Snow and I talked about the strangeness of this luggage routine and made sure we had pulled out clean socks, etc. I even mentioned to Phil that I needed to decide which pair of pants I was going to wear the next day, and thought about it and looked at a shirt too. We put the luggage out, got a good night's sleep, and got up at 6:00 A.M. for the buffet breakfast at the hotel before loading onto the busses for the ten-hour journey to New Orleans. After I showered and shaved (I had taken a few essential things out of my suitcase for shaving and teeth brushing), I got ready to get dressed. I soon realized that although I had thought about clothes for today, I had not taken a pair of pants or a shirt out of my suitcase before putting them out in the hall! I did have clean socks and shoes, but no pants or shirt!

"It was one of those situations where laughing and crying were both appropriate, but I really had a problem. I did have two things that could be a bad partial solution: the bottoms to black pajamas, and kind of a lightweight sweat suit—loose fitting, comfortable, but definitely not 'dressy casual,' the dress standard for traveling choir members. I also had a wrinkled white T-shirt with 'North Carolina Tar Heels' written on the front with a picture of the Tar Heels

Luggage is scooped up after midnight by volunteers from the Choir. The two-to-three-hour "pull" means that suitcases will be at the next hotel awaiting the Choir's arrival.

footprint. It was wrinkled because I had wrapped my camera in it and jammed it in my carry-on.

"I pictured myself waiting in our room for Phil to make an emergency run to whatever clothing place we could find open on an early Sunday morning—the busses were supposed to leave at 8:00 A.M.—or having the Choir leave without me, and locating clothes later in the day and trying to get a flight to New Orleans. I called the front desk to see if there was any place in the hotel where clothing could be purchased. The only place they had was a little gift shop, so I wasn't very hopeful. I tried on the black P.J. pants, the wrinkled Tar Heels T-shirt, and my black loafers. I was not a pretty sight, but I was presentable enough not to get arrested for wandering the halls. I bravely pinned my Tab Choir identifying pin on my T-shirt, and Phil and I set out for the gift shop. Phil tried to be encouraging, saying untrue things like 'You really look just fine' and 'Those pants are really not that bad,' but it would be an understatement to say that I was underdressed for the occasion.

"The gift shop looked encouraging, at least for shirts, but it wasn't open until 8:00 A.M., so we had to act casual for about fifteen minutes. When the gift shop opened, I made a beeline to the shirt department and purchased the only shirt that might fit, a light-blue denim long-sleeve shirt on display in the window. It had a small 'Ft. Worth' with a flag over the pocket, and it cost fifty dollars. I wasn't dickering. There were no pants, so I was stuck with my PJs.

"A real test was when we were waiting for the elevator with a group of choir people, and choir president Mac Christensen (owner of a very successful chain of men's clothing stores) walked up to catch the elevator. He glanced at my pants, but he didn't get any expression on his face like 'What's up with those?'"

The Choir's tour concluded at Tanglewood, the mecca of American music festivals and a first for the Choir. The Choir had performed one program on tour, but Tanglewood called for something special.

AS A FORMER CHOIRMASTER, I KNEW THAT I COULD GET EVERYTHING THAT I ASKED FROM THE CHORUS IN SUCH A SHORT TIME, BECAUSE OF YOUR EXCELLENT PREPARATION. I WILL REMEMBER THAT PERFORMANCE AS ONE OF THE MOST MOVING CONCERTS I HAVE DONE. —*Rafael Frübeck de Burgos, Tanglewood*

Rafael Frübeck de Burgos conducted the Choir with the Boston Symphony Orchestra in Brahms's *Requiem,* sung in German. Jessop directed them in Leonard Bernstein's *Chichester Psalms.* Patrons poured into "The Shed," and rain poured all around them. With some clutching their music scores, these music aficionados came prepared, and they were not disappointed. This renowned Spanish conductor wrote a thank-you note to the Choir.

Touring. It has stretched the skills of choir members, gained them a list of newfound friends, and made a name for the Choir. It has given it place. "The Mormon Tabernacle Choir has become so much a part of America," says Charles Osgood, "I think of it as being like the Grand Canyon or Mount Rushmore." For more than 100 years the Mormon Tabernacle Choir has reached out with music and a message. They began at home—in America—and have taken their America to the world.

Though the voices are changing, the song's the same
As it sings from sea to sea.
And as long as the music is strong and clear,
We'll know that tomorrow will always be free.
America, America, and the dream lives on.
American, America and the dream goes on.

GENTLY RAISE
THE SACRED STRAIN

Radio's Longest
Continuous Broadcast

Gently raise the sacred strain,
For the Sabbath's come again
That man may rest,
And return his thanks to God
For his blessings to the blest.

O N APRIL 20, 2004, the National Association of Broadcasters inducted the Mormon Tabernacle Choir into their hall of fame. The Choir joined broadcasting legends Bob Hope, Edward R. Murrow, Bing Crosby, Benny Goodman, and Paul Harvey. The recognition was more than a listening legacy; it was also a phenomenon of broadcasting. For seventy-five years—nearly the lifetime of radio—the Mormon Tabernacle Choir has sung weekly without interruption, giving voice to peace, brotherhood, and the Spirit of God. President Gordon B. Hinckley, whose involvement with the Choir reaches back more than fifty years, says, "No medium has touched the lives of so many for so long as has the weekly broadcast of *Music and the Spoken Word*."

Ed Payne, producer of the weekly broadcast for the past twenty years, has taken cues from the CBS radio network: "Don't change the format." Bonneville International,

The Choir's 300 members practiced for a month before the first live broadcast, holding a final "radio dress rehearsal" the week before. The chief divisional engineer of NBC called it an "epic" event, with 10,000 radio fans eagerly awaiting the program. In the early broadcasts, the announcer would aim the one microphone in the direction of whichever section was singing at the moment.

LDS-owned broadcast company, has listened. What has changed is the input the Choir has in the broadcast. Twice a month the choir management meets with Payne and other Bonneville staff members to review tapes and discuss ideas for upcoming broadcasts, and everyone agrees the collaboration has made a difference.

The Choir joined the airwaves on July 15, 1929, with a program of inspiration from the Tabernacle, what was later termed the Crossroads of the West. Salt Lake City radio station KZN temporarily went off the air that Monday afternoon while its only microphone was shuttled one block to Temple Square's Tabernacle, a 6,000-seat hall built for religious convocations. By today's broadcast standards, the scene was makeshift at best.

Perched atop a fifteen-foot ladder, nineteen-year-old Ted Kimball held aloft the microphone for the full thirty minutes to pick up the organ, the entire choir, and his announcements. Said young Kimball, "We are reminded of a phrase from Milton's *Paradise Lost*, 'And let your silver chime move in melodious time, and let the voice of heaven's deep organ blow.' And now, the 'Aria' from the *Tenth Concerto,* by George Frederick Handel, presented by Tabernacle organist Edward P. Kimball."

Edward P. Kimball, his father, was seated below him at the keyboard. "He was more concerned with the job that I would do than he was with his own part in the broadcast," Kimball later recalled, noting that he approached the "tremendous" task "with some trepidation." No one imagined the Choir's remarkable run through one century and into another.

LDS Church president Heber J. Grant first caught the vision of radio broadcasting. On May 6, 1922, at 8:00 P.M., he inaugurated radio broadcasting in Salt Lake City on radio station KZN, the forerunner of KSL. The station, a stepchild of the Church-owned *Deseret News*, was housed in a tin shed on the roof of a building in downtown Salt Lake. Grant's counselor, Anthony W. Ivins, said on that occasion, "When the 'Mormon' pioneers entered the Salt Lake Valley, in 1847, at which time the Pony Express was the most rapid means of communicated news from one point to another, they little dreamed that before a period of seventy-five years had passed, their children would talk to the world by wireless."

President Grant encouraged the Choir to get on the airwaves. The first venture was timid; the Choir produced a local program that showcased the Thursday-night rehearsals. The response was marginal. Still, Earl J. Glade, pioneer broadcaster

In 1922 a mix of American businesses, organizations, and individuals launched 500 radio stations in what was considered a "broadcasting boom." In 1927 LDS Church officials encouraged the operation of a local station. Its beginnings were in a shed on the top of a building.

and later executive vice-president of KSL, lobbied officers of NBC to launch the show coast to coast. NBC had been operating for three years, CBS for two. Both felt great responsibility to use the radio industry for the good of the nation, for cultural and uplifting programming. Previous national broadcasts of a series of symphony performances had been well received, which suggested success for a choir program. It was an ambitious undertaking from what many considered a remote mountain hamlet. Choir leader Anthony Lund expressed his concern: "We can't sing with this great choir and have it come over a little kitchen radio." Worry about the acoustics prompted radio technicians to hang a huge red curtain in the Tabernacle and drape the first ten rows with old carpeting from the radio station's offices.

A technician, positioned on the basement stairs so he could see both the Choir and the radio operator seated below the Choir, signaled Kimball when to begin. The audio engineer, a block away at the station, was cued by telegraph from NBC headquarters in New York. Thirty radio stations received that first NBC transmission.

The Mormon Tabernacle Choir touched the hearts of many on their first visit to Russia in 1991. The 13 concert tour opened in Frankfurt, Germany, and included Switzerland, Hungary, Austria, Czechoslovakia, and Poland. Previous tours to Europe were made in 1955, 1973, 1982, and later in 1998.

The unsophisticated sound system picked up the errant shuffling of feet and the tapping of the conductor, but more serious was the line-hum, which prompted some of the stations to cut off early from the debut broadcast. A Connecticut report stated, "This joint Choir and Organ recital began auspiciously enough, and the mammoth organ sounded particularly beautiful on the air. . . . But the eastern stations in the network had to be cut off because of the bad connection somewhere along the trail." By the next week, the problem had been solved, and this public-service program began to secure its place and prompt the far-flung audience to wish for more.

The 300-voice choir, many on lunch breaks from work, opened with the 1835 refrain "Gently Raise the Sacred Strain," which has been a hallmark of the broadcast ever since. That first program included six selections; the Choir and organ alternated as follows:

Chorus from *Die Meistersinger*, by Wagner

"Sonata in B-Flat Minor," first movement, by Boslip

"The Morning Breaks," by Careless

"An Old Melody," arranged by Kimball

The finale from *Elijah*, by Mendelssohn

"The Pilgrim's Chorus," from *Tannhäuser*, by Wagner

NBC president M. H. Aylsworth wired congratulations: "Your wonderful Tabernacle program is making great impression in New York. Have heard from leading ministers. All impressed by the program. Eagerly awaiting your next."

One year later the New York City Telegraph praised the Choir's program: "Somewhere in the world there may be more than one brilliant choral organization other than the Mormon Tabernacle Choir, but there is no broadcasting in America today to equal the one that comes from the air over the National Broadcasting System."

The lone microphone was used until the late 1930s, when Dr. Leopold Stokowski, conductor of the Philadelphia Orchestra, was presenting a concert in the Tabernacle and suggested that multiple microphones were being used to pick up his large orchestra at home. Maestro Stokowski pointed choir officials to Dr. Harvey Fletcher, who was experimenting with radio broadcasting at Bell Telephone Laboratories. Dr. Fletcher, coincidentally a member of the LDS Church, was invited to Salt Lake City and oversaw installation of a multiple-microphone system. Balance of the choral parts was difficult: too much soprano, too much bass. For ten days, technicians tested placement of

Richard L. Evans was the right man to shape the Spoken Word. *"Everyone has worries," he would say. His weekly task of writing the* Spoken Word *script drew from all around him. He sought a universal approach, a timely message, a promise of hope. The writing was unrelenting. Week after week he would craft his thoughts, which took him about three hours. But the editing of his initial fifteen- to twenty-minute commentary to two or three minutes was even more difficult. Often the sermons reflected famous names or experiences from history, but for the most part the words were classic Richard L. Evans.*

the microphones as a group of eight singers repeated the measures of the same song from various positions in the choir loft. By 1939 the Tabernacle had a fully equipped control booth with six microphones, one for the announcer, one for the organ, and one for each choir part, providing "greater clarity, intimacy, and eloquence." Over the years, improved equipment both at the Tabernacle and in homes produced increasingly better sound.

"It always intrigues me that the Choir has been on the cutting edge of sound reproduction from the very beginning," Tabernacle organist John Longhurst observes. "When stereophonic sound came along, the Choir was a natural. And how are we broadcasting now? Well, we are in high-definition TV, and we're in surround-sound. With every innovation in

broadcasting, the Choir has been right there at the forefront."

"You tune into that broadcast, and it is almost like coming home," says conductor Jerold Ottley. "You feel like you're family, and within certain parameters you know what you're going to hear. It's soothing, it's relaxing, it's spiritual, and I think it just strikes a welcome chord, a welcome response, within many, many people."

"The broadcast is a representation of America's own image," former *Music and the Spoken Word* announcer J. Spencer Kinard suggests. "It is a reflection of national moods, needs, and aspirations."

Letters have poured in from all over. A resident of Wasilla, Alaska, wrote, "Last evening, your Tabernacle Organ Program came over FINE. We also heard the many letters and messages read. We hear your programs often now. Kindly dedicate a number to the Wasilla Radio Fans."

The program aired in various midweek slots for three years until KSL moved to the CBS network and took the choir broadcast with it. At the

I HAD THE JOY OF HEARING THE CHOIR SING IN THE TABERNACLE ON ONE OF THEIR RADIO BROADCASTS, AND IT MOVED ME SO MUCH TO HEAR THEIR EXTRAORDINARY SOUND. THEY KIND OF GET UNDER YOUR SKIN, AND YOU JUST WANT TO BE AROUND THEM. THEY EXUDE SO MUCH WARMTH AND LOVE AND SUCH A WONDERFUL SPIRIT OF GIVING.

—*Angela Lansbury, guest artist, Christmas 2001*

time, CBS had 100 station affiliates. On September 4, 1933, the broadcast began its Sunday morning run and over the years has outlived many favorites of the time: *Amos and Andy, Ozzie and Harriet, Myrt and Marge,* and *The Lone Ranger.* By 1940 *Music and the Spoken Word* was the longest-running broadcast in radio history. It has never relinquished that place. A New Jersey newspaper said of the choir program, "Those who imagine because this feature comes from a house of worship that sacred music is the rule and therefore fail to tune it in, are making a mistake."

Time was when the program was monitored "long distance" by remote control from the KSL studios. One microphone connected to KSL by a single circuit. By 1946 program technicians C. Richard Evans, Stanley Rees, or one of their coworkers sat at the custom-built radio panel in the booth at the southwest end of the Salt Lake Tabernacle with eleven microphones, combining the best tonal modulations for the radio audience. On Sunday morning the technician watches the musical score and continuity as closely as any of the musicians; at Thursday rehearsal, he makes notes for the Sunday broadcast.

Young Ted Kimball announced the first four broadcasts and then left for an LDS mission to France. The microphone was passed around for 10 months until twenty-four-year-old Richard L. Evans received the assignment. Early on he established a poetic style that has never been altered: "Sunday morning on Temple Square brings us once more together at the Crossroads of the West, in the valley-lands of the everlasting hills, where sermons are preached in music and where the thoughts we think, the songs we sing, and the words we speak are given background by the time-mellowed voice of the organ." Just four years later he was named best radio announcer in the country.

In the 1930s, the choir broadcast adopted its present format of *Music and the Spoken Word* with Richard L. Evans as producer, announcer, and writer. He also traveled with the Choir across the country and around the world. But he was more than a radio personality and executive. For forty-one years he was the shepherd of *Music and the Spoken Word.* Famed Tabernacle organist Alexander Schreiner said of him, "He was the Choir's patron saint." Church authority Hugh B. Brown called him "the heart and soul of the broadcast."

Initially, Evans's part was simple—to introduce the upcoming compositions and the station identification—but he soon began to embellish with a thought or moral value. His sermonettes were pithy, eloquent, and disciplined. They never detracted from or upstaged the essence of the program—the Choir. In a few short minutes, he capsulized universal truths that focused on character, family, friendship, honor, respect, and simple goodness. The *New York Times* commented, "In print these broadcasts reveal an Addisonian charm that lifts them into literature."

Fan mail was often addressed to "Preacher of

THE CHOIR WOULD NOT BE WHERE IT IS TODAY IF IT WEREN'T FOR THE BROADCAST. IT WOULD BE A GREAT CHOIR IN UTAH, BUT IT WOULDN'T BE WORLD FAMOUS AND IN THE CONSCIOUSNESS OF THE WORLD. IT'S THE BROADCAST THAT GETS THE CHOIR INTO PEOPLE'S MINDS AND HEARTS.
—*Lloyd Newell, announcer,* Music and the Spoken Word

Opposite: On July 23, 1962, the Choir flew—a first for the Choir—to Mount Rushmore, South Dakota, to be featured in the "Pioneering around the World" broadcast by Telstar satellite.

CLIMB EV'RY MOUNTAIN

JoAnn Ottley has watched the Choir consume her life and, more so, the life of her husband, Jerold, who retired as the Choir's conductor in 1999. So many people over the years would ask Jerry, "Well, what do you do the rest of the week, Brother Ottley?" Conducting the Mormon Tabernacle Choir was not a full-time job, she contends; it was their life.

Dr. Jerold Ottley never intended to lead a choir. He filled in for Richard Condie while studying at the University of Utah for a master's degree in music, but he was firm in his intention to be a music educator and administrator. "I made up my mind at that point in time that I wanted nothing to do with conducting the Choir. It was just too high powered," says Ottley. "It's such a big choir!"

In 1974 he was asked to be associate conductor to Jay Welch, which was "comfortable," but within the year he was named conductor. He directed the Choir for the next twenty-five years.

LDS Church president Spencer W. Kimball counseled him at the time, "Take a close look at everything that the organization stands for—all of its traditions, all of its habits, all of its dreams and hopes for the future, and try to massage them so that they will fit the world in which we are now living."

The Mormon Tabernacle Choir, Ottley says, was very much a nineteenth-century concept in terms of its organization, its size, and the way it functioned. "We were entering a time when universities and community choirs and symphony choirs were coming onto the scene in droves. And I could see that the Choir could not maintain a national reputation living in the past, so we needed to start doing some things that would move it into a more contemporary status."

Jerold D. Ottley refined and shaped the traditional tone of the Choir into a more flexible, precise, and energetic sound, one capable of expressing the subtleties of the finest choral literature.

President Kimball also asked him to establish an equitable retirement policy for choir members. "At the time I assumed control of the Choir," Ottley says, "there was a man in the Choir who had sung for fifty-two years. The process of auditioning people and retiring people from the Choir was rather chaotic and had caused some deep feelings, schisms, problems." Ottley's assignment was to take the emotion out of the end of service in the Choir.

After much study, he proposed that members retire at sixty years of age or after twenty years of service, whichever came first. "We stuck with that policy religiously so that everyone knew it was coming," he explained. "It worked." But not without hard feelings. For some, the change "psychologically was horrific."

And Ottley had to cut deeper. "The Choir was really more a social organization than it was a musical organization at that time," he says. "They partied together, had Sunday School class on the Square together—many of them had no other church attendance." And that was President Kimball's next grave concern. "We began a process of interviewing and requiring qualification for a recommend to attend the temple, attested by the local bishops." That changed the Choir.

And then Ottley took on the sound of the Choir. "When we began to massage the sound of the Choir, to give it more capabilities, we had to take all the tootie-fruitie out of it, bring it back to vanilla, and rebuild it." He occasionally took the organ out from under the Choir, creating a "fresh and vibrant sound." He changed the seating policy. For years, members had sat in a fixed position with each having his or her own chair. Someone had to retire for singers to move up from the back row. "I took their seats away and began mixing them up and moving them around."

And over time it paid off. "Everybody was becoming more professional in the choral world," Ottley adds, "even though most choral work is done on an amateur basis."

The spiritual dimension of the Choir, too, became important to Ottley. "We realized, too, that the spiritual powers of the Choir meant increasing the spiritual power of the individual." Ottley added to the audition process an evaluation of who these people really were—not just musically but also as Latter-day Saints. "The Choir turned into a powerful spiritual organization."

It was the hand of Jerold Ottley, the heart of Jerold Ottley, that moved the Choir to a new level of music and service. Said Choir conductor Craig Jessop, who served as Ottley's assistant, "You can liken our personal lives, or the institutions to which we choose to dedicate our lives, to a cathedral. We each place a brick or add our contribution. Many of the great cathedrals of Europe took 100 or more years to build. Every generation added its part to the structure. In the institution of the Mormon Tabernacle Choir, Jerry and JoAnn Ottley have put in more than a brick; they've put in a couple of giant marble columns. There has been no one else like them, and probably never will be."

the Church at the Crossroads of the West." His name, his voice, and his wisdom left an imprint on the broadcast that will never be supplanted. Evans continued his work with the Choir even after his calling as a member of the Quorum of Twelve Apostles. Said President Hinckley of his associate, "Never missing a Sunday, his hopeful tones joined the hearts of America with music made by people who love their Maker."

"This Sunday morning program is our church service," wrote one woman who had begun listening with the first broadcasts, "and while my husband is not a church-going man, he never fails to listen to *Music and the Spoken Word*. He feels that there is more in those five-minute messages than most ministers say in an hour."

Richard L. Evans died unexpectedly in 1971 at age sixty-five. It was fitting that in tribute to Evans and his years giving counsel from a microphone to the world, one of his Church associates stated, "We know that there are heavenly choirs, and maybe they needed an announcer, and one to give the Spoken Word."

J. Spencer Kinard

J. Spencer Kinard, then news reporter at KSL Television, became voice for *Music and the Spoken Word* in February 1972. He recalls the dilemma: "I was reporting murder and mayhem Monday through Friday and preaching peace and love on Sunday." That soon changed. Just months after his appointment, he was made news director at the station.

Selected from many who auditioned, Kinard remembers then Elder Gordon B. Hinckley's counsel: "Remember, we are not asking you to start over the way that Richard Evans did; we are asking you to pick up where he left off." The frightening part, Kinard soon realized, was "not the delivery, but the content. What to prepare? What to write? What to say?" He wrote the sermonettes for the first few years and later brought in skilled writers to assist. The challenge was writing "something short and concise with a powerful message." Kinard began to understand "the words of Alexander Pope, who wrote a letter to his son and at the end said, 'Forgive me for writing such a long letter. I didn't have time to write a shorter one.'" For the next nineteen years, Kinard opened and closed the Sunday broadcast sharing wisdom born of his own experience and building upon the pattern of the first four decades of the broadcast.

Like Evans, he was young, just thirty-one, when he stepped out onto the Tabernacle stage. He, too, understood the connection between music and the Divine, as he elaborated in one broadcast:

"Most religious music deals with our relationship with the Lord. 'I waited for the Lord,' we sing. 'He inclined unto me. He heard my complaint.' While we may sing of these things, do we really believe they are so? Does the Lord, in fact, hear our complaints—both our significant and our sometimes petty human problems? Can the being who created the universe be bothered with the pitiful lament of a lonely soul on a tiny world on the edge of this galaxy? The answer is yes. But it is easy to feel insignificant before the Lord, even though he has assured us that is not how he feels toward us. The Lord said, 'Call unto me, and I will answer thee, and shew thee great and mighty things, which thou knowest not.' (Jeremiah 33:3.) It does not diminish the divinity of God to believe that he can incline toward the least of his creations. Quite the contrary—God hears and empathizes with us not in spite of his greatness but because of it, because

> THERE ARE CERTAIN WONDERFUL LANDMARKS THAT ONE HAS IN ONE'S CAREER, SORT OF THE BRASS RING, AND I WOULD SAY ONE OF THE TOP BRASS RINGS IS TO BE ABLE TO SING WITH THE MORMON TABERNACLE CHOIR. —*Frederica von Stade, guest artist, 2003*

his is a godly greatness founded on eternal principles of infinite love."

Lloyd Newell took over the microphone in 1991, having served as Kinard's backup for almost a year. A former news anchor, Newell performs his announcing role as a volunteer. "Everyone that comes close to this program and is involved in it is better," he states. "If you asked the Choir, 'How many of you are in favor of being paid right now?' most of them would say, 'No, the broadcast is a gift.' It's the same for me with the Spoken Word. Being paid would somehow diminish the opportunity."

For Newell, the program is not just a broadcast. A former anchor for CNN, at the end of the news day, he would take the newscast script, wad it up, throw it away, and start on tomorrow's program. He says of his stint at CNN, "I never got a letter from anyone saying, 'Your news touched my heart' or 'Your news made a difference in my life' or 'Your news brought me closer to God.' Never did." In contrast, Newell has boxes of letters that gratefully point to the choir broadcast as bringing hope: "I didn't know how I was going to deal with this" or "I just lost my job" or "I feel forgiven" are treasures to him.

Sweetly swells the solemn sound
While we bring our gifts around
Of broken hearts, Of broken hearts,
As a willing sacrifice,
Showing what his grace imparts.

When Newell began his service with the Choir, President Hinckley counseled him to make each message "a gem." He remembers the advice; he thinks of that all the time. "We try as best we can to make them little nuggets, gems. In a world where there is so much noise and confusion, despair, concern, worry, to be able to go to a place that's been around all these years, that's old enough to be our great-grandfather, that's safe, reliable, you can trust it, and it's not going to ask you for money or make you feel guilty, that's a tricky line to walk. To inspire and motivate and yet not make you feel discouraged," he states, "the message has got to come from the heart. The broadcast is like a trusted friend to people. I go forward each week

with faith, and at the same time I consider what went before."

He looks back to Richard L. Evans often. "I still get letters about him, and he died thirty years ago. He was an uncommon preacher, an institution that helped people see the best in themselves and the best in others. I still hear his smooth intonation, 'Again we leave you . . .'"

As soon as one broadcast is completed, the next is looming. Explains Newell, "You never have time to savor the moment." Yet the moments keep coming.

In seventy-five years of broadcasting, the Choir has taken *Music and the Spoken Word* on the road as it has toured, from the base of the Great White Throne at Zion National Park in 1937 to the Red

GIVE MY REGARDS
TO BROADWAY

In 1983 when Ed Payne began producing *Music and the Spoken Word*, the broadcast was filmed with a crew of ten, using three fixed cameras. At Bonneville he worked with veterans like Dick Alsop, who had helped guide the program for decades. The crew list today has expanded to twenty-five. Cameramen work from five to nine cameras; each one moves, including the jib-arm added when the Orchestra at Temple Square was organized. We are probably looking at close to five-hundred man hours that go into the half-hour program," Payne explains. "If it was a typical pre-recorded production, we would do a lot of editing and things like that, but we don't. What the people see is what they would experience if they were in the Tabernacle." He continues, "Every time we ask CBS about changes, they come back with, 'This program is an anchor in an extremely changing world. If you change it, you are going with the flow of the world. Don't change it.' People know that's what is coming." So the format has changed little in the past seventy-five years, but the pace of the television broadcast since the early 1960s has picked up considerably. The average shot-count twenty years ago for the thirty-minute program was about 65. Today, that number has doubled to 130.

Just being in the broadcast booth is a marked contrast to the sweet tones lilting to heaven: Directors and technicians in headsets. Hands flying. No hushed tones here. "Camera 2, you're up next. . . . And dissolve. . . . Camera 4. . . . Cue Lloyd. . . . Tell him we're over. . . . There's a camera in the shot. . . . And dissolve." And so it goes.

"What I like most about the Choir is being part of the impact they make," Payne explains. "The Choir carries with it such a legacy, not just with musicians but also with broadcast. We are a part of that. It's fun. It's serious work. It makes a difference."

In addition to the broadcast, Payne has also produced specials and documentaries for the Choir, including *The Wonder of Christmas*, with Frederica von Stade and Bryn Terfel; *Historic Visit to Nauvoo; The Joy of Christmas*, with Angela Lansbury; *Silent Night, Holy Night*, with Walter Cronkite; and an earlier production, *In a Land Called Israel*.

Ed Payne

Rocks Amphitheater in Colorado in 1956 and 1984; to the National Auditorium in Mexico City in 1972; to the Michael Fowler Center in Wellington, New Zealand; and the Opera House in Sydney, Australia, in 1988; to the BYU Jerusalem Center in 1992; to Royal Albert Hall in London and the Palau de la Musica in Barcelona, Spain, in 1998; and to the steps of the Nauvoo Temple in 2002.

Closer to home, the Choir crosses the street to the Conference Center to originate seven or eight broadcasts a year. But the Tabernacle is home. "I know this building," Craig Jessop says of the Tabernacle. "I love this building."

In addition to radio and television, the Choir performs for a host of conventions, conferences, and special guests. "The weekly broadcast alone is more than enough to keep you going," associate director Mack Wilberg states, "let alone all these tremendous projects that we do in addition. And by projects I mean singing for the National Governor's Conference, the National Association of Broadcasters—many groups knock on our door." Even before broadcasting, the Choir and organ were lifting the spirits of visitors to Salt Lake and other locales seeking a "show-stopper." But the ultimate was the two weeks of international visitors for the 2002 Olympic Winter

Games. The Choir presented four special concerts to showcase both themselves, the Orchestra and guest artists.

Other special broadcasts over the years have spoken to the hearts of the citizens everywhere. In 1934 a special choir broadcast was beamed to Admiral Byrd and his expedition to the South Pole. In 1942 devastated Americans at Pearl Harbor received a special transmission. In 1943 the Choir reenacted a segment of the dedication of the Salt Lake Temple over local radio station KSL; the Choir had sung at the occasion in 1893. The announcer stated, "Today's Tabernacle Choir, under the baton of J. Spencer Cornwall with Alexander Schreiner at the organ, will reenact most of the musical program of fifty years ago, as the temple anniversary is observed on Tuesday, April 6. Present-day war conditions have prevented the assembling of people in Salt Lake to note this anniversary." (The Tabernacle was closed to the public though the Choir continued to broadcast from there.) In 1945 the nation mourned with the Choir at the death of President Franklin D. Roosevelt. The words of Richard L. Evans spoke of the solemnity of the time: "Again we have solemn cause to know that death comes in the overruling purposes of God, when and to whom it will. That this day it came to the president of the United States of America, at a time when world-shaping issues are being weighed in the balance, is profoundly sobering to us and to all people." During the Cold War, Radio Free Europe carried *Music and the Spoken Word* to isolated nations. In 1986 a special choir tribute aired following the Challenger disaster. The evening of 9/11, the Choir sang comfort and faith to a stunned nation.

"I think it is difficult to put into words what it

Charles Osgood

is that makes one musical performance better than another," veteran news reporter and lyricist Charles Osgood states. "But in 1976 I was doing a piece for *60 Minutes* about the Evelyn Tripp Piano Awards here in New York City, and Rudolf Serkin, the great pianist, was one of the judges. The judges decided not to give an award, and I asked him why; the performers all sounded like they had wonderful technique to me. He said, 'Oh, technique was wonderful; they all had marvelous fingers. But you know, you don't play the piano with your

fingers.' I said, 'Well, what do you play with?' He said, 'Your heart.' And that is, I think, why the Mormon Tabernacle Choir's performances are so great—because they sing with their hearts."

With each passing year, the Choir has marked a milestone on the calendar of broadcast: twenty-five years, fifty, sixty, and seventy-five. LDS Church president David O. McKay said of the Choir on its thirty-five years in broadcasting, its 1,770th program, "Congratulations to the most renowned musical organization in the world—the most influential, dignified, volunteer missionary influence in the history of the Church." At the half-century mark, conductor Jerold Ottley wanted to savor the sense of the Choir's history and pay tribute to the great and noble singers who had gone before. He invited former chief organist Alexander Schreiner and three former conductors to participate in the broadcast, including J. Spencer Cornwall, who led the Choir from 1935 to 1957; Richard P. Condie, 1957 to 1974; and Jay E. Welch, 1974. He acknowledged that from the beginning, the broadcast has always been about people speaking to people.

At the sixtieth anniversary in 1989, former choir members who had sung at the first broadcast were special invited guests. At the occasion, President Hinckley, said, "In seasons of conflict its voice has been one of peace. In times of doubt and cynicism it has brought reassurance and faith. To those in distress, in sorrow and in despair, it has given hope and strength and resolution. To a world at times unsure of God, it has spoken without equivocation and with certainty, singing His praises with majestic and moving power. In a culture of shifting values and changing tastes, it has won and held the love and loyalty of a vast audience, spanning the generations and reaching the continent and to foreign lands. It has become a most remarkable and valued national treasure, a vibrant part of the soul of our beloved nation."

At the ribbon-cutting ceremony of the LDS Church Museum of History and Art exhibit focused on the Choir's seventy-five years of broadcasting on November 21, 2003, Elder Robert D. Hales of the Quorum of Twelve Apostles fondly recalled his own experience as a child lying on the floor in the front room listening to the broadcast with his family. That picture of a family gathered around listening to music and words of wisdom is less repeated today—but not less needed.

The Choir changes lives and gives direction. Westin Noble became fascinated with the Choir in high school in the late '30s. In the '40s, after the war, he said, "I would go to bed on Sunday night, turn off the lights, and listen to the Mormon Tabernacle Choir." Today he is director of the Nordic Chorus at Luther College and has been a guest conductor with the Choir.

Sweetly swells the solemn sound
While we bring our gifts around
Of broken hearts, of broken hearts.

COME UNTO HIM

Lloyd Newell—today's voice of the weekly broadcast—claims he "is a different man because of his work with the Choir." He explains, "You can't prepare these messages for thirteen years and not be affected by them and by the Choir." Often the messages he writes reflect his own experiences.

"This is the most fulfilling thing I have ever done," says Newell, "and the irony is, I'm not paid for it. I get letters that say, 'I can make it through another week.' 'This program is exactly what I needed.' Or, 'I was so discouraged.' That never happened on the news desk when I was at CNN."

"It's not unusual to have someone stop me in the Tabernacle and say, 'This message was just for me.' Thirteen years ago, the message was different. I am different. I see life differently, I've known a fair amount of heartache and grief. I bring something different to the broadcast because I am a different person."

When asked to speak about his choir experience, he leaves his audience with a promise: "The groups you are listening to right now, in five years, won't be here. But the Mormon Tabernacle Choir will be here fifty years from now with its timeless music. You can count on it. You can almost set your watch by the Choir's Sunday morning performance. In this world of shifting values, we need things we can hold on to. The Choir is that trustworthy friend. It's not going to change dramatically; it's not going to ask for money. It can touch your life—daily—if you let it."

From *Music and the Spoken Word*, October 6, 2002, by Lloyd Newell

In every age, to every people, God opens His arms to His children. With all the love of a tender parent, He invites us to come unto Him. But He never forces or manipulates. He respects our agency and allows us to choose whether or not to receive His offering and feel His love.

In the parable of the great supper (Luke 14:16–24), Jesus likens the kingdom of God to a delicious dinner that has been carefully and lovingly prepared. When all is ready, the master sends his servant to gather the invited guests, but each is too preoccupied to attend. "They all . . . began to make excuse[s]" (v. 18). One said that he had just bought "a piece of ground" and needed to oversee it. Another was busy with his "five yoke of oxen." And the third had recently been married and wanted to stay close to home. They had just been offered the feast of feasts; bounteous servings of love, peace, and joy were on the table; but each who was invited was too encumbered by the cares of the world to even taste the heavenly offerings.

Upon hearing this report, the master quickly sends his servant out to "the streets and lanes," the "highway and hedges" to invite the poor, the maimed, the halt, and the blind to eat the food, still steamy hot and uneaten on the table. These meek and humble people gratefully respond to the invitation and enter the kingdom of God.

Oftentimes, what keep us from God are many of the "good" things he has given us: the land, the oxen, the relationships that can consume our time and prevent quiet reflection or personal worship. Hopefully, the ease and security of such good things will not distract us from that which matters most, from feeling the need to seek God and respond to His invitation to everlasting life. The Lord's promise is certain: He is "gracious and merciful, and will not turn away His face from you, if ye return unto Him" (2 Chronicles 30:9).

GLORY! GLORY! HALLELUJAH

Top of the Charts

Mine eyes have seen the glory of the coming of the Lord;
He is trampling out the vintage where the grapes of wrath are stored.
He hath loosed the fateful lightning of his terrible, swift sword:
His truth is marching on.

WHEN PRESIDENT MAC CHRISTENSEN and Craig Jessop approached Harvard Business School graduate and marketer Scott Barrick with an offer to join the Mormon Tabernacle Choir management in 2001, he asked what they had in mind. President Christensen responded, "We're sitting here in my office with five gold records and two platinum on the wall. It's been a long time since we've had another one, and we want to change that."

With more than 150 recordings to its credit, the Choir took a dramatic step on March 17, 2003, launching its own record label, "Mormon Tabernacle Choir." The Choir partnered with Deseret Book to distribute and market the new label. "It was a match made in heaven," Barrick chuckles. The first CD, *Consider the Lilies*, was released weeks later. A second recording, *Spirit of America*, followed in just a few months. The most recent relaese is *Peace Like a River*.

The Choir recordings over the years have come out under several labels, including Columbia, Sony, and Telarc. "Over the years, the recording industry's balance of power has shifted from the companies to the artists," Barrick explains. "The shift has enabled the artists to control the repertoire and to receive enhanced financial returns." The "Mormon Tabernacle Choir" is a brand name with recognition and acceptance that has been built for many years. "It only made sense to use our brand name as our label."

The biggest challenge the Choir faces is to have the world hear the Mormon Tabernacle Choir and the Orchestra on Temple Square. President Christensen states, "If they hear them—even better, if they hear them and see them—the Choir will touch their hearts." The Choir will make a little money on the recordings, but that's not why it's in the business. "What we really want is for people to *hear* our new recordings," he says. "They are out of this world."

Their target market is everybody. In the past, Barrick says, "people had Mormon Tabernacle Choir works in their homes, but I don't think that is necessarily the case anymore. We intend to reverse that trend." With the growing number of private labels, the music industry's distribution system has shifted, enabling new labels to get into the stores. "Ours is one of those," says Barrick.

"We come across people, organists, who cut their teeth on either the broadcast or recordings of the Choir," organist Richard Elliot observes. "During that period, the Choir was really the only national entity that was doing sacred music."

Choir leader Craig Jessop was one of those who grew up listening to recordings of the Tabernacle Choir. His friends were collecting Beatles albums, and he was collecting Tab Choir. He still has them all. "It may have been fourth or fifth grade," he explains, "that I really was aggressively seeking the Choir, listening to the broadcast, purchasing records." His first record was *The Lord's Prayer,* with Ormandy and the Philadelphia Orchestra, Richard Condie and the Mormon Tabernacle Choir. "I can almost tell you the songs cut-by-cut on both sides and their order," he says. "I wore it out and had to buy another."

Recording marketing consultant Bob Garcia, who has been taking the pulse of the recording industry for decades, has always kept track of the Choir since his youth in New York City. Now a Southern Californian and two-time president of the National Academy of Recording Arts and Sciences, Garcia works with the Choir just as he does with rock and pop stars. "This is the *Good Housekeeping* brand of choirs," he states. "Of groups of that size, there is nobody else." As Garcia has promoted the Choir's two recordings under the new label, he has found it has "pop" appeal. He worried that the very first CD that people latched on to, *Consider the Lilies,* might be too religious for their taste. "Not so. They found music of Rutter and others that has positioned the recording to be 'big.'" The pieces are short, easy for a station to

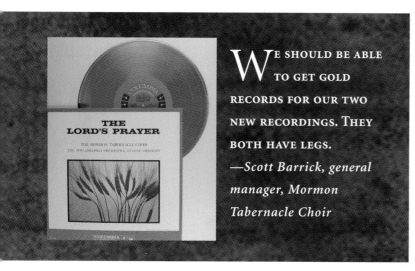

WE SHOULD BE ABLE TO GET GOLD RECORDS FOR OUR TWO NEW RECORDINGS. THEY BOTH HAVE LEGS.
—*Scott Barrick, general manager, Mormon Tabernacle Choir*

program. "I was surprised and elated for the Choir," Garcia says, adding that the Choir is back on track for recognition: gold and platinum records, the industry's measure of success.

"It will continue to be America's Choir; it will continue to do a mixture of shows, patriotic and what I call 'old war horse' hymns," he observes. And he sees new horizons. "This choir and its directors have too many ideas to lounge in territory where they are most famous. I see them going to an extended repertoire."

Today's Mormon Tabernacle Choir does not have a new sound, just an updated one. "We are trying to do music that has a broad appeal," Barrick explains, "but does not lose the heritage the Choir has built over time." What has the Choir recorded? Hymns, anthems, symphonies, requiems, marches, ballads, patriotic songs, Christmas carols, folk songs, oratorios, show tunes, opera selections.

The Choir and organ began their recording career on September 1, 1910, with Columbia Phonograph Company. The acoustical recording process used large horns to gather sound vibrations and focus them on a tight, pliable diaphragm. Secured to it was a needle that sat on a wax disc rotating on a turntable, making impressions. For that first recording, thirteen pieces were recorded, including four by the organ, two with choir and soloists, and seven by the Choir alone. Evan

Scott Barrick manages the "business" of singing for the Mormon Tabernacle Choir. "If we can give the Choir and conductors more information, help them get things done quicker and easier, help them retain the vision of what the Choir is, then we've helped in the creation of the music. We've given them more time, and their spiritual energy can focus on the music."

Stephens conducted, with John J. McClellan at the organ. However, Joseph J. Daynes set aside retirement to play one of the organ selections. The sounds closest to the large horns along with the middle frequencies dominated. Hence, the altos and tenors sounded much better than the sopranos and basses. The Choir gave the impression of a "well-trained revival chorus," while the organ receded into an "overgrown calliope" because the acoustical process could not grasp the resonance of the room. Still, Stephens had produced music that thrilled listeners.

"Every time we have a rehearsal, a recording session, or a concert, we have a prayer," President Christensen explains. "Our secretary gives me the choir member's name who will pray, and then people in the Choir and the Orchestra come up and put names on my little yellow pad, and sometimes they tell me why. One said, 'This person is a mother of three. She is full of cancer; she has maybe two weeks to live.' And then the choir member says the prayer and includes each name. To listen to those people pray is one of the most spiritual experiences we have."

Dear choir,

Remember when you prayed for me? Because of my tumor? Well now my tumor is gone, thanks to you. It was a miracle. My favorite songs are "Cindy, Joshua fit the Battle, Betzaleta ved." I still like the other songs too. Just to let my dad know I think it's cool that my own dad gets to be on T.V.!
Love,
Janessa Furness

The Choir made a wax recording of Evan Stephens's "Let the Mountains Shout for Joy" in 1910. In 1926 Anthony Lund conducted the Choir in a recording of "By the Waters of Minnetonka." In 1988 the Choir toured Australia, the land down under. In 1995 the Choir recorded "Waltzing Matilda" for the 100th anniversary of the song and a special broadcast.

The Choir and its leaders were encouraged: "Considering that this is the first time anything of this kind has been attempted, the results may be considered marvelous, and such criticism as is offered is only to point out ways for improvement on these initial experiments, in looking for more effective results." When Columbia president Arthur Hull Hayes presented two gold record awards to the Choir in 1964, he noted that the Choir reached back the furthest of any of Columbia's recording clients.

In 1927 the Victor Company of New Jersey pioneered an electric recording process using a new device—the microphone—using amplifiers to harness the musical tones and convert them into electrical impulses. The process was vastly superior in sound and fidelity to the acoustical system, not to mention simpler. In addition, the new technology captured how the Choir and organ actually sounded. The music showcased the conducting skills of Anthony Lund. Later, Dr. Harvey Fletcher from Bell Telephone Laboratories, who also consulted on the recording in the Tabernacle, introduced stereophonic sound.

In 1934 the Grambaugh Company began recording the weekly CBS broadcast "off line," and

CONSIDER THE LILIES

Consider the lilies of the field;
How they grow, how they grow.

The Mormon Tabernacle Choir has grown from a small community choir to a world presence in the recording industry. Their music is more than notes on a page; it is also an expression of faithful hearts handing "some of heaven" to mortals. Saints and angels sing when they record.

When a recording is in process, the Tabernacle is converted into a most unusual studio. Microphones are everywhere, pointing at odd angles at a choir loft filled with everyday folk who can sing. Any sound but voices stops everything.

"It's all about capturing the focus, feeling proud about what you have done for years to come," Bruce Leek, sound engineer, tells the Choir before they start. Intermittently he or his associate Fred Vogler stride to the podium and give a thumbs-up or a pep talk to the artists—for that's what they are.

IT'S A VERY BIG CHALLENGE TO RECORD IN HERE.
IF WE GET LUCKY TONIGHT WE MAY GET SOMETHING DOWN.   —*Craig Jessop*

In a back room Mack Wilberg sits with headphones and a television watching, listening, the score spread out in front of him, his red pencil circling a note here, a rest there. The sound engineers, up from Los Angeles and the best in the business, Craig Jessop says, have their stations as well. Headphones. Listening. Leek intermittently jabs the air with excitement—displeasure. "Take that again." "And again."

It takes three nights and one Saturday to lay it down. And then weeks to mix it. The result is a CD that walks off the shelves because the Choir not only has followers but also a voice that is alone in the market— singing of God, patriotism, civility, and grandeur, the best of the past and toe-tappers from the stage.

"I knew Mack Wilberg had to be here, I just knew it. There was no doubt in my mind," Jessop states. "I sat by Mack's side when the Choir did the Come, Come Ye Saints *CD in 1997, and we recorded two of his songs; Jerry conducted one and I conducted one. While Jerry was out on the podium, I was sitting at the table by Mack, and I felt that energy flow. It wasn't that easy to convince him to leave a very secure and prestigious position at Brigham Young University to come here as a second chair. But I can tell you this, I would have been his second chair in a heartbeat."*

With its own label and its marketing arrangement with Deseret Book, the Choir is releasing two CDs a year.

The Choir received a Grammy for "Battle Hymn of the Republic" and sang on the Grammy Awards program in Hollywood on November 29, 1959. The recording hit the top twenty in national record sales and continues to be a crowd-pleaser.

soon enterprising amateurs were "pirating" the Choir's program. When a young man approached Cornwall for permission to record, the conductor was intrigued that he might be able to "hear" the broadcast. The next week, Cornwall and others jammed into a room littered with broadcast paraphernalia, an unprofessional setup at best.

"We walked over to the recording studios, climbed the old stairs, and were ushered into a room divided into two compartments by heavy cardboard. A loudspeaker was placed in the upper part of the cardboard wall. The recording apparatus was placed in the inner compartment, and it was arranged so that listeners could hear from the outer compartment. The young recording technician started the record of the broadcast."

Cornwall was stunned by the inconsistency of the volume, and worse, he couldn't understand the lyrics. The controls for the broadcast were in the Union Pacific Building, a block from the Tabernacle. Then things changed—the Choir purchased a recording machine. In a short time, a recording booth was built inside the Tabernacle, once an architect assured Church authorities that "he could build the booth on one side of the Tabernacle in such a way that it would not destroy the symmetry." The necessary apparatus was moved from KSL to the broadcast booth, and technicians began making recordings off the air for the choir directors to study.

Updates to the broadcast booth have kept it current with innovations in the industry. When the

Conference Center was completed in 2000, the production of the broadcast shifted to the state-of-the-art audiovisual center in the new facility. But the broadcast booth in the Tabernacle continues to house an important part of the operation.

The Choir recorded its first LPs in October 1949, with Cornwall conducting and Frank Asper at the organ. The title of the ten-inch record was simply *The Mormon Tabernacle Choir of Salt Lake City—Volume 1.* A year later, in 1950, volume 2 was produced, with Alexander Schreiner at the organ. The records featured hymns and short oratorio selections. The *Saturday Review* in its May 6, 1950, issue said of the recordings, "These volumes are as fine choral recordings as have yet been done, in spite of the echo in the Tabernacle. Fine presence, nice clarity of diction, good balance. This huge Choir is highly musical, and sings circles around some plusher, less spontaneous groups."

By this time, Tabernacle technician Stanley Rees had developed a sound system for the broadcast that was used for recordings as well. Microphones close to the chorus and an omnidirectional microphone suspended out in the hall produced an even blend for voices and also drew in resonance from the room. The Tabernacle gained the reputation as "one of the toughest places in the world to do a recording, but also one of the loveliest."

By 1955 recording technology had so advanced that the Choir made new recordings of some of the same pieces, including "O My Father," with future conductor Richard Condie as soloist. The Choir also became popular with the armed forces and prepared a series of recordings for the radio and television divisions of the Department of Defense.

I have seen him in the watchfires of a
hundred circling camps;

I CAN'T BELIEVE HOW THEY MAKE THESE AMAZING SOUNDS . . . AND DO IT WITH SUCH HEART AND SOUL. —*Frederica von Stade, 2002 Cultural Olympiad*

They have builded him an altar in the
evening dews and damps.
I can read his righteous sentence in
the dim and flaring lamps;
His day is marching on!

Winning a Grammy Award in 1959 for "Battle Hymn of the Republic," the Choir established that it was not a force only on radio, in distant concert halls, and at home in the Tabernacle but also in the recording business. In November 1959, the Choir stepped onstage at the National Academy of Recording Arts and Sciences with Frank Sinatra, Ella Fitzgerald, Bobby Darin, and James Drift-wood. These were unlikely partners for a chorus whose repertoire was, for the most part, sacred and classical music. Filling in for the Philadelphia

JESU, THE VERY THOUGHT IS SWEET

"Talent that eclipses most anything seen in the LDS Church," choir members state. "His abilities are from another world." "The greatest choral arranger ever," Dennis Buehner, retired bass singer claims. "His music says what my heart feels," says Kathy Chandler, soprano. "A great human being" says Larry Riddle, bass. "Unbelievably talented and so humble," Susan Newland, alto, adds. "Humility that is Christ-like," says June Allred, alto. "Simply a genius," says Stanford Smith, baritone.

A composer and conductor who grew up in the rugged Utah mining and farming town of Castle Dale, Mack Wilberg found treasure not only in the hills and desert but also in his mind. "Music comes down to him from the sky," claims his wife, Rebecca, an accomplished musician herself. He would tell you that it comes sometimes when he's mowing the lawn or sweeping the floor. But composing and arranging, he's quick to add, is long, hard work, and much of it. "He's transformed the technique of the Choir," says Julie S. Sessions, soprano. "He can turn any tune into a masterpiece," says Jay Harding, tenor.

"A Mack Wilberg comes along once in a century," Craig Jessop states. "He's a gift. One hundred years from now his music will still be inspiring everyone. 'Jesu, the Very Thought Is Sweet' will get him into heaven."

Dr. Mack Wilberg composes in an unfinished room surrounded by stacks of mismatched boxes containing ornaments, garlands, and bows in the basement of his home in Draper, Utah. He claims it is a step up from his former digs in his Provo home, where he composed in the fruit room.

For fifteen years after receiving master's and doctorate degrees from the University of Southern California, Wilberg taught at Brigham Young University and directed the Men's Chorus, which became a premier vocal performance group under his tutelage. Training singers comes naturally to him; hence, he oversees the Choir's Training School and the Temple Square Chorale, and he conducts them in concert.

"I love the Mack Wilberg arrangements," says Meredith Campell, concertmaster for the Orchestra at Temple Square. "He takes a hymn and imbues it with strengths that characterize the best of classical music. When the hymns are arranged by Mack, they come up to the level of Chopin, Brahms, and Mozart, and as you play, you feel musically fulfilled."

He doesn't draw attention to himself, choir members agree. But Michelle Cox adds, "He can be a bulldog when it comes to making music beautiful."

He gives new meaning to "ears to hear." Put him in the recording booth during a taping session, on the podium in a rehearsal or concert, or in the studio composing or arranging. He, like his music, has many parts going at once. He gets weary of his pieces and thrives on the new. It's all part of the process.

Wilberg is intense in an unassuming way, yet he is passionate about music, precise in his conducting, pastoral in his own presence. Kind. But "for all his quiet," Jessop says, "he is a tower of strength."

Craig Jessop says a Mack Wilberg "comes along once in a century, if that. He is probably the most fertile musical mind I have ever been around and the most complete musician I have ever known—composer, arranger, pianist, conductor, vocal coach. This man is honest to the core, and that is reflected in his music. His arrangements never interfere with the integrity of the original; he enhances it. His writing has such subtlety, such small changes of harmony, that the trained ear will hear and be astounded, but average listeners will just be enveloped in the beauty of it. They don't know why they like it, but they know they like it."

Orchestra, the studio musicians began a slow marching beat punctuated by far-off trumpets when the doors of the resplendent stage parted to display the 300 singers of the Mormon Tabernacle Choir and their conductor, Richard P. Condie.

Between 1958 and 1970 the Choir partnered with the Philadelphia Orchestra under the baton of Eugene Ormandy, who praised the Mormon chorus as "the greatest choir in the world." The two groups joined together for fifteen separate recordings under the Columbia label as well as sharing the Grammy honors for "Battle Hymn." The single 45-rpm record of "Battle Hymn" was a favorite on jukeboxes and with disc jockeys across the country, prompting one reviewer in 1960 to describe the Choir as "winging its way to unprecedented national attention via its recordings."

The Choir's rendition of Handel's *Messiah* also brought rave reviews, including Ormandy's own assessment that he only wished "Handel were alive to hear them." Many of the recordings, *The Lord's Prayer* and *The Beloved Choruses* in particular, hit the top of the charts in the classical category and sold more than four million copies. And they stayed there. *The Lord's Prayer* sat atop the best-seller list for more than two years. "The Mormon Tabernacle Choir," noted one reviewer, "often without honor in its own country, particularly among the intellectual-sophisticated-beatnik-type music devotees, is definitely on an elevator named 'up,' and nothing can retard its acceleration to greater worldwide recognition."

When Richard Condie took over, he was suited

Over the years, the Choir has used a variety of seating arrangements. The men have sat across the bottom, the women across the top. They have sat in no order at all; in quartet formation; and in the current pattern, women on one side, men on the other. For recordings, modifications are made with microphone placement rather than seating.

to the times. While Cornwall had meticulously and artfully prepared the Choir for its growing visibility and the attendant need for proficiency, Condie brought to the Choir an energy and tenacity that opened new doors.

While on tour in Mexico in 1972, the Choir recorded an album of Spanish and Mexican folk songs. The recording sessions were held in the mammoth 17,500-seat national auditorium in the historic Chapultepec Park. All selections were sung in Spanish, including the Mormon classic "Oh Rey de Reyes, Ven"—"Come, Come, Ye Saints."

From 1983 to 2000, the choir cut nineteen more recordings. It was just a beginning.

*I can read his righteous sentence in
the dim and flaring lamps;
His day is marching on!*

GOD BE WITH YOU
TILL WE MEET AGAIN

Encore
Fond Farewells

IN THE TABERNACLE and in great halls around the world, the Mormon Tabernacle Choir has a tradition of closing with the familiar strains of "God Be with You." When Richard P. Condie concluded his seventeen years as conductor of the Choir (1957–1974), he initiated a new tradition for the much-loved concluding song. Condie gave the Choir the downbeat, and then, with no fanfare, simply set down his baton, stepped down from the podium, and walked out of the Tabernacle. Since that day in 1974, the conductor, at the conclusion of each performance, has put down his baton, turned to the audience, and joined the Choir in singing those poignant words, "God be with you till we meet again." Guest conductor Westin Noble said of his experience at the conclusion of a guest-conducting appearance, "I would have loved to have gone to heaven right then. The feeling went deep into my heart." Noble spoke for the many millions who have been touched by that tender musical farewell, who have felt the Spirit penetrating, lifting their very souls. Christine Schumann, soprano,

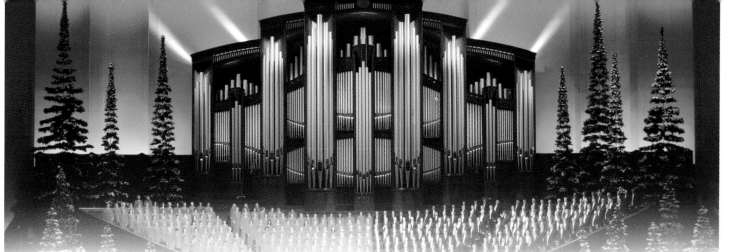

considers the closing "God Be with You" each Sunday, "fifty-two Sundays a year, as the personal expression of hope to each listener, and it brings healing to my own soul."

People are different because of their association with the Choir. Walter Cronkite, guest artist for the 2002 Christmas program, described his three days performing with the Mormon Tabernacle Choir as "a thrill in a thrill-filled life." Bryn Terfel, Welsh baritone soloist in 2003, remarked, "I turned around after I finished my first verse just to listen to this heavenly choir, and everybody in that Choir was looking down and smiling. That is the first impression that I had, and the pure enjoyment just flowed from that height in the hall down through the orchestra, past the

WHAT CHOIR IS BEST KNOWN IN AMERICA? THE MORMON TABERNACLE CHOIR. I CAN'T THINK OF ANY OTHER THAT WOULD EVEN COME CLOSE.
—Don Mischer, executive producer of 2002 Winter Olympic Games

conductor, past the soloists, and into the audience, and that is what music-making is all about."

People come to hear the Choir and leave with renewed peace and strength. Ask the Choir and they will say, as does alto Jeri Howard, "It's like I am singing with the angels in heaven." Ask the parka-clad visitors who bustle into the Tabernacle on Sunday morning, dressed more for a winter walk than a concert, how they feel, and their words are telling: "Grateful." "Resolved to do better."

"Surprised at how much I liked them." The Choir is an American institution, an icon for those looking to find their way. "They can be trusted," one man commented. "They've been around a long time, and I think they're here for a while more."

THE MORMON TABERNACLE CHOIR IS A TREMENDOUSLY BEAUTIFUL PERFORMING ORGANIZATION AND IS RECOGNIZED AS SUCH AND VALUED AS SUCH. IT IS DEDICATED PEOPLE WHO GIVE OF THEIR TIME AND THEIR ARTISTRY AND THEIR STRENGTH. I THINK IT IS THE FINEST CHOIR IN THE WORLD, AND I BELIEVE THAT I CAN SUSTAIN THAT OPINION. —President Gordon B. Hinckley, The Church of Jesus Christ of Latter-day Saints

The Choir represents a type of cooperation and goodwill that has few parallels. Those who come close to the Mormon Tabernacle Choir are changed. They are different because the Choir has offered what they themselves prize: the spirit of singing, the spirit of hope and goodness, the spirit of God. This luminous body of faithful Saints—and angels—leaves a message with all:

> God be with you till we meet again;
> By his counsels guide, uphold you;
> With his sheep securely fold you.
> God be with you till we meet again.
> Till we meet, till we meet,
> Till we meet at Jesus' feet,
> Till we meet, till we meet,
> God be with you till we meet again.

TAKE TIME TO BE HOLY
Mormon Tabernacle Choir Time Line

1834—*Choir schools established in Kirtland.*
1836—*Choirs sing for Kirtland Temple dedication.*

EVENTS

PRE-CHOIR

1835—*First Hymnal compiled by Emma Smith.*

1849—*John Parry named choir conductor.*
1850—*Welsh singers arrive in Salt Lake Valley.*
1851—*First Tabernacle completed.*

August 27, 1847—*First performance of what is today the Mormon Tabernacle Choir.*

October 1867—*Choir of 150 sings for General Conference in newly constructed Tabernacle.*

July 4, 1873—*First Mormon Tabernacle Choir concert presented in Tabernacle.*

October 9, 1875—*Tabernacle dedication.*

1880—*First trip away from Salt Lake City, to American Fork, Utah. Ebeneezer Beesley named choir conductor.*

1889—*Evans Stephens named choir conductor.*

September 1893—*Choir's first out-of-state tour, to Chicago World's Fair.*

1896—*Statehood celebration.*

1903—*Choir sings for President Taft.*

1909—*First noon organ recital.*

September 1, 1910—*First recordings of Choir for Columbia Phonograph Company.*

1916—*Anthony C. Lund named choir conductor.*

July 15, 1929—*First nationwide broadcast of Choir from KZN, predecessor of KSL radio.*

1935—*J. Spencer Cornwall named choir conductor.*

April 1940—*Choir gives first public demonstration of stereophonic sound from Carnegie Hall.*

January 16, 1944—*Choir's first broadcast overseas to U.S. Army Special Services in Great Britain.*

1948—*Tabernacle organ rebuilt.*

1949—*Choir's first commercial recording.*

August 1955—*Choir's first tour of Europe, with performances in Scotland, Wales, Denmark, Germany, Switzerland, and France.*

1957—*Richard P. Condie named choir conductor.*

November 1959—*Choir receives Grammy award for "Battle Hymn of the Republic."*

October 14, 1962—*First televised broadcast of Music and the Spoken Word.*

1964—*First of five gold records.*

January 1965—*Choir performs at inaugural of President Lyndon B. Johnson.*

January 1969—*Choir performs at inaugural of President Richard M. Nixon.*

1975—*Jerold D. Ottley named choir conductor.*

July 1976—*Choir tours Philadelphia, Boston, New York City, Washington, D.C., and its home state, Utah, for nation's bicentennial.*

1980—*Music and the Spoken Word receives Freedom Foundation Award.*

January 20, 1981—*Choir performs at inaugural of President Ronald Reagan.*

1987—*Choir wins Emmy award for "Christmas Sampler" with Shirley Verrett.*

January 1989—*Choir performs at inaugural of President George H. W. Bush.*

1991—*First of two platinum records.*

January 1999—*Formation of Orchestra at Temple Square and Temple Square Chorale.*

1999—*Craig Jessop named choir conductor.*

January 2001—*Choir performs at inaugural of President George W. Bush.*

February 8–24, 2002—*Choir performs twenty times for 2002 Winter Olympic Games in Salt Lake City, including opening ceremonies and Tabernacle concerts.*

June 27, 2002—*Choir returns to its roots, singing at dedication of rebuilt LDS Nauvoo Temple.*

March 2003—*Choir establishes its own recording label—Mormon Tabernacle Choir.™*

November 2003—*Choir awarded National Medal of Arts in White House Ceremony.*

July 18, 2004—*The Mormon Tabernacle Choir celebrates seventy-five years on the air, the longest continuous program in broadcast history.*

IT IS WELL WITH MY SOUL

Choir Volunteers

The following have served as members of the Mormon Tabernacle Choir, since its beginnings in pioneer times to the present, and with the Orchestra at Temple Square since 1999. The names, drawn from records of the Choir and the Orchestra, may not be complete. If you have additions, please contact the Mormon Tabernacle Choir historian, Marene Foulger, who has prepared this list, at foulgerm@ldschurch.org.

• A • Julie Aamot, Charles Abbott, John Abbott, Louise Clarke Abegg, John Charles Abercrombie, Don Abernathy, (?) Adair, Ann Rogerson Adams, Beth W. Adams, Clara Adams, Don L. Adams, Elias Harris Adams, Homer E. Adams, James (Jim) Adams, Joseph Adams, Lucy Adams, Nancy May Ferrin Adams, P. Adams, Paul Adams, Selia Adams, Tamara F. Adams, Corinne Adamson, Edith Adamson, Helen Adamson, John C. (Jack) Adamson, Sherry Rae Pratt Adkins, Anthon Ahbrichs, Eva W. Aird, Jack A. Aird, Kathy R. Airmet, John Akert, Edna L. Alba, May Albecht, Thomas H. Albisten, May Albrecht, Christine Albrechtsen, Florence H. Alder, Mae C. Alder, H. M. Aldous, Janet (Jan) Condie Aldous, Melba Aldrich, Susan Alldredge, Adele Allen, Arintha Allen, Brent Allen, David Allen, Dorothy Allen, Elaine Allen, Hal J. Allen, Julia Allen, L. Lynn Allen, Mary E. Allen, Patricia Allen, William F. Allen, Marcie Alley, Stephen L. Alley, H. J. Allgaier, Bessie Dean Allison, C. Evan Allred, Dorothy Allred, G. Hugh Allred, Garth W. Allred, June Allred, Karen Leishman Allred, Kathleen Allred, Viola May Blunck Allred, Donna Allsop, Becky Almond, Max E. Almond, Reese M. Almond, Lydia Almstead, Dean Alsop, Donna Alsop, T. H. Alviston, Catherine Ames, George Ames, Mark Ammons, Robert D. Amott, Eugene Amundsen, Yvonne Anastasiou, Henry Edward Anderegg, Montess (Monty or Tess) Miller Anderegg, Nephi Andersen (or Anderson), Fred Y. Andersen, Grace Andersen, Laura Andersen, Pearl Andersen, Vinnie Andersen, Agnes Anderson, Alex P. Anderson, Alice Bickerstaff Anderson, Allison Anderson, Anamae Anderson, Andrea Whitney Anderson, Anna Anderson, Barry Anderson, Beverly Anderson, Christine Anderson, Darrell Lewis Andy Anderson, David P. Anderson, Doyle R. Anderson, Elaine Card Anderson, Elizabeth G. Anderson, Elna Jean Anderson, Eunice Nanie Whipple Anderson, Frank Charles Anderson, Fred Y. Anderson, Grace Anderson, Howard Anderson, Howard T. Anderson, Ivy Anderson, James S. Anderson, Joan Ellen Fox Anderson, Joseph Moroni Anderson, Kathleen Anderson, Lawrence Dick Anderson, Marc Wright Anderson, Marilyn Anderson, Mary L. Anderson, Melba Anderson, Norma Anderson, Patricia A. Anderson, Phil Anderson, R. L. Anderson, R. Udell Anderson, Richard Anderson, Richmond M. Anderson, Robert L. Anderson, Rose Anderson, S. W. Anderson, ShaRee B. Anderson, Sheldon Anderson, Ted L. Anderson, Lila Harvatin Anderton, Lila Harvetin Anderton, Norma Christensen Anderton, Norma E. Anderton, Una Andreasen, Teenie Andrew, John W. Andrews, Ilene Andrus, Roman Raphael Andrus, Arthur Angel, Truman O. Angel, Alice Angell, Stella Angell, Betty Angerbauer, Alisha Ard, Arreva Armistead, Nellie Armitage, (?) Armstrong, Jed Armstrong, Mary Armstrong, Vilate Smith Arnold, A. L. Around, Thomas Ash, Bonna Ashby, Carl L. Ashby, Edna Ashby, Loren G. Ashcraft, Alice Ashton, Ann Clark Ashton, Elizabeth Ashton, J. W. Ashton, Louise Keddington Ashton, Mark Ashton, Norma Ashton, Eladia Ashworth, Thomas Ashworth, Frank W. Asper, Rebecca Aspinal, Margaret Aste, Debra Astin, J. N. Astin, Patyra Astin, Vivyenne Astle, Norma Aston, Scott Jay Aston, Donald Richard Athay, Bernard F. Atkinson, Deanna Atkinson, Earl Donald Attridge, Luana Au, William Aubrey, John Auden, Robert Aupperle, Gordon (Gordy) Peery Austin, R. F. Aveson

• B • G. H. Backman, Mary Jean Backman, Esther Bacon, Lindsay Baddley, Marie Baddley, Mary Lynn Pearce Baddley, Doris Martin Badger, A. Marie Bagley, Estrid Fors Bagley, Marie Brown Bagley, Anna Fugal Bailey, Esther Bailey, J. W. Bailey, Lauralee Moody Bailey, Liole J. Bailey, Rachel Whittaker Bailey, Laura G. Bair, Kristine Baird, Carlyle Baker, Claire Moss Baker, John W. Baker, Lola P. Baker, Moneta S. Baker, H. J. Ball, Lucille Ball, Natalie Ball, Elizabeth Ballantyne, Seth Ballard, Adam Ballif, Charles Balmforth, Cora Barber, Fern Barber, H. D. Barber, H. E. Barber, Stephen J. Bardsley, Allan H. Barker, Joanne Barker, Karen Weed Barker, Meredith Barker, O. Barker, Jean Palmer Barks, J. M. Barlow, Jane Barlow, Lillie Barlow, Thelma Barlow, Eva Lund Barnes, Richard Lloyd Barnes, Trudy Barnes, Joyce R. Barney, Richard Barney, Clyde R. Barraclough, H. G. Barraclough, Harold F. Barraclough, Alice Barrell, C. H. Barrell, E. Barrell, Elihu Barrell, H. Charles Barrell, A. W. Barrett, Ellen Barrett, Scott Barrick, Fred Barrows, Naoma Barrus, Naomi Barrus, Ralph M. Barrus, Alice Falkner Bartholomew, (?) Barton, Amy Barton, Anne Barton, David L. Basinger, Donald Basinger, E. K. Bassett, Maggie Bassett, Almon Bate, Blair Bateman, Harold E. Bateman, Mary F. Bateman, Ryan James Bateman, Deraold E. Bates, Edward Fetzer Bates, Elizabeth Fetzer Bates, George T. Baugh, Gwenneth Bauman, G. Bawles, Mary Baxter, Phyllis Baxter, Sandra Johnson Bayles, Emma Bayliss, Lois Beach, Lois Olson Beach, David Beal, Evan Bean, Virginia Bean, William Beasley, N. Ross Beatie, Ross Beatie, Sue Smith Beatie, Dorothy Ence Beck, Donald (Don) L. Becker, Peggy Becker, Bruce Beckman, Patty Beckman, Lee A. Beckstead, Maurine Beckstead, Arnold A. Beckstrand (or Bickstrand), Arnold A. Beckstrand, Ronald Beers, William L. Beers, Adelbert Beesley, Diane C. Heder Beesley, Diane Heder Beesley, Ebenezer Beesley, Ella Beesley, Evangeline (Vange) T. Beesley, F. Beesley, F. (female) Beesley, Fred Beesley, Frederick Beesley, Garratt Thomas Beesley, William J. Beesley, Gaylene Beeson, Ruby S. Beeston, Emily Beezley, Emily Cooper Beezley, James (Jim) R. Behling, Kaye Behling, J. Ray Behnke, Clarnell Behunin, George Frank Behunin, Joan Pitts Behunin, Lynda Behunin, Ruby Behunin, Jean Beisinger, Daniel Belgique, Bonna Bell, H. V. Bell, Judy Bell, Almina Bellamy, Elizabeth Bellamy, John R. Bellamy, Donna Belliston, Beatrice Bennett, Christopher Bennett, Fred Bennett, Lily Bennett, Peter H. Bennett, (?) Bennion, Carolyn Vance Bennion, Donald Bennion, Karla Bennion, Merrill Bennion, Wilma Bennion, Otto Bensch, Amy Benson, Elda Benson, Larry Benson, Ralph Benson, Clifford Bentley, Frank Bentley, Joseph Bentley, Janet Marie Jenkins Benzley, P. Robert Benzley, Mae V. Berg, Andrew Bergenson, Karen Maloy Bergeson, Cora Berghout, Aleen Berlin, Rose Berlin, William Bernards, Harry Bernstrom, A. G. Berrett, Reed B. Berrett, Charles L. Berry, Ellen Berry, Kathy Best, Richard Best, Wendell Best, Doris Bettridge, Eva May H. Bettridge, Eva May Henderson Bettridge, James Bettridge, Annalyn Beus, F. Bevis, Terry Bexell, John Beyer, Lucile Cardall Beyer, Lucille Cardall Beyer, Tony Beyer, Bonnie Rae Gardner Bigler, David Bigler, Eugene (Gene) Bigler, Gordon O. Bigler, Hazel A. Bigler, Jeffery Bigler, L. Burt Bigler Jr., Larry Bigler, Robert M. Bigler, Bryce Bingham, Keith J. Bingham, Leslee Steadman Bingham, Peggy Bingham, Alice Reid Bird, C. W. Bird, Charles E. Bird, Charles R. Bird, Clara M. Bird, Dwight Bird, Gale Bird, H. B. Bird, Hazel S. Bird, Heber G. Bird, Janet C. Bird, Lillian J. Bird, Marian Bricker Bird, Walter Birkedahl, Erling Birkeland, Arvilla Birrell, Alice Birt, Cohleen J. Bischoff, Carolyn C. Bishop, Jay Bishop, Klar Bishop, Lynn Bishop, Mariam D. Bishop, Marva Bishop, Marvin Bishop, Mary Joy Bishop, J. A. Bistline, Charles Bitter, Carol Jean Bittner, Libbie Bittner, May Bittner, Hertha Bixby, Lela Bixby, Marie Black, A. L. Blackburn, Douglas Blackhurst, Jonathan G. Blackhurst, Richard Blackhurst, L. A. Blackner, Reva Brown Blair, Erma Ridges Blakemore, Eric Blanchard, Kiersten Blanchard, Lorin R. Blauer, Louise Bluhm, Herbert Bluke, Olive Boatright, W. D. Bocker, Christine Bockholt, Rachel Bodell, Carolyn Bodily, Keith Bodily, Ramona Bogardus, A. D. Boice, G. F. Bolto, Clair Kent Boman, Connie Bond, Richard G. Bond, Jason Bonham, Nettie M. Bonner, Phillip Bonney, Mariner A. Bons, Peter Bons, Elizabeth A. Booth, Eva Booth, H. E. Booth, J. Kaye Booth, L. H. Booth, LaVern Booth, Melba Woodbury Booth, Nan Chipman Booth, Rebecca Booth, J. V. T. Borgeson, Nettie Borgeson, Rhoda Borgeson, Dora V. Borgquist, J. R. Bost, Dianna Boulter, George E. Bourne, Helen Whitney Bourne, Robert Bowden, Betsy Ila Bowen, Garrick Bowen, Lucile Ross Bowen, Lucy Gates Bowen, Lyle Bowen, Wesley Bowen, Alfred Bowers, Carma Douglas Bowers, David J. Bowers, Ida C. Bowers, Ioa Rowena Bowers, Levi Bowers, Louis Bowers, Mildred Bowers, Orlando Bowers, J. Bowler, John Bowman, Lorraine Bowman, Nina N. Bowman, Bertie Bowring, Maud Bowring, W. D. Bowring, E. D. Boyce, Carl Stephen Boyd, Kathleen Carter Boyd, Walter E. Boyden Jr., Vivian Boyer, A. E. Braby, M. (Mamie?) Braby, Ida Bracken, Barlow Bradford, Daron Bradford, Lillie Bradford, Lisle Bradford, Ray W. Bradford, Dyca Ann Frisby Bradshaw, Frank M. Bradshaw, William Bradshaw, Ethel Bradson, Jean Brady, Neil Brady, Carol Louise Brain, E. J. Brain, Brent Braithwaite, Linda Braithwaite, Tom Brandon, Arnold Branham, Beth Breinholt, L. P. Brewerton, Laurinda Brewerton, Lucile Brewerton, Maggie Brewester, Beth Stevenson Brewster, Bonnie Brewster, Kyle Hayes Brewster, Betty Ann White Dawson Johnson Bridgeforth, Amy Bridges, Robert Briggs, John Wesley Bright, Melody Brighton, Barbara Hoppie Brimley, George S. Bringhurst, Bonna Ashby Brinton, Sally Peterson Brinton, Janet Parry Broadbent, Stephen Reed Broadhead, Gayle Brockbank, H. D. Brockbank, LaVon Brockbank, Adelia Broderick, Haru Janu Speer Bromley, Sandra Brooks, Heidi Russon Broschinsky, Eugene E. Brough, Norma G. Brough, Patricia (Pat) P. Brough, Joy Brower, Brian Brown, Calene Brown, Calvin Reed Brown, Darrell Z. Brown, David Brown, Diana Brown, Dianne Brown, Donald Redford Brown, Dorothy Brown, Drusilla Brown, Elsie Brown, Emily Brown, George C. Brown, Gerty Brown, Jason Brown, LaPrele S. Brown, Mary Ellen Brown, May Brown, Milo Brown, Nathel Brown, Nephi Brown, Newel Kay Brown, Reed Brown, Richard Brown, Ruth Brown, S. F. Brown, Shirley Johnson Brown, Thelma C. Brown, William Brown, Bessie Browning, Michael Browning, A. V. Brownson, Bonnie Jean Bruce, Mika Brunson, Richard Brunson, Wessman Brunson, Dan Bryce, Jeannine Buckley, Richard Grant Buckmiller, S. Elliott Budge, "T" Buehner, Dennis Buehner, Michael Buehner, Ismae Buie, Hy Bull, Hyrum J. Bull, Gene Bullock, Mary Louise Bult, June Burbidge, Marjo Carroll Burdette, Lurrine Burgess, Roy Burgess, Claron D. Burgon, Caseel D. Burk, David Burke, Bruce E. Burkhart, Karla D. Burkhart, Kenneth L. Burnett, Barbara Burnham, Perry H. Burnham, Cecil Burns, Hattie Burns, Linda Burns, Arthur L. Burrell, E. Burrell, Sharon Faye Odell Burt, Rachel Burtch, Annette Jean Burton, Edith Burton, Fred Burton, Jacob Burton, Janene Burton, Jay P. Burton, Julia Burton, June Barlow Burton, Mabel Wood Burton, Nelson Burton, Robert S. Burton, Shipley D. Burton, Harley M. Busby, David Bush, Derilys Rowe Hill Bush, John Bush, Lily Bush, W. Sterling Bush, Rex Bruce Bushman, F. Butler, Lloyd Butler, Stanley Butler, Susan Fugal Butler, Thomas Butler, Edward or Edwin Butterworth, Mary Buttle, Richard Bytendorp, Diane Jarman Bytheway, Laraine Boehme Bytheway, Loraine (Leah) Boehme Bytheway, Donna J. Bywater, Lizzie Bywater

• C • Gomez B. Cahoon, Mary Ellen B. Caine, Alice Bourne Calder, Maurice Hammond Calder, Melvie Calder, Myrna J. Calderwood, Alfred Caldwell, Ann Caldwell, Ella Williams Caldwell, Nettie Caldwell, Shirley Ann Caldwell, L. A. Calkins, Carol Jeanne Bjorndal Call, Della H. Call, Nina R. Call, O. Jay Call, William G. Call, Genevieve Johns Callister, Emma Calton, George A. Calton, J. Calton, W. Calton, D. E. Cameron, Leah Halliday Cameron, Anne Brown Camomile, Glen R. Camomile, Bettie Camp, Mildred Camp, Virgil Camp, Aggie Campbell, Annie Campbell, Boyce Campbell, Jay Campbell, Karen Miller Campbell, Louis Campbell, Meredith Campbell, Robert Campbell, Ruby Campbell, Serge B. Campbell, Ales Canepari, Peggy Cann, Amelia Cannon, E. Cannon, Elias M. Cannon, Flora Mathews Cannon, Frances Cannon, Gary Cannon, Hester Cannon, Ida Cannon, Janath Russell Cannon, Joseph Cannon, Margaret S. Cannon, Theodore L. Cannon, Tracy Y. Cannon, Victor E. Cannon, W. Cannon, Ronald Cantera, Albert Maurice Capson, Elaine Anderson Card, George Edward Percy Careless, Lavinia Careless, Beatrice (Bea) Carey, Doris P. Carey, Thain Carlisle, Jean T. Carlson, Richard L. Carlson, Suzanne Sanborn Carlson, Jeanie Allen Carnahan, Agnes Carner, Haven R. Carr, Ruth F. Carr, Marjo Burdett Carroll, Hazel Carson, Bertha Carter, Clorence C. Carter, Florence N. Carter, Hattie Carter, Stephen Carter, Valeen B. Dummer Carter, Wayne Carter, Agnes V. Carver, Pamla Carway, Stephen T. Case, Michael Case, Gayle Cassidy, Mr. Castler, Charles Castleton, David B. Castleton, Grant A. Castleton, John B. Castleton, L. G. (Jerry) Castleton, W. C. Castleton, Katherine Celaya, Eunice Chace, Jennie Chalmers, Aaron Chamberlain, Amanda Chamberlain, Bessie Chamberlain, Carrie Chamberlain, John H. Chamberlain, Joseph Chamberlain, Thomas Chamberlain, Deanne Chandler, Kathleen Chandler, Priscilla Chandler, Ray Chandler, Rose Chandler, June Pehrson Chapman, Vernon Chapman, Joseph Pymm Chartrand, Judith Baur Chartrand, Richard N. Chatelain, Val J. Chatfield, Carolyn Sue Chatterton, Ollie Jean Cheapella, Millie Foster Cheesman, Mildred Cheney,

James (Jim) D. Cheshire Jr., Kim Clark Cheshire, J. H. Chester, Ollie Jean Chiapella, Mark Child, Nola Child, Ramon M. Child, Alta Victoria Childs, Catherine Childs, Bertha Chipman, Betty Jean Saville Chipman, Betty Jeanne Saville Chipman, Davis H. Chipman, Mildred Chipman, Nan Chipman, Joy T. Chisholm, Augusta Christensen, Clara Christensen, Dorotha Christensen, Ellen Christensen, Mac Christensen, Gordon Merwyn Christensen, H. J. Christensen, Harold C. Christensen, Hazel Nelson Christensen, Hugh Wilford Chris Christensen, Hy J. C. Christensen, JoAnn Williams Christensen, Kate Christensen, Katie M. Christensen, Lela G. Christensen, Lillie Christensen, Linda Christensen, Marlene Hewlett Christensen, Mary Ann Clyde Christensen, Milton Christensen, Opal Christensen, Paul Christensen, Rudolph Christensen, Susan Christensen, Trent Christensen, William (Budge) L. Christensen, Patricia Jean Babb Christenson, Joy Mimi Thalman Christholm, Wyoma Christian, Clay Christiansen, Frances Christiansen, James C. Christiansen, Joseph Christianson, Willard Christoperhson, Anna Christopher, Irene S. Christopher, M. A. Christopher, Raymond Christopher, Dagmar Christopherson, E. Christopherson, Lamar S. Christopherson, M. Christopherson, M. E. Christopherson, Victor Christopherson, Willard Christopherson, Jewel Chryst, Robert (Bob) Vernon Chryst, Salvatore (Sal) Ciccarello, (?) Clapham, Charles Clapham, Elizabeth Clapham, George Herbert Clapham, Gudrum Lillewick Clapham, (?) Clark, Annie Clark, Arvilla Clark, Dolores Seal Clark, Elayne Bright Clark, Elliott Clark, Elmer Lucius Clark, Grace Clark, Helen Elliott Clark, Jacquetta Johnson Clark, Jacquita Johnson Clark, Jane Clark, John Clark, Joyce Murray Clark, Karen Clark, L. S. Clark, L. W. Clark, Mary R. Clark, Osborne Clark, Owen Clark, Percy G. Clark, Ruel Clark, Shane Clark, VeAnn Clark, Louise Abegg Clarke, Evelyn Clawson, Orin Clawson, Ruth J. Clawson, S. H. Clawson, Sue Clawson, Thomas A. Clawson Jr., Fred E. Clayson, Belle Clayton, C. M. Clayton, J. L. Clayton, John L. Clayton, Leland Clayton, Martha Clayton, Maurice Clayton, Patricia J. Clayton, Robert (Bob) Ellis Clayton, Sarah Clayton, Susan Clayton, Vera Clayton, Vinnie Clayton, Will Clayton, Ruth Clegg, Betty Clements, C. Roland Clements, Elizabeth Clements, W. E. Clements, Richard W. Clinger, Shauna C. Clinger, W. Cordell Clinger, William C. Clive, Susan Reed Clough, Fergus Coalter, J. Kent Cobb, Raydell S. Cobia, Albert E. Cocking, John Colbert, Nellie Colebrook, Jacquelyn Coleman, Ruth Coleman, Richard C. Collett, Jeffrey L. Colletti, Gladys E. Collier, Gladys M. Collier, Gwladys E. Morgan Collier, Gwladys Eileen Morgan Collier, Kathryn Collier, Vernon Collier, Sonya Collins, David Combs, Douglas Condie, Gertrude Condie, Richard P. Condie, Joanne Conrwall, May Converse, Elease Cook, Elsie Cook, Janeece Cynthia Bush Cook, John H. Cook, Mary Ann Cook, Patricia K. Cook, Susan B. Cook, Nina Richards Cooke, Sarah A. Cooke, D. W. Coolbear, Nellie Coomans, Barbara Coombs, Jesse R. Coombs, Marian S. Coombs, Eldruna W. Coon, Edna Cooper, Hattie Cooper, Lizzie Cooper, Mabel Cooper, Emma Cope, F. W. Cope, Wilfred O. Copling, Kathleen Butler Coppin, Edith Corless, Pamela Cormay, Allen Cornwall, Bonnie Cornwall, Joseph Spencer Cornwall, Joanne A. Cornwall, Marian Cornwall, Mary H. Cornwall, Melvin C. Cornwall, Millicent D. Cornwall, Oscar Cornwall, Shirl Cornwall, Shirley Westover Cornwall, N. L. Cottam, Minerva Cotton, H. Coulam, Beulah Hinckley Coult, Fergus Coulter, R. H. Cowburn, Gae Cowley, LaVon C. Cowley, Lisa Cowley, Donna Cox, Gaylen J. Cox, Michelle Cox, William M. Cox, Victor J. Coy, Helen Cozzens, Duane Cradall, Fay Cram, Alice M. Crandall, Don A. Crandall, Peggy Joy McCandless Crapo, Ronell Crapo, James Crawford, Thomas C. Crawford, Will Crawford, Jesse Crisler, Lou Ann Crisler, Carol J. Crist, Robert H. Crist, Frances Critchlow, Patricia Critchlow, Kenneth B. Crocheron, Edna G. Crocker, Mathew Croft, Connie Consoer Crofts, Ray John Crook, Eve Crookston, Deon P. Cropper, Alan Croshaw, Ada Cross, Bonita Cross, Lily May Crotch, William Crotch, LaRena Crow, Fay Croxford, Emily Crumpton, Vinnie Cufflin, Ambrose Jericho Munson Cuison, Patricia (Pat) Culverwell, Birdie Clawson Cummings, Joye Jensen Cummings, Annie Cummock, John B. Cummock, Ione Cuncan, Betsy Cundick, Robert Cundick, Robert Cundick Jr., Thomas Cundick, Brandt B. Curtis, Dorothy Curtis, Eldra or Elda W. Curtis, Elsie Curtis, Janice Curtis, Matthew Curtis, L. Cushing, Lilly Cushing, Myrtle Cushing, Jewel Cutler, Lila B. Cutler, Lucy Cutler, Sue Cutler, Winfried Czerny

• D • Blair P. Dahl, Curt Dahl, Francis F. Dalby, Olive Dalby, Maxine H. Dale, Hyrum C. Dalgleish, Amy Dalton, Donna Dalton, Adrienne Dangerfield, Layne Dangerfield, Alice Daniels, Tasma Dansie, Mary Danzig, Peter Danzig, Peter (Pete) A. Danzig, Arlene B. Darger, Stanford (Stan) P. Darger, Yvonne Darke, Roy Maughan Darley, Della Darne, D. Kent Dastrup, Erva Dean Dastrup, Kathleen McKee Dastrup, Travis Dastrup, Calvin Davenport, Ira Davenport, Dorothy Davies, Henry Davies, John Davies, William Davis (or Davies), Alice Stephens Davis, Anita Hyatt Davis, Blanche Davis, Busly Davis, Carol Davis, Christine Davis, Christopher Davis, Edward Davis, Elizabeth Davis, Esther Davis, Faye Davis, H. Davis, Hannah Davis, Hazel Davis, Karri Davis, Kathleen Davis, Kerrie Davis, Lotta Davis, Marilyn D. Davis, Melvin E. Davis, Merlin Davis, Pearl Kimball Davis, Reed Davis, Reid H. Davis, Robert L. Davis, T. Davis, Toni Rae Davis, Vaudis Davis, Vickie Lou Umberger or Ungerman Davis, Arthur Day, W. Daniel Day, Della Daynes, John Daynes, Joseph J. Daynes, Robert Daynes, Robert F. Daynes, Robert (Bob) F. Daynes, Lineu (Lin) de Paula, Sharon Z. de Paula, Arden Dean, Bessie Dean, Leo A. Dean, Lizette Dean, William J. Dean, Lucy Deane, Leonore E. Debendiner, Enid Nelson Ogaard DeBirk, Martine DeBruin, Kirke M. Decker, Louise Lees Decker, Noram Decker, Deborah Egan Dedekind, C. DeGooyer, John DeGooyer, Selina DeGray, John Egbert DeHaan, Eda Dehlin, Aleaha Delaney, Cornelius DeLang (or Delange), Cornelis Den Ouden, William Denkers, Sarah I. Dennison, David Denniston, Fred Earl Densley, Christine L. Deppe, Richard Derby, Ella Derr, F. Derrick, Frankie Derrickson, Cleo DeSpain, Gertrude Despain, Gerald E. Deters, Karl Devenport, Wayne N. or M. Devereaux, Lewis Henry DeYoung, Richard S. Dick, Margaret Diehl, Conrad Dietz, Clive Lyon Dill Jr., Merrill Dimmick, Marilyn Louise Dinger, Annette Dinwoodey, Flora Dinwoodey, Alma Dittmer, Sam Divett, Crissie Dixon, Dennis M. Dixon, Kelly Dixon, Roger Louis Dock, Beatrice Dodworth, G. Dodworth, Girard Doezie, Jacob Doezie, Carrie Donaldson, Edna C. Donaldson, G. Kent Donaldson, Mamie Donaldson, Kathleen Donalson, Irene Done, Ivy Done, Otto Done, Earl Donelson, Laura Donelson, Richard Donelson, John Dories, Nora Dorius, R. E. Dorius, R. Joel Dorius, Claudio M. dos Santos, Claudius Doty, H. Doubleday, Henry Doubleday, Harlan Doud, Stella Doud, Hugh Dougall, Williams (Bill) E. Dowse, Bill Doxey, Cynthia Doxey, Nina Doxey, William Doxey, Lori Drake, Melba Draper, Harold W. Drawe, Arnold O. Drews, Shirley Driscoll, Wilma Drorbaugh, James H. Duckworth, Joseph S. Dudley, Fred Duersch Jr., Eliza Dunbar, James T. Dunbar, D. Duncan, Homer Duncan, Hortense Hinckley Duncan, Ione Duncan, Jean Duncan, L. C, Duncan, L. C. Duncan, LaMar Duncan, LaMar Bill Duncan, Leah Shinder Duncomb, M. Diane Dunford, A. Dunn, Charlene M. Dunn, M. Dunn, Melvin Westwood Dunn, Phillip Dunn, Thomas Dunn Jr., Victor Dupuis, Thomas (Tom) L. Durham, C. J. Durrams, S. T. Durrant, Vera Durrant, Verna Durrant, A. Porter Dutson, Edna Dwyer, Kate Dwyer, George Dyer, Mary S. Dyer, May Dyer

• E • Janine McBride Eames, Oliver D. Eames, Suzanne Gilmore Earl, Hattie Earnshaw, Betty Hyde Eastman, Betty Ivins Hyde Eastman, R. C. Easton, Marjorie Eberhart, Albert Eccles Jr., Albert Eccles Sr., Caroline T. Eccles, Faye S. Eccles, Minnie Eckard, Janet Sue Whitman Eddington, Louie Eddington, Rose Eddington, Charlina Edholm, Lizzie Edmunds, Lizzie Thomas Edward, Craig M. Edwards, Edna Edwards, Lizzie T. Edwards, Mae Edwards, R. Edwards, Dick Howard Egan, Doyle Carlos Egan, L. M. W. Egan, Mary Jane Egan, Shirley Peterson Egan, Jeanett Whipple Eggett, Donald Rufus Egginton, Shirley H. Christensen Egginton, Susan N. Egli, Mark E. Eisley, Hildur or Hildbar M. Ekberg, Marva May Saunders Young Elggren, Olive Hickman Rich Elggren, Olive N. Hickman Rich Elggren, Leone H. Eliason, Clara Elieson, Marilyn Elison, Rachael Elison, Alma Elkins, John Elkins, Billie Dean or Deen Ellett, Nola G. Elliott, Richard Elliott, Alice Ellis, James Ellis, Robert J. Ellis, Susan Ellis, Susie Ellis, Suzanne Ellis, Hazel Ellison, Alice Ellsmore, Ellen Ellsmore, Emily Ellsmore, Julia C. Ellsworth, Beth Monson Carver Elmer, John Elzinga, George R. Emery, H. Emery, Paul Enciso, Kristie B. Engar, Vera Engberg, Breck (Richard) England, Marie English, Jean G. Enniss, (?) Ensign, Albert L. Ensign, Elaine Pusey Ensign, Elaine Woodbury Pusey Ensign, H. Ensign, H. S. Ensign, Horace S. Ensign, Ivie J. Ensign, Martha J. Ensign, Mary E. Ensign, Rula Ensign, Amos Epperson, DeVere Erb, Carrie Erickson, Debra Erickson, Florence C. Erickson, Yvonne Marler Steiger Erickson, Lettie Erikson, Herbert Eriksson, Justus Ernst, Mary Jane Pidd Ertmann, LaMar C. Eskelson, Vera Monsen or Monson Espinosa, (Wayne) Kent Ethington, Mark Ethington, Mark Eubanks, Bruce Evans, Colleen Evans, Craig Evans, David William Evans, Edna Evans, Elizabeth Evans, George Davis Evans, Georgia Kanell Evans, H. T. Evans, Ivy Evans, Joan Evans, Joanne Evans, John Evans, Kenneth (Ken) R. Evans, Lynn B. Evans, Max Evans, Oakley S. Evans, Paul H. Evans, Richard L. Evans, T. Max Evans, Velma Evans, Vance Everett, D. Evertsen, Arthur G. Eves Jr.

• F • Chandelle Fairbanks, Craig Fairbanks, Fonda Williams Fairbanks, James Fairbanks, Ortho Fairbanks, Reed S. Fairbanks, Lily M. Fairclough, David Faires, Albert (Bert) D. Fallows, Lorna Lowry Fallows, Tom Fallows, Jane Fanning, Jacob Faragher, Brent Farley, Janene Farley, Elsie Farnsberg, Alma Farnsworth, Dean Farnsworth, Karl Farnsworth, Ovid L. Farnsworth, Douglas Farr, Lynn Farrar, Alice C. Farrell, Michael Farrell, Phyllis D. Mossing Farrell, Robert Michael Farrell, Mary Farrer, Helen DuBell Grubbs Fatten, W. Fatten, Annette Faux, Sheila Favero, Kenneth Fechser, David Feller, Russell Fellows, C. B. Felt, D. Felt, Harry Felt, Lizzie Felt, Minnie Felt, Richard N. Felt, Rita P. Felt, Wanda Harris Fenton, George C. Ferguson, Annette B. Fernley, Edward (Ed) R. Fernley, Clara Beatrice Seal Fernstrom, Dolores Seal Fernstrom, Loren W. Ferre, LuCretia Ferre, Dennis M. Ferrell, Desna Ferrell, May Ferrin, Minnie Ferrin, Mary Ferro, Richard W. Fetzer, Cecelia H. Fielding, Florence Fife, Winona Fifield, David P. Fillmore, Marilyn Pitts Fineshriber, Keith N. Finlayson, Luella Wheeler Finlinson, Bonnie Jo Fisher, C. Marianne Fisher, Donna Fisher, E. W. Fisher, Jon E. Fisher, Lon Fisher, M. N. Fisher, Merlin Fisher, Robert S. Fisher, Steven D. Fisher, Judith Fitzgerald, Michael Fitzgerald, Sheree Fitzgerald, Jane Ripplinger Fjeldsted, Twylla Gibb Flanders, Beverly Flandro, Rose Edith Flashman, Betty Lou Flemming, Leland E. Flinders, Eleanor Foerstl, S. W. Fogelberg, Cheryl Fogg, Laura Folkerson, Robert (Bob) Elry Folsom, Theron P. Folsom, Luna Fonnesbeck, Ludwig Forback, Mollie Forbes, Mary E. Forbush, Jacqulin Ford, Nellie G. Forman, E. Kaye Forsgren, Douglass Forsha, J. A. Fortie, Alice Foster, Aurelia Foster, Charles E. Foster, Doreen Lauder Foster, Frank Foster, George Foster, Millie Foster, William H. Foster, Josephene Chamberlain Foulger, Marene Foulger, Paul Adelbert Foulger, Annie Fowler, Esther Fowler, James Fowler, Tamara Fowler, Ann Schlofman Fox, Joan Ellen Anderson Fox, Kenneth Fox, Lillian Stokes Fox, Lucy Grant Fox, Wallace Fox, Jean B. Fraenkel, Delight Thomas Frampton, Elva Francom, Christine Franzen, Bluford Fraseur, Robert (Bob) Frederickson, Clara Fredrickson, Janalee Free, Archie Freeburn, Edward Freed, Nan Freeman, Ray Freeman, George Freeze, M. Freeze, Mr. Freeze, Jacqueline French, H. LeRoy Frisby, Orlene H. Frisby, M. Froisland, Frank Frost, Kathleen Frost, Mathilda P. Frost, Nettie Frost, Rosalie Richards Frost, Fred C. Fuller, Lael G. or J. Fuller, Lael K. Fuller, Marvin Fuller, Nida Fuller, J. M. Fullmer, Jeannette Fullmer, Maude Stepherts or Stephens Fullmer, Valetta Fullmer, H. Fulmer, Minnie Fulmer, George T. Furner, Douglas Furness, Emma Ellen Alder Furness, Joe Fyans, May Fyans

• G • Lulu Gagon, Lela Galbraith, Lela Lisonbee Galbraith, A. LeRoy Gale, Charlene Gale, Ella Gale, Jennie Gale, John Gallacher, James Gallagher, Bonnie W. Gallegos, Renee Gallegos, Virginia S. Gallup, Mihaela Ganea, Louise Garbe, Althea H. Gardiner, Amy H. Gardiner, Henry Gardiner, Aleen A. Gardner, Annette H. Gardner, Boneta Gardner, Claribel Gardner, Cora S. Gardner, Eileen Gardner, Harry Gardner, Joshua Gardner, Karma Gardner, Melodie Larsen Gardner, Olga Helen Dotson Gardner, Sally Louise S. Gardner, DeVal R. (or R. DeVal) Garff, Herschal V. Garff, Ellen Garner, Julie Garner, Violet Garner, V. Gwen Garrard, Jana Garrett, Lewis H. Garrett, Anna B. Gasser, Freda (Freddie) Nadine Gasser, Cecil Brigham Gates, Paul Gates, (?) Geddes, Charlotte Gedge, Margaret A. Gedge, Kenneth V. Gee, Jane Geertsen, David K. Gehris, Debra Gehris, Gustave A. Geis, Ruth Gensen, Floyd Blaine George, Bertha Gerrard, Loren W. Gerre, Marvin D. Gerstner, Carolyn Sue Gibbons, Harvey Gibbons, LeRoy Gibbons, LeRoy Gibbons III, Mildred Gibbons, William Gibbons, W. Sherman Gibbs, Ada R. Gilb, James Gilbert, Allen R. Giles, Carol Giles, Catherine Evans Giles, Georgene Giles, Henry E. Giles, Linda Giles, Merle Giles, Sarah Hague Giles, Sybil W. Giles, K. Gill, Gillespie, E. Gillespie, Moroni B. Gillespie, Irene Gillies, Jessie Gillies, Mark Givens, George L. Glade, Virginia Glade, Linda Hatch Glazier, J. W. Glenn, Darro H. Glissmeyer, H. August Glissmeyer, Jonathan Gochberg, Benjamin Goddard, Harold W. Goddard, Heber S. Goddard, Jeanne King Goddard, Stephen Goddard, A. J. Godfrey, C. Joseph Godfrey, Elaine Godfrey, Joseph Godfrey, Emma S. Godwin, Jeannine Goeckeritz, Elmina Gold, Nicholas B. Gold, Ruth Everton Gold, Diane Goldman, Jane Meyerhoffer Gonzales, Rolando G. Gonzalez, Bonnie Goodliffe, John Goodman, Thomas Goodman, Hyrum Goodyear, Lucille Goodyear, Sherry Sue Gore, Hortence Gorring, Linda Gorringe, Lucille Gorringe, Charlotte Goss, Frederick Goss, L. Goss, Edna Gotberg, Don

Edward Gottfredson, Don M. Gottfredson, Shawna Robin Struthers Gottfredson, Opal Gourley, Amy Gowans, Terri Graff, Fred C. Graham, William Grange, Beryl Granger, Hazel Granger, Augusta W. Grant, Catherine Harper Grant, David Grant, Heber J. Grant, Minerva Unice Grant, Patricia S. Ashton Grant, Richard Gibbs Grant, Michaelene Grassli, Joseph Graves, Joseph (Joe) A. Graves, Lanette Robinson Graves, Andrew S. Gray, Blossom N. Gray, G. R. Gray, Jessie Gray, Winnifred N. Gray, William Lloyd Greaves, Jacob (Jake) Greeff, Arnold Cornell Green, F. W. Green, Janine Green, John Fredrick Green, Jon Green, Lizzie Green, Marcia Vowles Crosby Green, May Green, Norma Green, R. N. Green, Susan Green, Vivian Green, William H. Green Jr., Kristine Greene, Norma Greene, Betty Greenhalgh, May M. Greenwood, Herold (Huck) L. Gregory, Joanna Gregory, Kate Gregory, Jennifer Gremillion, Jessie Ellen Grieve, Thomasina Grieve, Laura Griffeths, J. Marcus Griffin, Philip Gordon Griffin, Debbie Griffiths, Marian C. Griffiths, Thomas C. Griggs, Lee B. Groberg, Edna G. Grocker, Kate Groesbeck, Miss Groesbeck, Thomas Gronemann, Whitney Groo, Charles T. Gross, David Gross, Aaron Grossberg, Claire Grover, Kathy Grover, Marilyn E. Grover, Emily S. Grow, Henry Grow, Joseph H. Grow, Robert M. Grow, Sarah Grow, Helen DeBell Patten Grubbs, Igor Gruppman, Vesna Gruppman, Holly Gudmundson, Sidney Gudmundson, Norman Gulbransen, Debra Gull, Had Brinton Gundersen, Esther Louella (Lou) VanDam Gunderson, George D. Gunderson, Ruby Brown Gunderson, Mary Gundry, Fanny Louise (Lou) Gunn, J. T. Gunn, Mary Louise Gunn, Ronald Gunnell, Vicki Gunnerson, Marilyn Gutke, Nellie Gutke, Lola Ann Gygi, Ruth Gygi

• H • R. Haag, Marian Cornwall Hackett, Mollie Haddock, Sarah Haddock, Blake Elden Hadley, Erick or Erich P. Haertel, Elizabeth Halbrook, Cleve Hale, Brian Hales, R. A. Hales, Ronald Thane Hales, Susannah Hales, Joseph D. Halgren, Frances Hall, Hazel Hall, Jeni Hall, John C. Hall, Kyle Hall, Lucy Hall, Mina Hall, Patricia Hall, Rosalind Hall, Saundra Whipple Hall, John R. Halliday, Nina Halliday, Josie Halsett, Ruth W. Halsett, Gary Halversen, Deoine Halverson, Dorothy Halverson, Gary Halverson, Joseph Halverson, Ray Halverson, Edna MarGene Poulson Halvorsen, Barry Hamilton, Elna Hamilton, Calder M. Hammond, Joyce Hammond, Martha Hammond, Richard Mardell Hammond, Zora Hampton, Marcus Lee Hamson, Cheri Hancock, J. T. Hand, Jean Palmer Hanks, Paul Ashton Hanks, D. Hannabell, Michelle (Shelley) Hannig, Aaron A. Hansen, Donna Marie Kowallis Hansen, Francelle B. Hansen, Hans Hansen, Kenneth Hansen, Kent F. Hansen, Lola Hansen, Maurine Hansen, Rhonda Hansen, Robert N. Hansen, Roma Hansen, Verne Hansen, Walter H. Hansen, Golden K. Hanson, Julie Cawley Hanson, Roger Hanson, Shirley Hanson, K. Hantz, Virginia Harder, Wm. M. Hardiman, Jay (Fred) Harding, Betty Hardman, Esther Margetts Hardy, Kenneth K. Hardy, Lena Hardy, O. F. Hardy, Roy L. Hardy, Ray Harker, Gordon Harkness, Ida Harline, Ardythe Twitchell Harlow, Carolyn Taylor Harmon, Lester John Harper, Richard F. Harper, Ione Lunt Harrington, Betty Harris, Carl Harris, Clinton Harris, Colleen R. Harris, DeLora W. Harris, Edith Harris, Freda Henrie Harris, Gaylen Harris, H. Jarolde Harris, Leroy M. Harris, M. Harris, Preston Harris, Richard Carl Harris, Ruth Lillian W. Harris, Victoria Harris, Conrad B. Harrison, Edith Harrison, T. Harrison, Richard Harston, Camille Hart, Corine Larsen Hart, Janice Beesley Hartvigsen, Emma Haslam, James E. Haslam, Cora Beth Hassell, Myrth Hassell, Alena Hatch, Debra Belliston Hatch, Dorian Hatch, Luacine Hatch, Maureen Hatch, Richard Hauert, Rick Hauert, E. Rich Hawkes, Pricilla Hawkes, Vera Hawkes, Dale R. Hawkins, Lucille Hawkins, Merrill G. Hawkins, Nettie Hawley, Marie Haymond, Ida Hazen, Melvin Headman, Maureen C. Hearns, Luella Sharp Heath, Sasie Heath, Geraldine Hebdon, C. Heesche, Kate Heesche, Melva H. Heilson, Edith Adamson Heim, Gary Lee Heiner, Laura Shand Heiner, Lydia Heiniger, Joseph D. Helgren, John Walter Hellier, Clyde O. Helme, DoraDee Hemeyer, Mark Artie Hendersen, Ben Henderson, Bonnie Cornwall Henderson, Peggy Henderson, Steven Hendricks, Dorothy Kennard Hendriksen, Mark Hendriksen, Michael Hendriksen, Oscar J. Hendriksen, Lizzie Hendry, Leslie Henrie, Lula Marie Henriksen, John M. Henry, Eva May Henserson, Mary Heppler, Ida G. Hepworth, Joseph E. Hepworth, John R. Herbst, Amy Herrick, Linda S. Hess, Marjorie B. Hess, Susan Hess, Brookann Hessing, Barbara Clawson Hewlett, Charles Stewart Hewlett, Lester F. Hewlett, Margaret S. Hewlett, Peggy Brazier Hewlett, Kittie Heywood, L. Heywood, Randen Heywood, John Cameron Hibbard, Gilbert (Gil) W. Hibben, Ward M. Hicken, George Hickenlooper, Wilfrid (Bill) L. Hickison, F. L. Hickman, Eunice Salin Hicks, Judy Linn Hiebert, (?) Higgins, Elsie Higgins, H. D. Higgins, Rowland C. Higgins, R. Keith Higginson, Lucile Child Higgs, Twylla Higgs, Wallace E. Hight, Pamela Van Brocklin Higley, Gailya (Gay) B. Hildreth, David Hill, Edna M. Hill, Edythe or Edith Hill, Flora Shipp Hill, H. S. Hill, Houston Hill, J. Dean Hill, Jean Hill, Joseph S. Hill, Marlin V. Hill, Ruland Hill, Helen Russell Hillier, E. Hillstead, James Hillstead, Kevin Hilman, Delwin I. Hilton, Raymond Hilton, Lisa Kempton Hilton, Afton Hinckley, Clara Hinckley, Edith Hinckley, Gordon B. Hinckley, Hortense Hinckley, Ira Hinckley, Jaren Hinckley, Josie Hinckley, Lee Hinckley, Wave S. Hinckley, Elizabeth R. Hirsh, Thelma M. Hisatake, Mildred Hixson, May L. Hobson, R. H. Hodge, Jennie H. Hoel, Laura Hoff, Jennifer Hoffenreich, Gerald A. Hoffhiens, Lena Hoffman, Marie Hoffman, Lisa Hofheins, H. J. Hogensen, Johanna Hogensen, Julie Hogenson, Elmer Morris Hogge, Alice Holbrook, Esther Hogensen Holbrook, Everett Holbrook, Keith Holbrook, Robert B. Holbrook, Loren D. Holdaway, (Holding) W. S. Holdiway, Ann Holland, George T. Holliday, Laura Hollingsworth, Martha Hollingsworth, Helen Hollingworth, Jon Holloman, William Holman, Annie Holmes, Elizabeth (Lizzie) Griffiths Holmes, Hannah Holmes, J. Holmes, J. T. Holmes, John Holmes, John L. Holmes, Samuel Holmes, Sophie Holmes, Tecla Holmes, Josie Holsett, Karen P. Holt, Joseph J. Holyoak, Marilyn Holyoak, Alan Homer, Ann Homer, Brian Homer, Diane Homer, Gerald Lynn Homer, J. Russell Homer, Kathe Homer, Kay Honaker, Randall Honaker, Louise Hoofer, A. W. Hook, Ernest E. Hook, Carolyn Hooper, Emily Hooper, Helen P. Hooper, Thomas A. Hooper, Shawn Hoopes, G. W. (Bill) Hoover, M. J. Hopewell, Myriel Cluff Hopkins, Karen Hornberger, Clara Horne, Grant Horne, Jennifer Horne, Laura Horne, Leila Horne, Virginia Horne, W. P. Horne, Marie Hornes, Sara L. Horrocks, Adelina Horsley, Amy Horsley, T. W. Horsley, John L. Horton, Kate Houtz, Lester D. Hovey, Rosalie M. Hovey, Arthur (Art) Hovley, Carolyn Howard, Jeri Howard, Stephen (Steve) Thomas Howard, Thomas Howard, Virginia S. Howard, Alice Howarth, Lindsay K. Howe, W. Howell, Mary Henrietta Peirce Howells, Barbara Ione Hoyt, Timothy Hoyt, Susan Ying-Chi Hsieh, Helen Lee (Schueh-Mei) Hsueh, J. Hubbard, L. A. Hubbard, Layne Hubbard, Barbara Ann Huber, Delores Huff, Lora Lee Huff, David Hughes, Gary W. Hughes, A. Hulbert, Gertie Hulbert, M. Hulbert, Vivian Hulet, Maggie C. Hull, Thomas Hull, Marilyn Humpherys, Lee Humphries, Elmer P. Hunsaker, Judith Hunsaker, Mary Stewart Hunsaker, Scott Hunsaker, Sylvia Hunt, Jeanne C. Hunter, Steven Hunter, Delta Huntsman, Eric Huntsman, Ned Huntsman, Cecelia Jackson Hurst, James Hurst, Leland Hurst, Nancy "Duffie" Furner Fenn Hurtado, Victor A. Hurtado, Karl G. Hutchinson, Vera S. Hutchinson, E. Hyde, J. W. Hyde, Dave Hymas, David Hymas, Max Hymas

• I • Sione Ika, Max Ingalls, Virginia Duncan Ingalls, D. P. Ipson, Joseph Jared Ipson, Powell Ipson, Virginia Glade Ipson, Esther Irvine, Robert R. Irvine, LaVar S. Isaacson, Gladys Isom, Emma L. Iverson, Scott Iverson

• J • Ella D. Jack, Mary Rose Jack, Mary Ruthera Jack, David Jackman, John Fuller Jackman, Valerie Alice Jackman, Victor A. Jackman, Cami Jackson, Cecile Jackson, Jennifer Jackson, Marie Jackson, Ramona Jacob, Ruth S. Jacob, Lula Jacobs, Nona Marchant Jacobs, Veda Jacobs, Phillis Jacobsen, Richard D. Jacobsen, Jordan Jacobson, Joyce Jacobson, Kent Jacobson, Melvin (Mel) Jaensch, Darl Rhodes James, Darl Rohdes James, E. M. James, Frances James, John James, Minnie James, P. James, Prissie James, Dan Jansen, Carl W. Janson, June Jansson, Winnifred C. Jardine, Clarence E. Jarman, Vernon E. Jarman, Ronald Jarrett, Dora Jarvis, E. Jarvis, Carol Jefferies, Sarah Jeffs, Ann H. Jenkins, H. Jenkins, H. Barbara Jenkins, James S. Jenkins, James W. Jenkins, Leone Jenkins, Marvin Jenkins, Marvin L. Jenkins, Marvin Lindsay Jenkins, Maggie Jennings, Prissie Jennings, Anne Bennion Jensen (or Jenson), Allen Jensen, Alvin M. Jensen, Angelina Jensen, Belinda Jensen, Brian Jensen, Earlene B. Jensen, Erik Jensen, Felix Jensen, Harold H. Jensen, Hazel Jensen, Helen Jensen, Helen Hollingsworth Benard Jensen, Ilna Jensen, James Alvin Jensen, Jane Jensen, Joseph Jensen, Katherine Jensen, Marjorie or Marjory R. Jensen, Nancy Jensen, P. Joseph Jensen, Rita Jensen, Tonia Lee Stallings Jensen, Valorie Jensen, Vera Jensen, Zina Jensen, Martha S. Jenson, Richard Jenson, Helen Jeppsen, Christine Jeppson, Jon M. Jeppson, Saylor Call Jeppson, Karen Jepson, Paul Weinreich Jespersen, Oscar Jesperson, Craig D. Jessop, Yvonne Jessop, J. Delos Jewkes, Jennie Joel, Hildur Fluge Johansen, Margaret Johansen, Moani Johansen, Ruth Astrid Johansen, Margaret Johanson, W. M. Johns, Ferris M. Johnsen, Vard L. Johnsen, Patricia Johnson, Ann Johnson, B. Johnson, Bethanie Joy Johnson, Beverly Johnson, Brian Johnson, Carma Johnson, Charles L. Johnson, D. Jeanne Johnson, Dale G. Johnson, Donna Johnson, Ernest H. Johnson, Frieda Wescke Johnson, Glenn H. Johnson, Grant Johnson, H. Johnson, Helen Beisinger Johnson, Hilda B. Johnson, Jackquita Johnson, James Johnson, Jean W. Johnson, Jeanne Johnson, Jeanne Cowley Johnson, Jim Johnson, Jolene Johnson, Joy Holladay Johnson, Kenneth Johnson, L. Johnson, Laurence (Larry) M. Johnson, Linda Lee Lynn Morgan Johnson, Lois Johnson, M. Johnson, Mable Johnson, Mahlon Johnson, Mahlon G. Johnson, Mary Jane E. Johnson, Priscilla Davis Johnson, Ray H. Johnson, Reid H. Johnson, Richard D. Johnson, Shirley Johnson, Susanne Johnson, Tracy Lynn Johnson, Verna Swan Johnson, Viola Johnson, Wallace P. Johnson, I. L. Johnstone, David Jolley, Dorothy Thomson Jonas, Afton Jones, Anne Jones, Benjamin Jones, Colleen Keeler Jones, Darwin Jones, DeEtte Jones, Eleanor Jones, Elma Jones, Elsie L. Nilson Jones, Elsie Nilson Jones, Emma L. Jones, Geri Jones, Helen B. Jones, Joseph Elroy Jones, Judith (Judy) Anderson Jones, Kalleen Jones, Kenneth Jones, Kenneth (Ken) P. Jones, Mamie Jones, Mary E. Jones, Minnie Horne Jones, Patricia Jones, R. Lorraine Jones, RaNae Jones, Raymond P. Jones, Steven Jones, Thomas C. Jones, Vernon O. Jones, Voneta Jones, William X. Jones, Jane Hatch Jordan, Mark Jordan, Myra Jordan, William Smith Jordan, Josephine (Josie) Jorgensen, Lawrence Jorgensen, Craig Jorgenson, Osborn Jorgenson, Jeanette Clawson Judd, Lourie Judd, Loretta Julander

• K • Charles (Chuck) Kalin, Kay P. Kane, Roelof Kanon, Gus Karpolitz, James (Jim) Kasen, Claudia N. Kavanaugh, Tyler Kay, Wilma S. Kearn, Alvin Keddington, Dorothy Kimball Keddington, Hulbert Keddington, J. Harold (Hal) Keddington, John Keddington, Joseph Martin Keddington, LaRue Egan Keddington, Martin Keddington, Richard Keddington, Ruth Arlene Keddington, S. Richard (Dick) Keddington, Beth Keele, Frank A. Keele, Douglas Keeler, Kuing Keil, Helen Keller, Lillian Keller, John H. Kelly, Kathleen Kelly, Lillie Kelly, Roberta Kelly, W. J. Kelly, A. H. Kelson, Druce Kelson, Jack G. Kemker, Harry F. Kemp, Jesse Kemp, Sandra Kemp, Eleanor K. Kennard, Frank J. Kennard, Gary Kennard, James B. Kennard, Leonidas (Lon) H. Kennard, Roger Kennard, Rose Kennard, Florence Kennedy, Maud Kenner, Winifred Kenner, Alton J. Kent, Carol Kent, Charles B. Kent, Jack Kent, Wilma (Willy) Smith Kern, Gwen Kersell, Annie Wixey Kesler, Christopher S. Kesler, Ellen Kesler, Stephen F. Kesler, Clara Kessler, Jane Kessler, Vivian Kessler, Barbara Helen Key, Dorothy Killpack, Nancy Killpack, David Roy Kilpatrick, Ruby Mork Kilpatrick, Edward P. Kimball, Louie Kimball, Mattie Kimball, Ted Kimball, J. Spencer Kinard, Corinne King, Dale S. King, John Jospeh King, Mona Mann Hunter King, John Kingdon, Minnie Kingdon, Nina Kinghorn, Mary Kingsbury, H. A. Kirk, James E. Kirk, Kathryn F. Kirk, Mable Kirk, Marian Seare Kirk, Arno Kirkham, E. Dale Kirkham, Elmoine W. Kirkham, George Kirkham, J. M. Kirkham, James Arno Kirkham, Jelda Kirkham, H. Kirkman, Jacquelin French Kirkpatrick, Dago A. O. Klein, Carter Knapp, Ardelle Knibbe, Keith B. Knighton, Gene Belnap Knitzsch, Dorothy Knous, Dan Knudsen, Lillian Knudsen, Rosina Knuzles, Zether Koch, Sharon O. Koncurat, Ramona Leah Koop, Sharon Jones Koplin, Elsie Koras, O. W. Kotter, H. R. Krantz, Bente Kristiansen, Shirlee Anne Kropf, Emond Kruger, Martha Kruger, Ruth Kruger, Rebecca Krull, Willard L. Kunzler

• L • Bonnie Lack, Patricia Lake, A. Lamb, Jane Lamb, John Lamb, Peggy Lambert, Synthia Lambert, Charles Lambourne, Harry C. Lambourne, William Lambourne, Brook Lamoreaux, Lota Lamoreaux, Richard Lamoreaux, Verna Lamoreaux, W. S. Lamoreaux, D. R. Lamph, Nellie Lamph, Richard Lamph, D. J. Lang, Sarah E. Olsen Langford, Thella Langford, Lany Kate Henderson Langton, Dean Larkin, Mary Ellen Larkin, Alton R. Larsen, Arthur Larsen, Carole Larsen, Corine Larsen, Dora I. Larsen, Douglas Larsen, Earle Larsen, Ellen Larsen, Ethel Larsen, Patricia Tenney Larsen, Alton R. Larson, Amanda Larson, Arvid J. Larson, Gene M. Larson, Golda Larson, Lorraine Larson, Marie Larson, Mark H. Larson, Matthew Larson, Nadine Larson, Neil Larson, Melodie Brighton Laser, Amalia Lassig, Latimer, Emily G. Latimer, Helen E. Latimer, Hazel C. Laughlin, Leonard Laughlin, Martha F. Lauritzen, Emile Lauze, Ethel Law, Loraine Baird Law, Connie C. Lawrence, Richard Dwight Laws, Belle Lawson, Crissie Lawson, Hattie Lawson, Fred Laycock, Richard D. Le Vitre, Barbara F. Leatham, Bonnie Lee, Carol Ann Summers Lee, Carolyn Thompson Lee, Dan Lee, Golda A. Lee, James Lee, Kathleen Lee, Lizzie Earll Lee, Louene J. Lee, Mary E. H. Lee, Maurine Butterworth Lee, Morris F. Lee, Ralph Lee, Ronald (Ron) E. Lee, Sarah Lee, Virginia Lee,

Vesta Leek, Helen Palfreyman LeeMaster, Vernon LeeMaster, Milo Lefler, Louise Lehman, Carol Leishman, Marjorie Robbins Leishman, Robert Lentz, Leo Leonard, Leona Leonard, W. I. Lester, William Lester, Barbara J. Lewis, Emily Lewis, Gwendolin Lewis, Janet Shurtliff Lewis, John S. Lewis, Laura Lewis, Lizzie Lewis, Henry Leyland, Miriam Johanna Neiderhauser Lieber, Arlene Maughan Liechty, Marjorie Lignell, Sue Cutler Liljegren, Wilda Liljenquist, O. K. Lillewick, Viola Linberg, Marilyn Lincoln, Kathleen Lind, Erna Linde, Erna Gertrude Linde, Dana Linder, David Lindford, Annie Lindsay, Bertha Lindsay, Evelyn Stewart Lindsay, J. L. Lindsay, LaRae Lindsay, Maggie Lindsay, Mary Lindsay, Sharron A. Lindsay, Emma Lindsey, M. S. Lindsey, James (Jim) R. Lindsley, L. Reid Lindstrom, Carl Linn, O. S. Linsey, Harriett Little, Mary A. J. Lively, Wilma Gay Smith Livsey, W. E. Llewellyn, Barry Lloyd, Christy Lloyd, Lewis Haslam Lloyd, Lois Kimball Clark Lloyd, Max Lloyd, Erin Lochhead, Robert Lochhead, Erlynn Leidig Lofthouse, Margrit Feh Lohner, E. Londema, Patricia Long, Phyllis Long, John T. Longhurst, Blanche Stark Lord, Lawrence James Lord, Ralph K. Lord, Walter Lord, Richard Loutensock, Claude Elroy Love Jr., Ray E. Loveless, Velma Lovorsen, Garth R Low (or Lowe), Afton Lowe, Laurence Lowe, Saundra (Sandy) M. Kedd Lowe, Lola Lowry, Melba Knowles Lowry, Phillip Lowry, Hazel Loy, Joseph A. Lubbers, Beth Ludema, Eddie Ludema, Kathy Ludlow, Hazel Lugenbeuhl, Evelyn Luke, Virginia Luke, A. C. Lund, A. H. Lund, Anthony C. Lund, Cannon Lund, Cornelia Lund, H. Z. Lund, Irene Lund, Lexye Lund, Nancy A. Lund, Phyllis Lund, Ray Lund, Wilber Lund, Wildene Lund, Hattie Lundgren, Oscar Lundgren, Robert H. Lundquist, Ruth Lundquist, Jannette Lusk-Unterborn, Almon P. Lyman, Vint P. Lyman, Janet Condie Lynn, Lynne Lynn, Adele Lyon, Alice Lyon, Delia Lyon, Matt Lyon, Wanda Lyon

• M • Sara Maack, Taylor MacDonald, Olive Beth (Bobby) Kimball Mack, Annie MacKay, Janet Mackay, Kitty Mackenzie, John E. (Tim) Mackerell, T. J. Mackintosh, Reo Mackley, Rosalie Macmillan, John Williams Maddox, Alice Madsen, DeDee (Doralee) Madsen, Farrell Madsen, Frank Madsen, Jean Waterman Madsen, L. Madsen, Patricia N. Madsen, Phyllis Ransom Madsen, Rosalia Madsen, Karl G. Maeser, L. Maggley, James D. Maher, Judson M. Maher, Carol Mahlum, Darren Major, Rea Malin, (Dale) Cary Malmrose, Edith Mann, Michele Mann, Kathryne Manning, Bob Manookin, Dorothy Manookin, George Manwaring, Jesse Manwaring, Emily Marble, David Marcyes, Lottie Marcroft, Kate B. Margetts, Linda Margetts, Margot Marler, Addie Lund Marsden, Mary Louise Marsden, David Marsh, Myrtle Checketts Marsh, Ann Forsyth Martin, C. S. Martin, Charles C. Martin, Deborah Martin, Earl Martin, Mamie Martin, Raymond R. Martin, Wallace L. Martin, Wynetta J. Clark Martin, Arline Martindale, Reva Marx, Ida Marz, Nells A. Marz, Elizabeth Green Mason, Fay L. Mason, Reuben Mason, Wesley Laurence (Larry) Mason, Miriam Massey, Lois Massion, Edward Masterson, Josephine Masterson, Lois J. Matheson, Mary M. Haack Matheson, Wesley (Wes) A. Matheson, Bartly Mathews, Patricia (Pat) J. Mathis, Sipuao Josefine Matuauto, Wells Maudsley, Wells S. Maudsley, Denis Glen Maughan, Richard Maughan, Charlotte Maxfield, Neal Dean Maxfield, Nelden V. Maxfield, Rodney E. Maxfield, Art V. Maxwell, W. LeGrande Maxwell, James (Jim) A. May, Stanley P. May, Rosina Mayan, Hilda Mayfield, Jackie K. Maynard, John H. Maynes, Joseph W. Maynes, Craig McAllister, D. A. McAllister, D. H. McAllister, Dale A. McAllister, Duncan M. McAllister, Kate P. McAllister, Lucille McAllister, M. H. McAllister, Mamie McAllister, Wells Alder McAllister, Max McBeth, Marsha McBride, Kate McCallister, Helen McCausland, Tiffany McCleary, John Jasper McClellan, Myrtle McClement, Wallace (Wally) L. McCloy, Leslie McClure, Camille McClurg, Terrance D. McCombs, Gwen Wirthlin McConkie, James McConkie, Ramona McConkie, Peter (Pete) P. McCune, Donna J. McDonald, Helen McDonald, Russell F. McDonald, W. C. McDonald, William McDougal, R. T. McEwan, Arthur McFarlane, Ray McFarlane, Zola Jacobs McGhie, Thomas McIntyre, Heidi McKay, Lottie L. McKay, Beverly McKea, John W. McKea, Jon E. McKea, James McKean, Dianne Williams McKee, Marsha McKellar, Alice McLachlan, Rebecca Cluff McLaughlin, Mike McLean, Clara W. McMaster, Richard McMaster, A. McMurrin, Darlene Knitzsch McNeil, Michael McOmber, Frances McPhail, Marilyn Norma Jones McPhie, Walter (Walt) Evan McPhie, Carol McRae, Dave McRae, Maggie Richards McRae, Angela Meacham, A. Dennis Mead, Dennis Mead, Ed Meakin, Mr. Meakin, Bryce Mecham, Emily Mecham, Norma Weight Mecham, Stephanie Mecham, Lola Ethel Meehan, John K. Meibos, David Meidell, Elva Meiklejohn, Joann Mary Meitler, Martha Mellen, Melvin Cleone Memmott, Pat Menlove, Marion G. Merkley, Vera Merkley, Virginia Ann Merkley, Darleen Merrill Merrihew, C. Merrill, Carolyn Merrill, F. W. Merrill, Ione C. Merrill, Irene Merrill, Lester Merrill, Lynn Evan Merrill, R. C. Merrill, Sandra Merrill, Gabriel Mes, Minnie or Mimi Mes, Forest Z. Meservy, Iris Kunzler Meservy, Oliver Kingsbury (OK) Meservy, Lora Lee Metzler, Carol Rose Pulley Meyer, Douglas Meyer, George Wade Meyer, John M. H. Meyer, Lyle Saunders Meyerhoffer, Amber Meyers, Stanley R. Michaelson, Sylvia G. Mickels, Kathleen L. Mickelsen, Alice Midgley, Bertha Midgley, E. P. Midgley, Jemima Rushby Hough Midgley, Joshua Midgley, May Midgley, Sadie Midgley, Morris Miles, Rae Miles, (?) Miller, Alene Miller, Arnold Miller, Bonnie B. Miller, Charles Miller, Clifford Miller, David W. Miller, Dianne Marie Whitelock Burton Miller, Henry Miller Jr., Janet Dee Packard Miller, Karen Miller, Lavon Chipman Cowley Miller, Layne Miller, Lloyd Miller, Marie F. Miller, Marilyn Miller, Marion Toronto Miller, Martha L. Miller, Minerva F. Miller, Nadine Royle Miller, Roger Miller, Roger L. Miller, Scott Miller, Stella Frisby Miller, Vaneta Miller, Vernon "J" Miller, W. David Miller, Denton Millet, Diane Millett, Beth Milna, Anna or Annie W. Milner, Susan Minarchik, Loren Minert, Bartlett C. Mitchell, Betty Mitchell, Dorothy H. Mitchell, Kate Mitchell, Martha Mitchell, N. Lorenzo Mitchell, Rex C. Mitchell, William Dean Mitchell, Becca Moench, Tamara Moffat, Lavar J. Moffitt, Heidi Mogensen, Mogens Mogensen, Elizabeth Thomas Molinaro, James Moncar, Harry Mondfrans, Joseph Edward Monson, Lorna Monson, Margaret Erickson or Erekson Monson, Edgar F. Montague, Rachel Montague, Jennie Montgomery, Justin Moon, Alma Moore, Andrew Moore, Blythe Southern Moore, F. Michael Moore, Garth R. Moore, Joseph Oakley Moore, Matthew Moore, Linette Moreno, Edith Morgan, Emilee Neff Morgan, Eric Morgan, Evelyn Morgan, Fanny Morgan, Georgeva Giles Morgan, Ivy Morgan, James Morgan, John Morgan, Joseph R. Morgan, Julia Morgan, Linda Lee Johnson Morgan, Vernon Morgan, Alfheld Mork, Clarence Morley, Charlene H. Dunn Morr, Alexander C. Morris, Alexander R. Morris, Alfred (Bob) R. Morris Jr., Belle Morris, Bessie Marley Morris, Gary Morris, Ida Morris, Jenna Vee Morris, Mary E. Morris, Todd C. Morris, Victoria A. Whipple Morris, Violet (Vy) S. Morris, William Morris, Douglas W. Morrison, Shirley Anne Krapf Morrison, William Douglas Morrison, R. Morriss, Ruby C. Morriss, John D. Morse, Lorin Morse, Eva Mortensen, Jennie Mortensen, Sterling Mortensen, Andrew M. Mortimer, T. F. H. Morton, Thomas Morton, L. Cameron Mosher, Chelta Moss, D. Ray Moss, Debra Moss, Ruth Mouritsen, John T. Mourtgos, Sherry Mourtisen, Marie Mower, Dorothy Mowrey, E. Mozley, Hannelore Mueller, Richard J. Mueller, Joyce Terry Muhlestein, Anita Mumford, Elizabeth A. Mumford, Claire or Clara T. Murdock, Elva B. Murdock, George Murdock, John Murdock, Marjorie Murdock, H. Melvin or Melvin H. Murphy, Mamie Murphy, Paul H. Murphy, Charles Musgrove, Eva Musser, Jennie Musser, Wayne P. Musser, Amran Musungu, Marilou Dyreng Myers, Thomas Myers

• N • Robert Namanny, Richard B. Nameworth, Lynn M. Nance, Lydia Nasner, David Naylor, Elaine Ellsworth Naylor, Garth Laird Naylor, Rilla Naylor, Anna Neaff, David Michael Neal, Donna Janzen Neal, George Neal, Lloyd William Neal, Richard William Neal, Sarah Neal, B. Needham, Nellie Needham, Leah Neibaur, Alfred Neilson, H. Neilson, J. H. Neilson, James H. Neilson, Jesse Thomas Neilson, Naomi Neilson, Osborne Neilson, T. Moani Johansen Neimann, Steven Neiswender, Catherine (Cathy) Nelson, Charlotte Nelson, Dantzel White Nelson, Edward Nelson, Geraldine Nelson, James Nelson, John H. Nelson, Karl K. Nelson, Larry A. Nelson, Mary Nelson, Mary Redd Nelson, Michael Nelson, Nadine Nelson, Nyena Nelson, Osborne Nelson, Rebecca Nelson, Rene Nelson, V. Rene Nelson, Val A. Nelson, Victor J. Nelson, Zora B. Nelson, Thomas Nesbitt, Nellie Neslin, Blossom Ness, Raynor Ness, C. J. Nettleton, Marylin O. Neubert, Edna Lyle Jenkins Neuhart, A. Neve, Reed C. Newbold, Lloyd Newell, Joseph (Joe) M. Newey, Susan Newland, Ada C. Newman, Colleen E. Newman, Laurel Kay Kawk Newman, Leslie S. Newren, Loeto (Loey) Young Newren, Louise Brown Newren, May Newsom, Donald (Don) W. Newsome, Julie Newton, Kathleen Newton, Lizzie Parker Newton, S. E. Newton, E. H. Nichols, Maxine Nichols, Danny Nickle, Matt Nickle, Loretta Niebur, Carol Anne Nielsen, Ernest J. Nielsen, J. (Dr.) Nielsen, Julia Ann Nielsen, Lee Nielsen, Marilyn Nielsen, Ragna Nielsen, Sue Nielsen, Verda Nielsen, Elizabeth Nielson, Evelyn P. Nielson, James (Jim) Nielson, John Marlowe Nielson, Lorna Nielson, Malva Nielson, Marlin or Merlin A. Nielson, Mary Schindler Nielson, Verda Nielson, Alfred Nilsson, Ray F. Nilsson, Sven Osborne Nilsson, Wilford Nilsson, Melvin Nimer, DeAnn Nixon, Myrene Kemp Nixon, Claire Noall, Ethel Noall, Harold F. Noall, Ivy B. Noall, Matthew Noall, Wallace Ray Noble, Lynden (Lyn) R. Noe, William R. Nooley Jr., Christine Norbe, A. C. Nordberg, Elsie Harline Nordberg, Desna Ferrell Nordfelt, Curtis Norling, Ida Norman, Jess Roger Norman, Keith E. Norman, Marilyn L. Yuille Smith Norris, Ginny North, Vaughn North, Kent Norton, Celeste Noyes, David W. Noyes, Jan Camp Noyes, Lucian L. Noyes, Cecile Nugent, Jean Nyberg, Axel A. Nylander

• O • Allison O'Bryant, Dan O'Bryant, Daniel O'Bryant, Melvin (Mel) C. O'Donnal, J. P. O'Gorman, Donal Ray Oakden, Burke Oastle, Annie May Oborne, B. L. Oborne, Sharon L. Brimley Ockey, Christine Odell, Pearl Ofgreen, Joan Hoppie Ogden, Joseph Ogden, Larry Wayne Ogden, Scott Ogden, Hannah L. Oldroyd, Ricki Olmstead, Annie Olsen, Barbara S. Bybee Olsen, Bart Olsen, Birdie Olsen, Craig Olsen, Effie Olsen, Hyrum Olsen, J. J. Olsen, Kristen Olsen, Lettie Olsen, Mark B. Olsen, Orrin J. Olsen, Rosemary Nelson Olsen, Wanda S. Young Olsen, Patricia Olson, Susan Olson, Tracy Olson, Bradley Omer, Cherie Park Omer, Lizzie Openshaw, Mary Openshaw, Margaret Orahood, Julie Orchard, Alan Ord, Kathleen Ord, Amy Orgill, Joseph J. Orullian, Nelson Osborne, Iva LaRue Russell Osguthorpe, Iva R. Osguthorpe, Lola (Lolly) Amelia Sedgwick Osguthorpe, Russell Trent Osguthorpe, Mark Oshida, Matt Oshida, Julie Ann Oslett, Stephen D. Osmond, Fanny Ostler, O. R. Ostler, Mavis Oswald, Tamara Oswald, Paul Otterstrom, Helen Ottinger, Earl Ottley, Jerold Don Ottley, JoAnn South Ottley, A. R. Overlade, Peter M. Overson, Alvia C. Owen, John L. Owen, Kenneth Owen, William D. Owen, Hazel Owens, Margaret Owens, Rial Smith Owens, Kathy Oyler

• P • G. Arnold Pace, Laura Mae Pace, M. E. Pack, Onita Pack, Wallace (Wally) Dean Pack, Ward E. Pack, Clarence F. Packard, Jan D. Packard, Janie or Jane Packard, Lela Packard, Michael Packham, May Padgen, Lillie Page, Marian W. Page, Minnie Paine, Annie Palmer, David Palmer, Elizabeth Palmer, Sarah Palmer, Elizabeth Paniagua, Ruth Wilcox Papworth, Florence Pardoe, Isabella Brizee Pardoe, William Pardoe, Berniece Park, Hung Young Park, John Park, Steven Park, William Park, William L. Park Jr., Audrey M. Parker, Barbara Jean Gunn Parker, Jane Wirthlin Parker, John H. Parker, Kristine Parker, Lizzie Parker, Jane R. Parks, Peggy Jane Parks, John Parrish, Stanley Parrish, David Parry, Dick Parry, Dorothy Reid Parry, E. F. Parry, Edward (Ed) Parry, George Parry, Georgia R. Parry, Janet Parry, John Parry, Richard Parry, Tamara Parry, Verna Monsen Parry, Arthur Parsons, Nancy Parsons, M. Olive Partridge, Violet P. Passey, Sue Patchel, Carrie Thorne Patrick, Lizzie Patrick, W. Patten, Leila Bixby Patterson, Patricia Patterson, Bonnie Anderson Paulsen, Edward (Ed) J. Payne, Clara Peacock, Kelly Thayne Pearce, Mark Pearce, Beverly Ostler Pearson, Jeanette Condie Pearson, John Pearson, Karl Lorenz Pearson, Marlayne Pearson, Owen B. Pearson, Stewart E. Pearson, A. Byron Peart, Edna H. Peck, William Peck, Annie Pedersen, H. Robert Pedersen, Jeffrey Pedersen, Jennie Pedersen, Jenny Pedersen, Erma Pendleton, Laura Lee Pendleton, Virginia Pendleton, Karen Penman, J. E. Pennock, Ettie Penrose, Katie Penrose, Marjorie Penrose, Nellie Penrose, Jeffrey R. Peo, Helen Perkins, Freda Jean (Jeannie) Malmrose Perrington, David Perry, Hazel S. Perry, Janice Kapp Perry, Jeremiah Perry, Gerald (Jerry) Avard Petersen (or Peterson), Brent Petersen, Brian Petersen, Ethelyn Petersen, Everett Petersen, Jack Petersen, Janet Petersen, LaMar Petersen, Nora Petersen, P. Melvin Petersen, Robert K. Petersen, Thora Petersen, A. F. Peterson, A. W. Peterson, Andrew Peterson, Ann Peterson, Annie Peterson, Blaine A. Peterson, Brent R. Peterson, Carolyn Faye Peterson, Diana Peterson, Ebba Peterson, Ellen H. Peterson, Ervin Peterson, Ethel Peterson, Ferdinand E. Peterson, Gertie Peterson, Gunnel Peterson, Hilma Peterson, Kent Peterson, Melvin Peterson, Minnie Van T. Peterson, Nyla B. Peterson, Patsy Peterson, Rilla Wilxon Peterson, Virginia Isakson Peterson, Wayne Leo Peterson, Katie Pettit, Myrtle Pettit, Richard (Dick) N. Pexton, Ronald (Ron) Dale Pexton, Sherry Phair, J. Phillips, Jan Phillips, Lois Draney Phillips, Raymond (Ray) A. Phillips, Richard Phillips, S. R. Phillips, Sid Phillips, Josephine Picco, Lucy Picco, Charles Pickett, Dorothy Pidd, Harry B. Pidd, Eli H. Pierce (or Peirce), Carol Pierce, Ida Pierce, L. S. Pierce, Linda Elaine Grover Pierce, Ramona Pierce, Anna Piercy, Frieda Piesonotzki, Kathleen Pike, Malcolm (Mike) Davis Pike, Malcolm (Mike) England Pike, Malcolm Pike Jr., Sydney L. Gudmundsen Pike, Van Pilkington, George C. Pingree, James (Jim) Keith Pinkerman, Thomas G. Pinkerton, Patricia Pinkston, Alice Pinney, Josephine Pinney, Ida Pitt, Florence C. Pitts, Marilynn Kay Pitts, Gladys Fullmer Pixton, Richard N. Pixton, Thelma Pixton, Doreen Place,

Kenneth Plaizier, Alonzo Platt, Carlene O. Platt, Daniel Platt, Edward O. Platt, Irene B. Platt, Linda N. Simper Plouzek, Marilyn Joy Plowgian, Mildred W. Plummer, Norma R. Pocock, Elfriede Johanna Ehrier Poecker, Nona Politonicz, Brian Poll, Charles Poll, Farrell Poll, Joseph Poll, Peninah (Nina) W. Poole, Stanley S. Poole, Shirley Porath, Don LaMar Porter, Earl C. Porter, Elsie Porter, J. Earl Porter, Lyman Karl Porter, Thomas Porter, Karen Post, David Potter, Francine Potter, Genevieve Potter, Robert S. Potter, Pauline Poulsen, Udell E. Poulsen, Alton Monte Poulson, Florence K. Poulson, Scott Poulson, W. Howard Poulter, William I. Poulter Jr., Annie Poulton, Florence Poulton, J. T. Poulton, James H. Poulton, Louisa (Louie) Poulton, Walter J. Poulton, William Poulton, Andrea Elizabeth Stringham Powell, Clarnell B. Powell, Debra Ann Powell, John Powell, Lois Kristine Parry Powell, Dean Power, Loren John Prather, C. R. Pratt, Calvin D. Pratt, Donald Young Pratt, Dorothy Pace Pratt, Ida Pratt, Irvine T. Pratt, Margaret Pratt, Marilyn Inees Pratt, Marintha Pratt, Maude E. Pratt, Michael S. Pratt, Neva Pratt, Orson Pratt Jr., P. O. Pratt, Parley P. Pratt, Percy Wilcken Pratt, Viola Pratt, Winnie Pratt, Inez R. Preece, Marjorie Preece, Michael Preece, Kate Preston, May Preston, Kamber Price, Lynn Price, Mary Price, Melissa Price, Richard Price, Sidney Price, Grace Priestly, Mayna Prince, Robert Scott Prince, Bonnie W. Prizer, Beverly Probert, Beverly Smith Provost, Sterling R. Provost, Florence Stevens Prows, Joseph Prows, Joseph H. Prows Jr., Ronald S. Prows, Gene Puckett, Nellie Druce Pugsley, Marjorie D. Puriri, Martha Putnam, Alex Pyper, Emma Pyper, George D. Pyper, James M. Pyper, Paul G. Pyper, Ross Pyper

• Q • Gordon Myrl Quigley, L. Glen Quigley, Joseph H. Quillian

• R • Michael Raddatz, Stacie Raddatz, Stephen Raff, Nettie Raleigh, Marilyn Ramsay, Emma Rand, Beryl Amelia Randall, William (Bill) Randall, Mary Rankin, Jane Ransom, Kalevi A. Rasi-Koskinen, Dale Rasmussen, David L. Rasmussen, Elna Rasmussen, Mae Rasmussen, Sarah Rasmussen, Wyoma W. Rasmussen, Ann Brown Ravenberg, E. Rawlings, Ernest Rawlings, James Rawlings, Joseph S. Rawlings, Marie Rawlings, Melvie Rawlings, Murl L. Rawlings, William Rawlings, Melvia C. Rawlins, Murl L. Rawlins, Jane Rawlinson, R. Vernon Rawlinson, Margaret Y. Ray, LuJean Paterson Rayl, Dorothy Lee Raymond, Stephan L. Raymond, Earl Read, Joseph Read, Lucy Read, Rachael Barney Read, Fred Rease, Christina (Chris) Reber, Vera Lee Redd, Patricia Ann Clawson Redford, B. Redo, Arthur Reed, Florence Reed, John Grant Reed, Mattie Reed, Natalie Reed, Zina Bishop Reed, George Jesse Reeder, Tecla H. Rees, David Reese, Fred Reese, Fred E. Reese, G. R. Reese, Glenna L. Reese, F. A. Reeves, Reed L. Reeves, S. H. Reeves, C. W. Reid, Dorothy Reid, Florence Reid, Hellen Reid, Lidia T. Reid, Sinah Reid, Rilla P. Reiger, Ron Reimschussel, Winifred Kennard Remington, William Robert Reok, Bess Smith Rex, Carol W. Reynolds, Clifford (Cliff) M. Reynolds, Ina Reynolds, James Reynolds, Shirley M. Tame Reynolds, Theron Reynolds, Diana Rhodes, Ronald L. Rhodes, Tamra Rhodes, Rose E. Ribner, Leslie Rice, Ada Rich, Elsie Mae Rich, Gloria Rich, R. Dee Rich, Thethe Hardy Rich, Angie Richards, Beverly B. Richards, Claire Richards, Earl H. Richards, Emily Richards, G. William Richards, Janice Johnson Richards, Joel Richards, Joseph E. Richards, Laura Mae Penrose Pace Richards, Leslie Richards, Marjorie Jensen Richards, Melanie Richards, RoMay Richards, Stephen W. Richards, Vickie Richards, Virginia Richards, Beth Richardson, Ellen B. Richardson, Marjorie Thorson Richardson, Nora P. Richardson, Shirleen Richardson, Marjorie Riches, Virginia Riches, LaRue Baldwin Richins, Mary Ann Holladay Richins, Michael D. Richmond, Bradley Rickards, Kelly Ricks, Gordon L. Ridd, Lawrence Riddle, Susan Standing Rideout, Alvin Ridges, Claribel Ridges, Ella B. Ridges, Lance Ridges, Nellie Ridges, Rilla Rieger, Sonja Jean Riem, Carla D. Riethmann, Kate Rigby, Lester S. Rigby, Thomas (Tom) C. Rigby, Dyanne Riley, Cheri Lynn Oaks Ringger, Paula Riordan, Paula Riorden, Alice Elaine Bankhead Ripplinger, Cary Ripplinger, Donald (Don) H. Ripplinger, Hilton Ripplinger, Myra Ripplinger, Edna C. Ririe, Donna Ritchie, Vera Ritchie, Edith or Edythe C. Robbins, Richard L. Robbins, William Phillips Robbins, Arthur Roberts, Brian C. Roberts, Glenna Roberts, Ingrid Scherer Roberts, Kate Roberts, Lizette D. Roberts, Annie Robertson, Matt Robertson, Matthew Robertson, Ruth Bowers Robertson, Yvonne Drake Robertson, Ray Robins, (?) Robinson, Annie Robinson, Bonnie Dipo Robinson, Christine Robinson, E. J. Robinson, Ethel Louise Burks Robinson, J. P. Robinson, Jackie Herriman Robinson, John Robinson, Lincoln E. Robinson, Lynn Robinson, Melba or Melva Robinson, Nora Luke Robinson, Pearl Robinson, Richard Robinson, Samuel P. Robinson, Talmadge D. Robinson, W. F. Robinson, Ethel Louise Robison, Richard Robison, Vivien Robison, Harry Roby, Romania Young Roby, Nonna Rock, Volna Beatrice Cottrell Rockwood, Kale Rodabough, George B. Roden, Christine Rodgers, Joan Mary Williams Rodgers, Ralph G. Rodgers Jr., Rebecca Roessler, Aura Rogers, Carolyn Rudd Rogers, Chester Rogers, Clothield Newren Rogers, Ella Rogers, Fay Rogers, Lucille C. Rogers, Margaret Rogers, Venice Rogers, M. Kenneth Rogerson, Susanna (Sue) Rogerson, Thomas (Tom) Milton Rogerson, Julie Hedgepeth Rohde, Trudy Rohletter, Laurel Barker Rohlfing, Velma Rolfe, Leslie McKay Rollins, Ardelle Durrant Romney, Bryan Romney, Deborah C. Dedekind Romney, George R. Romney, Leona Romney, Mary Romney, O. D. Romney, Paul Romney, Sylvia P. Romney, Geraldine H. Roos, Walter K. Root, Monika Rosborough-Bowman, C. E. Rose, Elma J. Rose, Leona A. Rose, Lucile Rose, W. T. Rose, J Roseborough, Raphael Rosenbaum, Dorothy C. Rosenbraugh, Don Rosenfeld, Erma Rosenhan, Ida G. Rosenhan, C. J. Ross, David J. Ross, Jewell (Bud) Ross, Lucile Ross, Mary R. Ross, Stanford B. Rossiter, Ted Rosval, Cecile Humphries Rosvall, Oscar A. Roth, Glenna Roundy, Jon Rowberry, Joyce Yuvonne Evert Rowberry, Larraine Rowberry, Robert Lee Rowberry, Tracy Rowe, Boyd G. Rowley, Edwin J. Rowley, Lucretia Roylance, LaVon A. Woods Rudd, Pat Rudd, Robert Rudd, Walter B. Rudolph, Charles M. Ruff, Howard Ruff, H. E. Rumel, Emma Rushton, Virginia Rushton, Carolyn Russell, Dianne Russell, Eileen Russell, Frank Russell, Helen Russell, Jay M. Russell, Valoran Russell, William H. Russell, Heather Rust, Suzanne Rust, Charles H. Rutherford, Kathryn Ann Howell Rutherford, Georgia C. Shaw Rytting, Ralph Dean Rytting, Sandra Rytting

• S • June Hansen Wayment Sackett, Orvil DeLaun Sackett, John Sacks, Shirley Jeanne Sacos, Kaarin Joy Safsten, Ferren N. Sager, B. W. Sainsbury, Laura Sakulich, Shirley Salm, Belle Salmon, Elsie S. Salt, Mary R. Salt, Bertha Punaotala Samoa, Carl Samuelson, Leonora M. Sandall, Delores Wilde Sandberg, Louise Sandberg, Georgia Sanders, Leland Sanders, Virginia Sanders, Jennifer Sandland, Robert Sands, Eve Sanford, Delta H. Sanone, Lovena "Vinnie" Hill Sansom, Delta H. Sansone, Claudio M. Santos, Wany Thirkill Santos, J. C. Saulsbery, William Saunders, C. R. Savage, Fern Nelson Savage, Ione Saville, Fred Schade, Jane Coon Schaerrer, Ilene Schick, Karren Schick, Mary Schick, Alexander (Alex) E. Schmalz, Clara Schmidt, Johanne Ferdinand Schmidt, Ronald (Ron) Schneider, Anna M. Schoenhals, Carol Schoenhals, J. A. Schoenhals, Lizzie Scholes, Mary Ann Scholes, Morgan Schouten, Alceodene Hofer Schow, Andrew Schow, Margaret Schramm, Alexander Schreiner, Julianne Schreiner, Merle Astin Schreiner, Norma Schreiner, William L. Schreiner, Franz P. Schreyer, Allyn E. Schroeder, Bonnie Schroeder, A. Schulthess Jr., Arnold Schulthess, Jane Reed G. Schulze, Adell or Dell Schuman, Christine Wood Schumann, Miss Schwab, Beverly S. Schwendiman, Helen S. Schwendiman, Lillian Austin Schwendiman, Anna Louise Schwindling, StevenS. Scoffield, Susie Scofield, Vilate Scofield, Arline M. Scott, J. Russell Scott, Joyce A. Durrant Scott, Margaret Hansen Scott, Marie Scott, Nancy Rose Scott, Willard Scott, A. Seal, Beatrice Seal, A. J. Seare, B. A. Seare, Betty Angerbauer Seare, L. A. Seare, Lillie Seare, Marian Seare, Cristopher Searle, Shirley Jeanne Searle, Alan Sedgley, R. Sedgwick, Ella N. Seigmann, Daniel Sellers, Marian Sellers, Joshua Selley, G. A. Sells, Jane Selly, Leila T. Senior, Rowland C. Senior, Bertha Sessions, Julie S. Sessions, Richard Lee Shafer, Harvey Shank, Raymond Shanks, Annetta Sharp, Georgia R. Shaw, Janet E. Shaw, Laurence Shaw, Lawrence (Larry) F. Shaw, Nellie Sheets, William Sheldon, Millie Shelmerdine, Arthur Shepherd, Shannon Ripplinger Shepherd, W. N. B. Shepherd, Sarah Sansome Sheriff, Constance Sherman, Mary E. Ferguson Sherriff, Alice Sherwood, Blanche Shewell, Harry Shewell, Mary Shindler, Richard L. Shipley, Bardella Shipp, Mary E. Shipp, Ola Shipp, Holly Bateman Shirley, Ronald Shneider, Preston A. Shockley, Veneeta Sholyoak, Dell S. Shuman, Erin Shumate, Carolyn B. Shumway, James Grant Shumway, J. W. Shurtliff, Janet Shurtliff, Leona Shurtliff, Lillian S. Shurtliff, R. H. Siddaway, Barbara Morris Siddoway, Catherine Siddoway, Ella Neiderhauser Siegmann, Julia Silverwood, Gilbert Simmonds, Delilah Simmons, Hope Simmons, Louise Simmons, Nat Simmons, Stephen Simmons, Steven Simmons, Judith D. Simonds, Marjory Simone, Christa Bell Simons, Elizabeth Simons, Dale Simper, Robyn Simpkins, Edith Simpson, J. H. Simpson, Marie Simpson, Robert (Bob) Sink, James (Jim) Dawson Sinquefield, Marilyn Davies Sirrine, James Sitine, Kathy Skidmore, Jennie Skolfield, Orval N. Skousen, Glen Slight, Adrian M. or N. Slighting, Betty Ellison Sloan, Marjorie or Marjory B. Simons Slotboom, Beryl J. Smiley, A. Smith, A. F. Smith, A. L. Smith, A. S. Smith, Adelaid Smith, Albert Smith, Amy Smith, Andrew Smith, Angie Smith, Arline Ridges Smith, Bessie Smith, Beth Smith, Blaine Smith, Bona Bell Smith, Carolyn S. Smith, Carroll B. Smith, Charles Smith, Christian Smith, Cornelius Smith Jr., D. Smith, Daphne Smith, David A. Smith, Debra Smith, Donnetta O. Smith, Douglas H. Smith, Earl Smith, Edith Smith, Edith Ball Smith, Eliza James Smith, Emmeret C. Smith, Felice Swain Smith, Florence C. Smith, Gaylen Smith, George C. Smith, George H. Smith, George O. Smith, Gertrude S. Smith, Glenn Alan Smith, H. J. Smith, Hyrum J. Smith, Hyrum Manfred Smith, J. C. Smith, J. G. Smith, J. S. Smith, Jennie Smith, Jessie Evans Smith, John (Jack) Jones Smith, John H. Smith, John Y. Smith, Joseph Fielding Smith, Kelly Smith, L. Smith, Laura Nebeker Smith, Leon G. Smith, Lisa Anderson Smith, Lizzie Smith, Lorenzo Smith, Lyla J. Smith, Lyneer C. Smith, M. L. Smith, Mahala Smith, Manassa Smith, Margaret Smith, Margine Ann Smith, Marie Smith, Marilyn Smith, Mary A. Smith, Mary F. Smith, Mattie G. Smith, Maude M. Smith, Millie Smith, Minnie Smith, Naomie Smith, Patricia Smith, R. Gail Meyerhoffer Smith, Raymond Smith, Robb Smith, Robert Smith, Robert (Bob) E. Smith, Robert W. Smith, Sarah Smith, Sornelius Smith Jr., Stanford Smith, Sue Smith, Susie W. Smith, Sylvia Dean Smith, Thomas (Tom) G. Smith, Vickey Smith, Wilma Smith, Winnie Smith, Winslow Smith, Raelene Smithee, Rose E. Smithen, James Smithies, Wendell M. Smoot, Rhea Folsom Smurthwaite, A. C. Smythe, Lindsey Snarr, Claire SneIl, E. S. Snelgrove, H. Y. Snell, Nettie Snell, Barbara Snow, Charles Snow, Deneice Snow, Helen Snow, Philip Snow, Chelta Snyder, Nellie Solomon, Rosetta C. Solomon, Norma Kay F. Sonntag, Charles E. Sorensen, Clifford (Cliff) G. Sorensen, Erma W. Sorensen, Frederick C. Sorensen, Jon Craig Sorensen, Kathy P. Sorensen, Lillie Sorensen, Marvin A. Sorensen, Richard Scott Sorensen, C. R. Sorenson, Clifford Sorenson, Heidi Sorenson, John Sorenson, M. Sorenson, Mattie Sorenson, Paul Sorenson, Susan T. Sorenson, Jonathan Soules, Daniel Martin Soulier, Albert J. Southwick, Portia S. Southwick, David Spackman, Florence L. Spall, Bertha Chipman Spencer, Bessie Spencer, Chris Spencer, Christopher Spencer, Cora Spencer, David Earl Spencer, Ed Spencer, Katie Spencer, Maitland G. Spencer, Marjorie Mower Spendlove, Vaughn D. Spendlove, Annie Sperry, Arthur Sperry, H. Sperry, M. Sperry, W. A. Sperry, Christa D. Spilker, LaPrele Spratley, Andrew Spry, Gussie Spry, Samuel Spry, Carolyn Matthews Squires, Glacia Squires, Mary Rhodes Squires, Victoria Squires, Violet St. John, Cynthia Anne Staheli, Margaret Stahl, Florence Marie Stamm, LaVern Stamm, Melvin (Mel) Joseph Stanford, Leola Stanley, Amman Starr, Jeremy Starr, LaVern Stas, Scott Stayner, Calvin Mehr Steadman, G. Valerie Hancock Steadman, Kim Stanley Steadman, Meade Steadman, Richard (Rick) K. Steadman, Stanley Glen Steadman, Frank Wayne Steckler, Della McAnne Steed (or Steid), Jennifer Steed, Merle Steiber, Jerry R. Steiger, Yvonne Steiger, Arles K. Steiner, Eida Neves Steiner, Penny Steiner, Thelma S. Steiner, Marie H. Stenacher, Gerald Glen Steorts, Alice Stephens, Ann Stephens, Esther D. Stephens, Evan Stephens, Karen Anderson Stephens, Sybil C. Stephens, Wade N. Stephens, Craig Stephenson, Liz Sterling, Marie Diane Sterling, Craig Stevens, Debbie Stevens, Grayce Needham Stevens, Mark Stevens, Michael H. Stevens, Orvilla Allred Stevens, Robert Stevens, Robert (Bob) Stevens, Robert K. Stevens, Robert V. Stevens, Ruth Lang Stevens, C. J. Stevensen, E. Stevenson, Hilda C. Stevenson, Lizzie Stevenson, Elaine McRae Stewart, Irene Stewart, Isaac M. Stewart, Jonny Stewart, Katherine Romney Stewart, Lottie E. Stewart, Mary Stewart, Mary Jane Stewart, Mayda Stewart, Robert Stewart, Vera Stewart, Marie H. Stobbe, Carolyn Stock, Francis Stoddard, Ruth Swensen Stoddard, Barbara Green Stoker, Stephen Green Stoker, Terry Lynn Stokes, Marjory L. Stolk, Ena Stoneman, Jamesina Bannatine Stoneman, Ruth Gibbons Stoneman, William Harper Stoneman, Margaret J. Muggs Storrs, Margaret S. Jirovec Storrs, Norven or Norvin L. Storrs, Richard Storrs, Shirley Stone Storrs, Agnes Stout, Alta Stout, Kathleen McDonald Stout, L. Woodruff Stout, Madeline Wirthlin Stover, LeRoy Strand, Kerry Strauss, W. R. Strehl, Heather Streuber, Bruce Stringham, Dell B. Stringham, Joyce A. Stringham, Joyce H. Anderson Stringham, Richard B. Stringham, Shawn Stringham, Annie Stromberg, Nellie Stromberg, Rebecca Rose Strong, Roy Lee Stuart, Estella Clark Stubbs, D'Nel Stucki, Beverly Sudbury, Don C. Sudbury, Virginia Sudweeks, Bruce Sullivan, Kristy Western Sullivan, Beth P. Summerhays, C. E. Summerhays, J. Terry Summerhays, Joseph R. Summerhays, Lillian Summerhays, Margaret Summerhays, Mayme Summerhays, Marian Taylor Summers, Leonora

Sundall, Dewey Sundberg, Kathlyn Sundberg, Dorothy Sutton, A. R. Swain, Felice Swain, Emma Swan, Patricia Swanson, Ann Swensen Sweeny, Robert L. Sweeten, Alice Folland Swensen, Karl Jones Swensen, Paul Swensen, Annie Swenson, Erin Swenson, Lucile Burnhope Swenson, Mary Louise Cummings Swenson, Shirley Salm Swenson, Vernie C. Swenson, J. Swift, Ryan Swigert, Bronwyne Swiggert, Jason Swiggert, Lois Swint, Heidi S. Swinton

• T • Freda Tadje, Blanche M. Taggart, Elaine Taggart, Scott Taggart, Susan Linda Taggart, Hendrik (Hank) W. Tak, Ryo Takahashi, Dee Ann Talbot, Grace P. Talor, Marilyn Tanner, VaLeen Tanner, Lewis Tarbox, Lydia Davis Tarbox, Leon Tate, Sherman Tate, Suzanne Tate, Suzanne Jeppson Tate, Dawn L. Pratt Taylor, Eleanor Taylor, Ethel Taylor, Florence Taylor, Gary L. Taylor, Gloria B. Taylor, Grace Praker Taylor, J. Taylor, J. H. Taylor, Jabez Taylor, John Taylor, Kate Taylor, Katherine (Kay) Kelly Taylor, LaMar H. Taylor, Lizzie Taylor, Mamie Taylor, Marvin R. Taylor, Norman L. Taylor, Ralph Randall Taylor, Richard M. Taylor, Robert Taylor, Ruby Taylor, Sarah H. Taylor, A. Tayner, Kristyle Teasdale, Verl Teeples, Evelyn R. Teerlink, Marie Teerlink, N. Teirlink, Elvis B. Terry, Isabella A. Terry, M. A. Tester, Clara Teuscher, Barbara Tew, Fanny Young Thatcher, David C. Thayne, Berenice or Bernice Steele Theurer, Rhea S. Thiriot, Shalaun Thiriot, Agnes Thomas, Agnes Olsen Thomas, Alice Thomas, Charles J. Thomas, Claire Thomas, D. Paul Thomas, Delano Thomas, Ellen Thomas, Emma Lindsay Thomas, Evangeline Thomas, J. Thomas, Julian M. Thomas, Moroni J. Thomas, R. Craig Thomas, Sara Thomas, Sarah (Sadie) Ann Thomas, Shirlene Thomas, Stiles McLaughlin Thomas, T. R. Thomas, T. S. Thomas, Thomas V. Thomas, Vaughn L. Thomas, Warren John (Jack) Thomas, Dorothy Thompsen, Bessie Murk Thompson, Brad Thompson, Carolyn Thompson, Cordia Thompson, Dorotha C. Thompson, Edgar (Ed) Thompson, Edna Thompson, Fred Thompson, Hazel Thompson, Janet Thompson, John Thompson, Lillian Thompson, Lora Harmon Thompson, Orson D. Thompson, Robert (Bob) H. Thompson, Sam Thompson, Susan (Sue) D. Thompson, Cannon A. Thomson, Mina Thomson, Sarah Thomson, J. Thomstoft, Eric Thorkelson, Imogene Johnson Thorn, Scott Lee Thorn, Emily Thorne, LaMont Thornock, Genevieve Thornton, Carl Thornwall, Karl A. Thorson, Gail Throckmorton, Claudia Stokes Thurman, Henry Thygersen, Ruth Jensen Thygersen, Dorothy Tillbury, Christine Timothy, A. W. Timpson, G. W. Timpson, Jean Timpson, Melba Timpson, N. S. Timpson, Richard (Dick) H. Timpson, Laura Tingey, Mattie Horne Tingey, Charlene Tippetts, Marie Tipton, LaVon Tomander, Ida Grayston Tomlinson, J. W. E. Tomlinson, Matt Toone, Kathleen H. Topham, Norman W. Torgensen, Eric Torgersen, Richard C. Torgerson, John J. Toronto, Paul Toronto, Dee Marshall Tracy, Kristyle Tracy, Alfred Trauffer, Annabel Traynor, Nettie R. Treweek, Leah S. Tribe, George Triplett, Ardell Roberts Trottier, Karl Robert (Bob) Tschaggeny, Jessie L. Behunin Tucker, Julie Martha Brimm Tucker, Pat Tucker, Phyllis O. Clegg Tucker, A. Tuckett, Ethel Tuckett, H. A. Tuckett, Roger Tuckett, W. F. Tuckett, Abe Tueller, Arch Tueller, Linda Tuke, Julie Judd Turley, Wayne Turley, John S. Turnbull, Delma Turner, James (Jim) Clarence Turner, Kamber Price Turner, Maye Turner, R. Ann Turner, Raphael Tuten

• U • George A. Udall, Forest G. Umberger, Alison Unsworth, Galen Updike, Andrew Ure, James Ure, Lucinda Ure, William Ure, Elsie Urich, Francis Urry, Babe Lund Utter

• V • Deina Van Bezooyen, Ernest C. Van Bibber, L. E. Van Dam, Michael Van Dam, Melvin Van den Akker, Gerard Robert Van Dijk, Raymond (Ray) W. Van Dongen, Ronald Van Dongen, Teda Van Dongen, Jacob A. Van Duran, Agnes O. Van Duren, J. A. Van Duren, Jacob A. Van Duren, Bouke (Bob) Van Komen, Lorna Ellen Zielke Van Komen, Robert Van Komen, Ray Van Noy, Spencer Van Noy, Cornelius G. Van Os, Diena or Dena Van Tussenbroek Van Os, W. F. Van Os, Williams Van Os, Antonia (Toni) Van Otten, Arien or Adrien Van Roosendaal, Jane Van Roosendaal, Bertha M. Hunsaker Van Tussenbrock, A. Van Tussenbroek Jr., G. (Bert) Van Tussenbroek, Gerrit Van Tussenbroek, Joanna Van Tussenbroek, Minnie Van Tussenbroek, Musa Van Tussenbroek, Barbara Van Veen, Glen Elden Van Wagenen, Robert L. Van Wagenen, Carol C. Van Wagoner, Drew Van Wagoner, Gary M. Van Wagoner, Leland Van Wagoner, Lucile Van, Maggie Van, Marian Walker Vance, Oscar Vance, Robert Bliss Vance, Ellen VanDam, Jacob C. Vandervis, Johanna Vanderwiel, Frances Sugden Vane, Wayne VanTassell, Werner Varhaaren, Davis Vaudis, Razel Veasy, Aize Carl Veeninga, Nina Vickers, Frances Viehweg, Amy Villett, Eliza J. Vincent, Ina Reynolds Vincent, Irene Vincent, James or John Vincent, Phoebe A. Vincent, Kathryn Austin Visher, Carl Volmar, Bill Vonk, William Vonk, Gary Voorhees, Joanne Voorhees, Marie Vreken

• W • Julie F. Dowse Wade, Sherry or Sherrie Wadham, Marilla Sophia Wagner, James R. Wagstaff, Oralie Bailey Waite, Rulon W. Waite, Ann or Anne or Anna Wakefield, Garth Wakefield, Kay Lynn Wakefield, W. Mack Wakins, Yoshie Walbeck, Thomas (Tom) M. Waldron, H. J. Walk, L. Walk, Ada E. Walker, Albert C. Walker, DeAnne Walker, Elmo Lavelle Walker, Karl Reed Walker, Leslie Ann Walker, Lily Walker, M. Richard Walker, Marietta Walker, Mary Walker, Nedra W. Walker, Norlan G. Walker, Richard Walker, Ruth Walker, J. B. Walkley, Joseph E. Wall, Annie Wallace, G. Wallace, Hattie Wallace, Kathleen Wallace, Rose Wallace, Susie E. Wallace, W. A. Wallace, Rawn Wallgren, Barbara Lloyd Wallin, Kent Wallin, Kristine Wallin, Sidney Wallwook, Albert Walsh, Boyd Walsh, O. S. Walsh, Melissa Walstenholme, C. R. J. Walter, Todd Wangsgard, Fred Wanless, J. Wanless, Nora Warburton, Shane Warby, Tracy Warby, Esther Jane Ward, Evelyn G. Ward, Lucile Ward, Mondell K. Ward, Ray C. Ward, Rex Clark Ward, Hal J. Wardle, Calvin L. Wardrop, Todd Wardrop, Jack Ware, Patricia Waring, Betty Ann Johnosn Warner, Darlene Warner, Elizabeth Warner, Blaine Johnson Wasden, Douglas F. Wasden, Annie Waterworth, Jeanette Watkins, Pamela D. Watkins, Reed A. Watkins, W. Mack Watkins, Katherine Watson, Louise Watson, Werdna Watson, David Cyril Watt, Anna Watts, Barbara Watts, D. J. Watts, Don Watts, Kathie Watts, Ruth C. Watts, Alan Wayman, Lillian Weaver, Cleo Millet Webb, Grace Susanna Vanderhyde Webb, Walter Y. or L. Webb, Marie J. Webster, Helen B. Weeks, Carl Weenig, Karl Wegener, Carol Weibell, F. H. Weight, Ormon R. Weight, Pamela Weight, Maggie Weihe, Saundra Weihe, Willard E. Weihe, Kurt Weinzinger, Anna Weis, Violet Weiss, Arthur H. Welch, Catherine (Kay) C. Welch, Garth Larry Welch, Gertrude Welch, J. E. Welch, Jay Evard Welch, Kay Welch, Richard (Dick) E. Welch, Timothy Welch, Annie Bertha Bowring Welling, Carolyn O. Welling, Marjorie Welling, Jewell Wellman, Emma Wells, Louie Wells, Robert Faris Wells, Conrad Welti, Ruth Jensen Welti, Betty Ann Werner, Fred Wesche, Walter Wesche, Lee Wessman, Annette Sorensen West, Charles West, Cosette V. West, Eliza West, Fern Westenskow, Donald Western, Janice Western, Helen or Helene Westlund, Mildred Weston, Fred B. Wetherell, J. R. Wetherell, Virtue Wetzel, Bret Wheadon, Geraldine S. Wheeler, James Wheeler, D. Sterling Wheelwright, Edna Wheelwright, Grace Whipple, Inez Stout Whipple, Erma Whitaker, Martha Whitaker, Will Whitaker, Robert Whitchurch, Bonnie Jean Hebdon White, Clara White, Dorothy J. White, Elvira C. R. White, J. A. White, John B. White, Larry M. White, Lydia White, M. White, Mondell White, Nada Malette White, Oralie White, Ronald J. White, Verdi R. White, Robert Whitehead, Ruth Whitehead, Alicebeth Whiteley, Herbert G. Whitelock, Ingeborg Whitelock, Kenley Whitelock, Vanza Whitemore, Reed Burton Whitesides, Brent Whitlock, Morris Whitlock, Phyllis Whitman, Keith Lindsay Whitmore, Phyllis Burton Whitmore, Robert (Bob) S. Whitmore, Vonza Whitmore, Andrea Anderson Whitney, Florence Whitney, H. G. Whitney, Jennie Whitney, Katheryn Mayer Whitney, Keith Lynn Whitney, Laura Whitney, O. F. Whitney, Ralph E. Whitney, Fred Whittaker, Rachel Whittaker, Christine J. Wickens, Hendrika Wiegel, Marie Wiegel, Eleanor Wightman, Mack Wilberg, George Q. Wilcken, George W. Wilcken, Vera H. Wilcken, Cleone Wilcox, E. Wilcox, Helen M. Wilcox, Joyce Tate Wilcox, Matilda Wilcox, Jesse E. Wilde, George Wilding, Ethel Wilkin, Eva A. Wilkin, Frank Wilkin, G. R. Wilkins, LouAnn Wilkins, Rose Wilkins, Carol D. Wilkinson, Clytie Read Wilkinson, Dorothy Wilkinson, Geraldine J. Wilkinson, Kenneth (Ken) A. Wilks, Dorothy Beck Willardson, Alexander Willey, Anthony Willey, Elizabeth Willey, Emily Willey, Kristina Willey, Alfred Williams, Ann Bedford Williams, Annie Williams, Carol Williams, Carol Yvonee Williams, Charlie Williams, Deanna Williams, Denise Williams, Eleanor Williams, Emma Williams, Gina Ann Williams, Jeremy Williams, Jessie A. Williams, John Thomas Williams, Lyman S. Williams, Marilyn Richards Covey Williams, Marjorie Williams, Melba Williams, Millie Williams, Minnie Williams, Nelson Williams, Pauline Williams, Ryan Williams, Sherman A. Williams, Thomas Williams, Verona Williams, Ella Williamson, Emily Williamson, James Williamson, Jean Williamson, Jim Williamson, Bertram Willis, Eliza Willis, George Willis, Natalie Willis, A. F. Wilson, Al Wilson, C. E. Wilson, Kathy Wilson, LaRae Egbert Wilson, Margaret Wilson, Merrill L. Wilson, Miss Wilton, Louise J. Wimmer, Eva Winberg, Elizabeth (Bette) A. Edwards Winch, Quentin (Pete) C. Winder, Cindy Winegar, Mary Kathleen Shearer Winegar, Amelia Winkworth, T. Winkworth, Ernest Winn, Sam Winn Jr., Rick Winscot, Viola Winson, C. W. Winter, Sam D. Winter, F. Burton Winters, Joyce A. Winters, Susan Bennett Winters, Bonnie Winterton, Lonny Dee Winterton, Gwendolin Wirthlin, Thore Wiscomb, J. William Wiscombe, Debra Wise, Kenneth G. Wiseman, Analee Wiser, Elaine Witte, Donna Wittwer, E. G. Witzel, E. J. Witzel, Harold F. Wolfgramm, Melissa Wolstenholm, N. Joy Wonnacott, Dorothy Marie Wood, Elizabeth A. Wood, Evelyn Wood, George C. Wood, J. H. Wood, John Howard Wood, Lillian Wood, Lorena Wood, Lorreta S. Wood, Marvin F. Wood, Patricia Wood, Phyllis Wood, Rue Wood, Sarah H. Wood, Sarah L. Wood, Stephanie Wood, W. Wood, Becky Woodbury, Janice Condie Woodbury, Joseph Stephen Woodbury, May Woodbury, Norma Woodbury, Scott Woodbury, T. L. Woodbury, May Woodruff, Brenda L. Woods, Mary Woods, Ruth Wooley, Vaneta M. Woolf, A. M. Woolley, Bradley P. Woolley, E. Richard Woolley, Grace Welch Woolsey, PJ Woolston, Viola or Veda Worley, William R. Worley Jr., Ralph Worsley, Cherilyn Worthen, Mary Worthington, Britt-Marie Barnes Bryggman Wraspir, Amos Wright, Jeralynne T. Wright, Clair Ann Wright, Genaveve Wright, Geneva Ensign Wright, Genevieve Wright, George A. Wright, Jeralynn (Jeri) Topham Wright, Lana Wright, Lynn Ronald Wright, M. J. Wright, Matt Wright, Mode Wright, Nathan Wright, Steven Wright, William Dennis Wright, Hertha Wugk, Esther Wunderlich, Marybeth Wynder, Max Kendall Wynder, Irena W. Wynn, Sam Wynn

• Y • Susan (Sue) H. Yank, Dennis Yarrington, Joan Yarrington, Karen Adele Yearsley, Hans Ylst, Marjo Ylst, Charles Yost, A. P. Young, B. B. Young, Barbara H. Lambert Young, Betsy Ross Young, Clifford E. Young, Don C. Young, E. R. Young, Edith G. Young, Emma L. Young, Eveline Young, J. H. Young, James Lawrence Young, Janet Young, Jeanette Young, Katheryn Young, L. C. Young, Lillie Young, Lorenzo S. Young, Martha Hammond Young, P. H. Young, Rettie Young, Ruth O. Young, S. B. Young, Sonoma Young, Florence Cummings Youngberg

• Z • Bob Roland Zabriskie, Grant Rodney (Rod) Zabriskie, Jennie Zabriskie, Marba Zabriskie, Mary Zackrison, Rudy Zander, Emily Zappe, V. DeAnne Zarbock, Kenneth (Ken) L. Zeeman, Linda Anderson Zeeman, Margarite Zeender, Wolfgang Zeisler, Jerry Zenger, Robert Pingree Ziegler, Leland (Lee) Zurligen

When sorrows stir the water
Like winds across the sea,
In ever-swelling billows that roll
repeatedly.
Whatever fate befalls me,
whatever is my lot,
Thou gave me strength and courage
And taught me how to say,

"Yes, it is well within me, well
with my soul;
Just like a peaceful river deep in my soul."

And Lord, haste the day
When our faith shall be sight,
The clouds be rolled back as a scroll.
The trumpet shall resound
And the Lord shall descend;
Even so, it is well with my soul.
It is well, it is well with my soul.

PRAYER OF THANKSGIVING
Acknowledgments and Sources

In the life of a book there are those whose quiet imprint makes all the difference. My heartfelt thanks to Lee Groberg for the opportunity to write the documentary *America's Choir* and this companion book; choir president Mac Christensen, Craig Jessop, and Mack Wilberg for their vision and support; and Scott Barrick for his remarkable foresight, precision, and friendship. Many thanks for the direction and encouragement of Sheri Dew, president of Deseret Book; the coordination and commitment of Jana Erickson, project manager; the thoughtful work and generosity of editor Jack Lyon; and the artistic brilliance of art director Richard Erickson.

BOOKS

Ashton, Wendell J. *Theirs Is the Kingdom.* Salt Lake City: Bookcraft, 1970.

Beesley, Sterling E. *Kind Words: The Beginnings of Mormon Melody.* Salt Lake City: Genealogical Research Foundation, 1980.

Calman, Charles Jeffrey. *The Mormon Tabernacle Choir.* New York: Harper and Row, 1979.

Cornwall, J. Spencer. *A Century of Singing: The Salt Lake Mormon Tabernacle Choir.* Salt Lake City: Deseret Book Company, 1958.

———. *Stories of Our Mormon Hymns.* Salt Lake City: Deseret Book, 1968.

Dennis, Ronald D. *The Call of Zion: The Story of the First Welsh Mormon Migration.* Provo: BYU Religious Studies Center, 1987.

Hicks, Michael. *Mormonism and Music: A History.* Urbana: University of Illinois Press, 1989.

Kinard, J. Spencer. *A Moment's Pause.* Salt Lake City: Deseret Book, 1989.

Holzapfel, Richard Neitzel. *Every Stone a Sermon.* Salt Lake City: Bookcraft, 1992.

Maeser, Karl G. *School and Fireside.* Salt Lake City: Skelton and Co., 1898.

McDaniel, E. A. *Utah at the World's Columbian Exposition.* Salt Lake City: Salt Lake Lithographic Co., 1894.

Russell, Margaret. *Biography of John Parry.* Self-published.

Scraps of Biography. Salt Lake City: n.p., n.d.

Thomas, Warren John "Jack." *Salt Lake Mormon Tabernacle Choir Goes to Europe 1955.* Salt Lake City: Deseret News Press, 1955.

PERIODICALS AND ARCHIVES

Deseret Evening News, October 6, 1867; October 29, 1880; August 22, 1883; February 6, 1910; August 13, 1955; January 13, 1960.

Hicks, Michael. "Beginnings of the Mormon Tabernacle Choir." *Pioneer,* Spring 2003.

Improvement Era, July 1905; January 1912; June 1914; June 1922; June 1938.

LDS Church News, July 22, 1989; October 3, 1992; September 4, 1993.

LDS Conference Report, April 1939, April 1952, October 1955; October 1994.

Mormon Tabernacle Choir historical files: minutes, letters, news clippings, and periodicals, *Keeping Tab, The Tab.*

"The Salt Lake Mormon Tabernacle Choir." *The American Organist,* December 1988.

Utah Historical Quarterly, Fall 1981.

Young Woman's Journal, December 1905.

INTERVIEWS

Barry Anderson, Scott Barrick, Rafael Frübeck de Burgos, F. Mac Christensen, Clay Christiansen, Sue Coblentz, Walter Cronkite, Gabriel Crouch, Richard Elliot, Dana Gioia, Gordon B. Hinckley, David Hurley, J. Spencer Kinard, Angela Lansbury, Phillip Lawson, Keith Lockhart, John Longhurst, Craig Jessop, Don Mischer, Lloyd Newell, Charles Osgood, Jerold Ottley, Ed Payne, Paul Phoenix, Wendell Smoot, Bryn Terfel, Frederica von Stade, Mack Wilberg, John Williams, Barbara Turner, various choir members.

MUSIC

"America, the Dream Goes On," Alan and Marilyn Bergman.

"As the Dew from Heaven Distilling," Thomas Kelly.

"Battle Hymn of the Republic," Julia Ward Howe.

"Call of the Champions," Olympic Motto.

"Come, Thou Fount of Every Blessing," American folk hymn.

"Come, Come, Ye Saints," William Clayton.

"Gently Raise the Sacred Strain," W. W. Phelps.

"God Be with You," Jeremiah Rankin.

"Goin' Home," William Arms Fisher.

"Hymn for America," Michael Dennis Browne and Stephen Paulus.

"I Sing the Mighty Power of God," Isaac Watts.

"It Is Well with My Soul," Horatio Gates Spafford, additional lyrics by Michael Davis.

PHOTOGRAPHS

We would like to thank photographers Marene Adler, Gerry Avant, Craig Dimond, Marene Foulger, Debra Gehris, Lee Groberg, Gordan Huston, and Jonathan Swinton.

Front cover: Marene Foulger
Back cover top: Craig Diamond, © Intellectual Reserve, Inc.
Back cover bottom: Gerry Avant, © *Deseret Morning News.*
Author photo, Jonathan Swinton.

Marene Adler: page 11 bottom left.

Bancroft Library: 34, 43 top.

Corbis Images: 87.

Denver Public Library © 2004: page 128 bottom right.

Deseret Book: page 37 painting by Del Parsons.

© *Deseret Morning News:* pages vii, 2, 3 top and bottom shaded, 4 bottom right, 6 bottom, 11 top left and bottom right and shaded background, 14, 15 bottom, 17 top left, 18 top, 21, 23 middle left and bottom left, 29 bottom shaded, 32 top, 42 shaded background, 52-54, 84, 85 bottom left, 92, 95, 96, 108 bottom left, 112 shaded background, 115 shaded background, 116, 119, 121 top, 123, 124 bottom, 124, 129 bottom.

Lee Groberg: pages 3, 15, 29, 33, 43, 72, 94, 105, 109, 112, 113, 115.

Gordon Huston: pages v, vi, vii, 51, 58, 100.

Keystone-Mast Collection UCR/California Museum of Photography: 73.

Official White House photos: pages 8, 9, 42.

Paul and Alice Swenson: page 11 top right, 78.

Jonathan Swinton: page 124 top.

Utah Historical Society: page 28 top, 29 top, 30, 31, 32 bottom, 35 top, 36 middle, 40, 41, 62, 64.

All other photographs © Intellectual Reserve, Inc.: LDS Church Historical Department, Visual Resource Library, Museum of Church History and Art, Tabernacle Choir Archives.

Editor: Jack Lyon
Art Director: Richard Erickson
Designers: Barry Hansen and Shauna Gibby
Typesetter: Tonya Facemyer